NATIONAL GEOGRAPHIC
Student Atlas
of the World

NATIONAL GEOGRAPHIC SOCIETY
WASHINGTON, D.C.

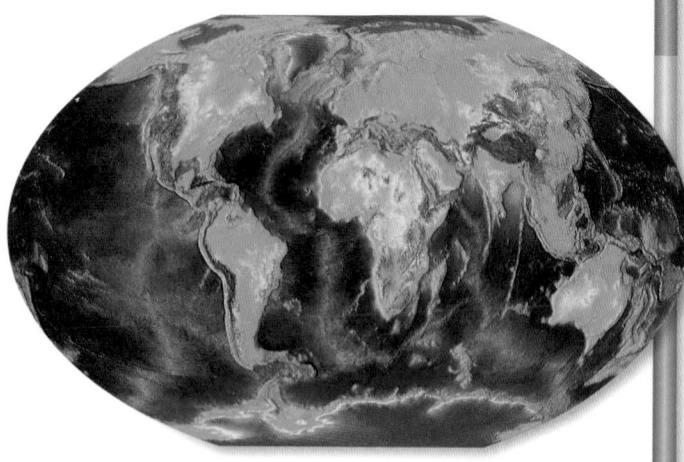

About the Earth

The Continents

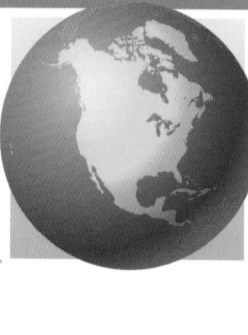

40 North America

56 South America

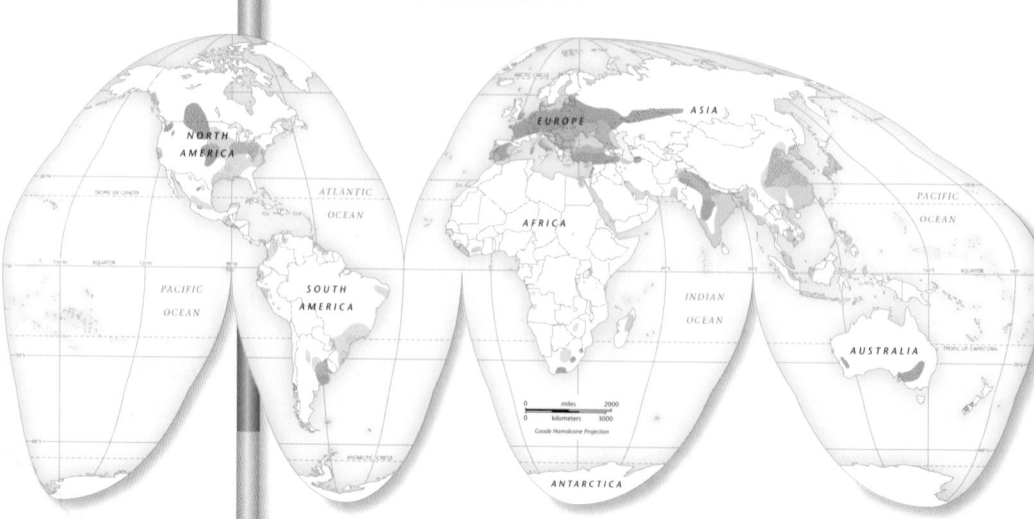

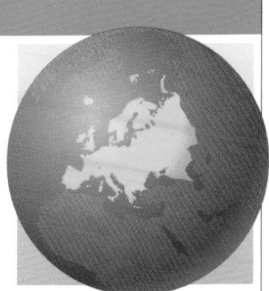

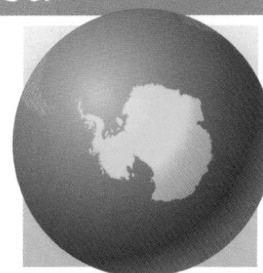

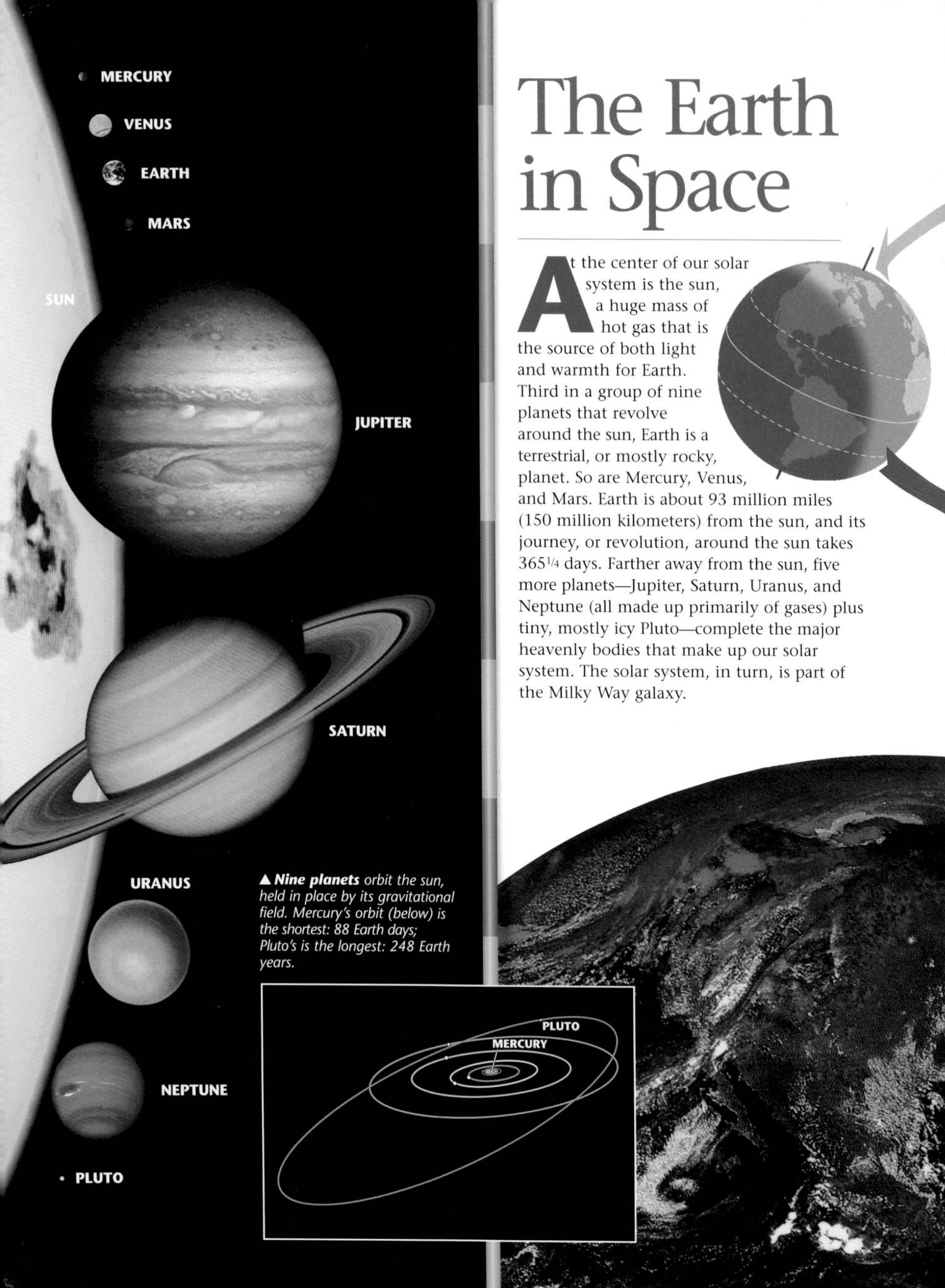

MERCURY

VENUS

EARTH

MARS

SUN

JUPITER

SATURN

URANUS

NEPTUNE

• PLUTO

The Earth in Space

At the center of our solar system is the sun, a huge mass of hot gas that is the source of both light and warmth for Earth. Third in a group of nine planets that revolve around the sun, Earth is a terrestrial, or mostly rocky, planet. So are Mercury, Venus, and Mars. Earth is about 93 million miles (150 million kilometers) from the sun, and its journey, or revolution, around the sun takes 365¼ days. Farther away from the sun, five more planets—Jupiter, Saturn, Uranus, and Neptune (all made up primarily of gases) plus tiny, mostly icy Pluto—complete the major heavenly bodies that make up our solar system. The solar system, in turn, is part of the Milky Way galaxy.

▲ *Nine planets* orbit the sun, held in place by its gravitational field. Mercury's orbit (below) is the shortest: 88 Earth days; Pluto's is the longest: 248 Earth years.

PLUTO

MERCURY

ARCTIC OCEAN

E U R A S I A N   P L A T E

ALPS

Plate boundary (uncertain)

Plateau of Tibet

HIMALAYA

PACIFIC OCEAN

ARABIAN PLATE

INDIAN PLATE

PHILIPPINE PLATE

PACIFIC PLATE

A F R I C A N   P L A T E

Great Rift Valley

SOMALI PLATE

EQUATOR

OCEAN

MID-ATLANTIC RIDGE

INDIAN OCEAN

AUSTRALIAN PLATE

A N T A R C T I C   P L A T E

	miles	2000
0	kilometers	3000

Winkel Tripel Projection

Plate Tectonics

- Divergent boundary
- Convergent boundary
- Transform zone
- ○ Notable earthquake of the 20th century
- ∘ 20th-century quake greater than 6.5 magnitude
- ▲ Notable volcanic eruption of the 20th century
- ▲ Known volcanic eruption during the past 10,000 years
- ○ Hot spot

◀ **Tectonic boundaries** mark areas of geologic change in ocean floors, along continental margins, and even through continents, as in East Africa's Great Rift Valley. Clusters of volcanoes and frequent earthquakes signal areas of instability.

▶**Eve of Destruction.** By 65 million years ago, continents were moving toward their current positions. The impact (✱) of an asteroid in the Gulf of Mexico probably extinguished the dinosaurs and many other species.

NORTH AMERICA · EUROPE · ASIA · ATLANTIC OCEAN · PACIFIC OCEAN · PACIFIC OCEAN · SOUTH AMERICA · AFRICA · AUSTRALIA

▶**Deep Freeze.** By 18,000 years ago, the continents resembled their current shapes. A great ice age had the far northern and southern regions locked under huge ice sheets.

NORTH AMERICA · EUROPE · ASIA · ATLANTIC · AFRICA · PACIFIC OCEAN · PACIFIC OCEAN · SOUTH AMERICA · OCEAN · AUSTRALIA · ANTARCTICA

EARTH'S LAND & WATER FEATURES

The largest land and water features on Earth are the continents and the oceans, but many other features—large and small—make each place unique. Mountains, plateaus, and plains give texture to the land. The Rockies and the Andes rise high above the lowlands of North and South America. In Asia, the Himalaya and the Plateau of Tibet form the rugged core of Earth's largest continent. These features are the result of powerful forces within Earth pushing up the land. Others, such as canyons and valleys, are created when weathering and erosion wear down parts of Earth's surface.

Dramatic features are not limited to the land. Submarine mountains, appearing like pale blue threads against the deep blue on the satellite map, rise from the seafloor and trace zones of underwater geologic activity. Deep trenches form where plates collide, causing one to dive beneath the other.

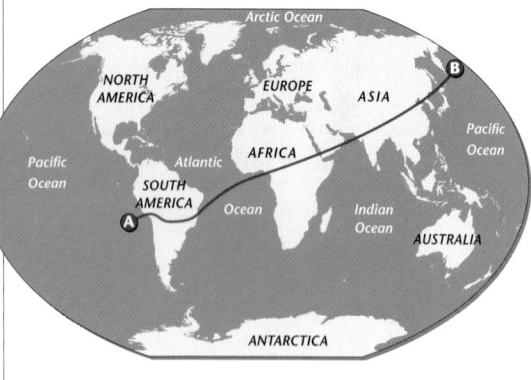

▼ A Slice of Earth.
This cross section of Earth's surface extends from Lake Titicaca near South America's Pacific coast to the Kuril Islands in the North Pacific Ocean. It shows towering mountains, eroded highlands, broad coastal plains, and deep ocean basins.

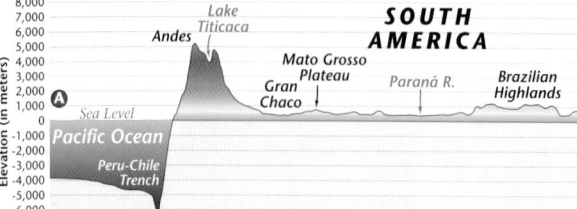

Physical Systems
Earth's Land and Water Features

Elevation
Meters
Feet
5,000
16,400
3,500
11,480
2,000
6,560
1,000
3,280
500
1,640
Sea Level
-500
-1,640
-1,500
-4,920
-3,000
-9,840
-5,000
-16,400
-7,000
-22,960
-9,000
-29,520
-11,000
-36,080

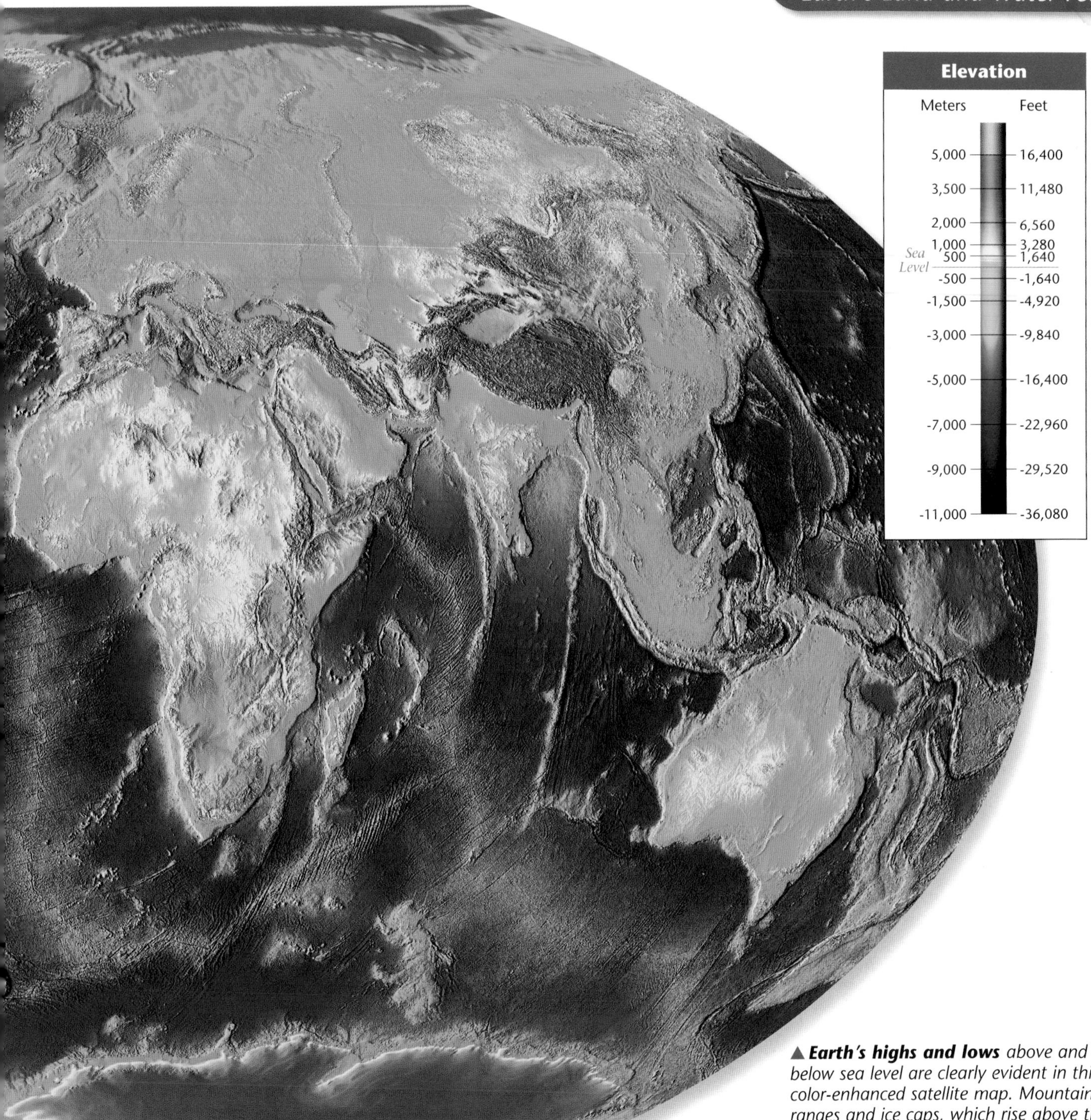

▲ ***Earth's highs and lows*** *above and below sea level are clearly evident in this color-enhanced satellite map. Mountain ranges and ice caps, which rise above the land, stand out in shades of red; broad expanses of lowlands are shown in green. Pale aqua marks shallow seas along continental margins and over peaks and ridges rising from the ocean floor.*

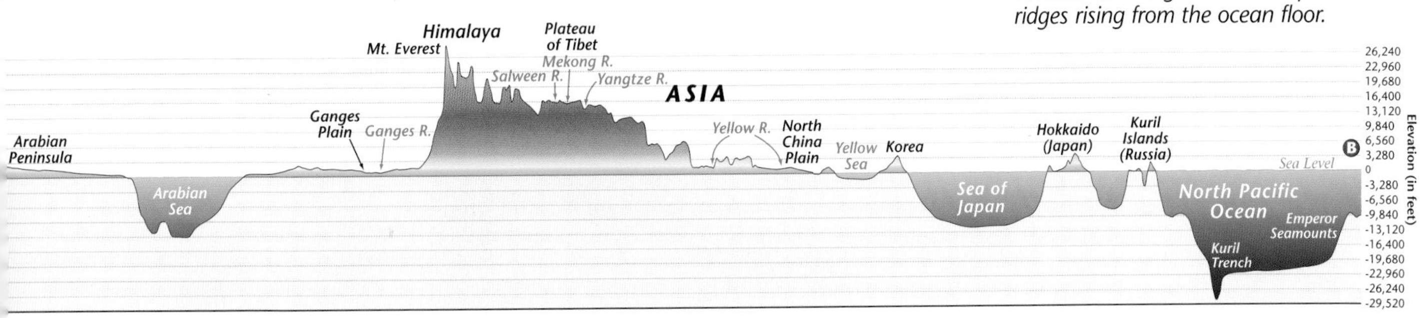

Himalaya
Mt. Everest
Plateau of Tibet
Mekong R.
Salween R.
Yangtze R.
ASIA
Ganges Plain
Ganges R.
Arabian Peninsula
Arabian Sea
Yellow R.
North China Plain
Yellow Sea
Korea
Sea of Japan
Hokkaido (Japan)
Kuril Islands (Russia)
Sea Level
North Pacific Ocean
Emperor Seamounts
Kuril Trench
B
26,240
22,960
19,680
16,400
13,120
9,840
6,560
3,280
0
-3,280
-6,560
-9,840
-13,120
-16,400
-19,680
-22,960
-26,240
-29,520
Elevation (in feet)

EARTH'S CLIMATES

Climate is not the same as weather. Climate is the long-term average of conditions in the atmosphere at a particular location on Earth's surface. Weather refers to the momentary conditions of the atmosphere. Climate is important because it influences vegetation and soil development. It also influences people's choices about how and where to live.

There are many different systems for classifying climates. One commonly used system was developed by Russian-born climatologist Wladimir Köppen and later modified by American climatologist Glenn Trewartha. Köppen's system identifies five major climate zones based on average precipitation and temperature, and a sixth zone for highland, or high elevation, areas. Except for continental climate, all climate zones occur in mirror image north and south of the Equator. Web Link

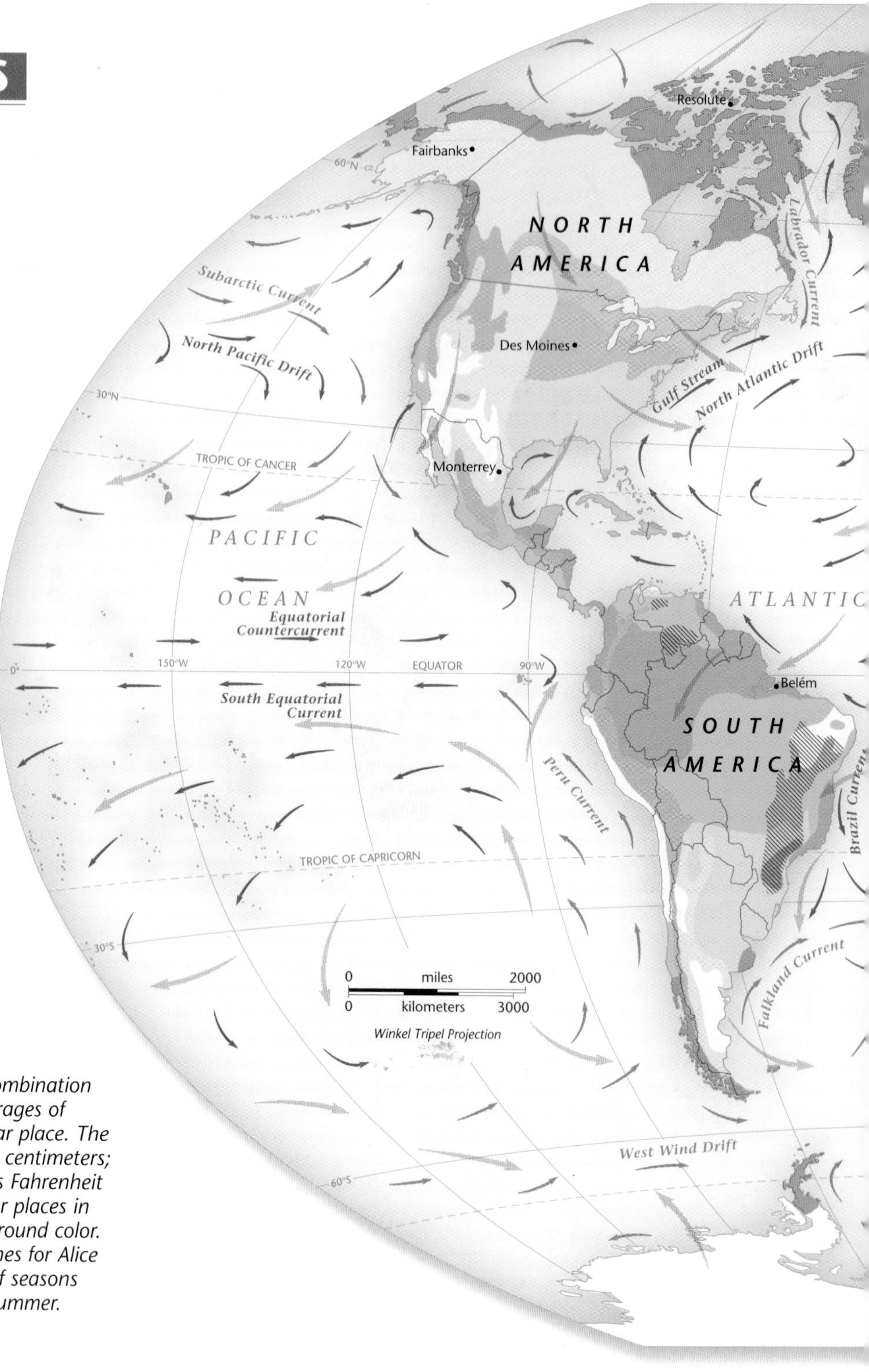

▼ **Climate Graphs.** A climate graph is a combination bar and line graph that shows monthly averages of precipitation and temperature for a particular place. The bar graph shows precipitation in inches and centimeters; the line graph shows temperature in degrees Fahrenheit and Celsius. The graphs below are typical for places in the climate zone represented by their background color. The seeming inversion of the temperature lines for Alice Springs and McMurdo reflects the reversal of seasons south of the Equator, where January is midsummer.

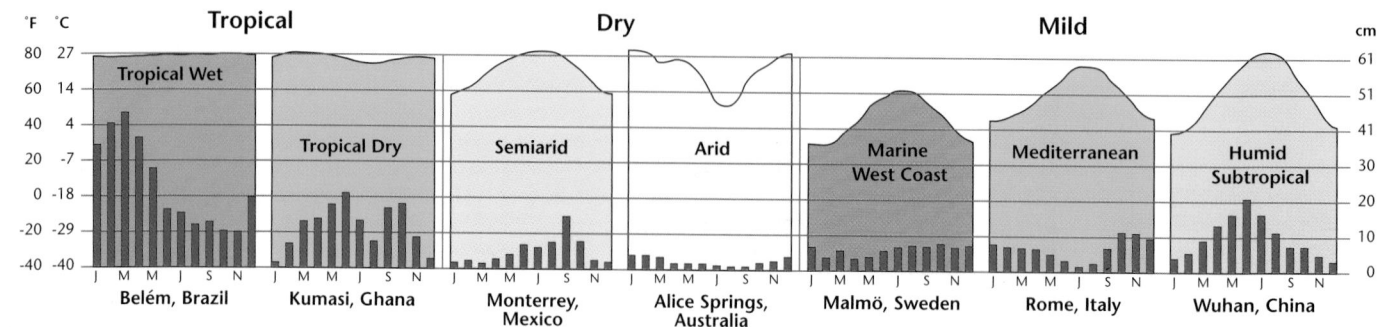

Tropical		Dry		Mild		
Tropical Wet	Tropical Dry	Semiarid	Arid	Marine West Coast	Mediterranean	Humid Subtropical
Belém, Brazil	Kumasi, Ghana	Monterrey, Mexico	Alice Springs, Australia	Malmö, Sweden	Rome, Italy	Wuhan, China

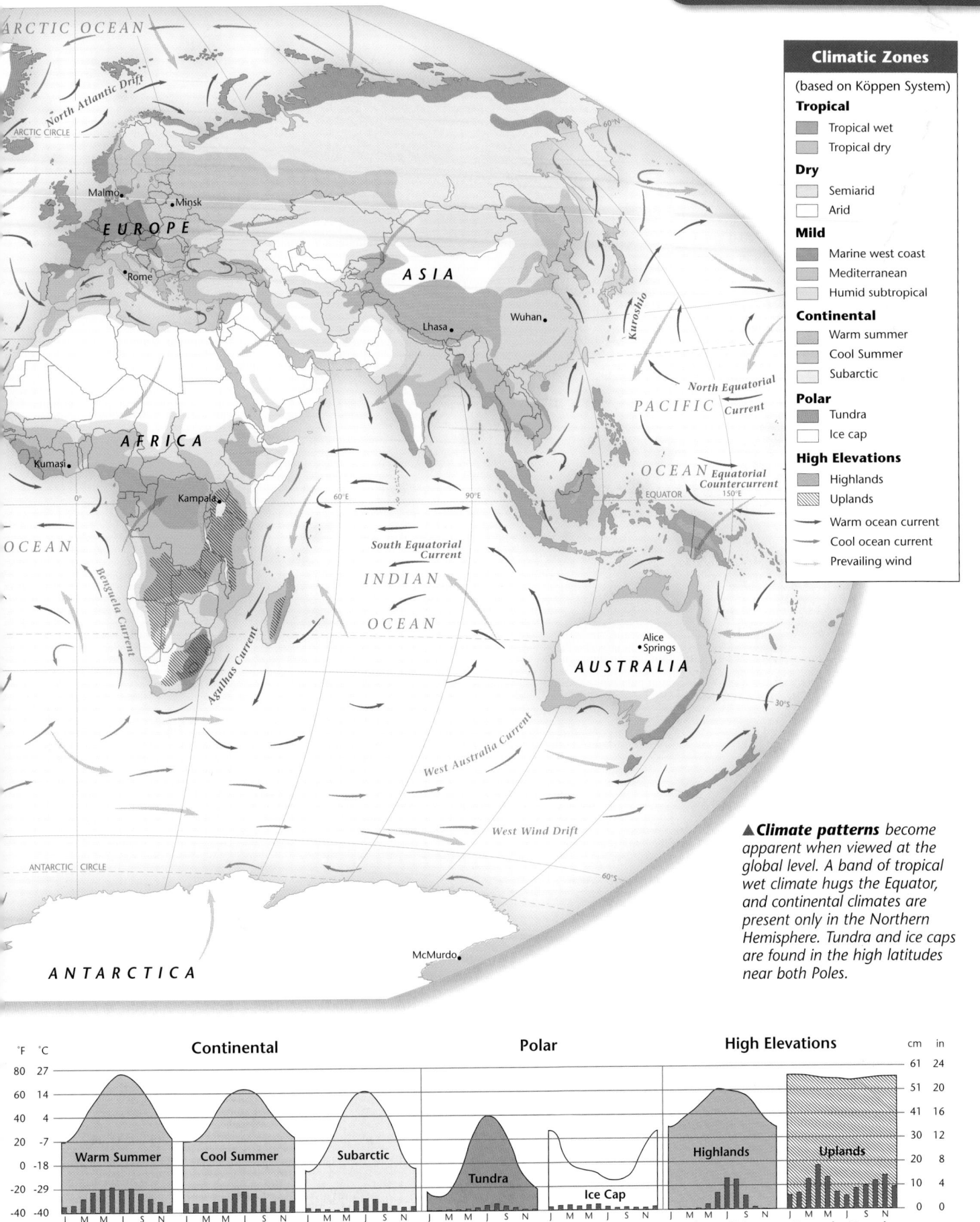

Climatic Zones

(based on Köppen System)

Tropical
- Tropical wet
- Tropical dry

Dry
- Semiarid
- Arid

Mild
- Marine west coast
- Mediterranean
- Humid subtropical

Continental
- Warm summer
- Cool Summer
- Subarctic

Polar
- Tundra
- Ice cap

High Elevations
- Highlands
- Uplands
- → Warm ocean current
- → Cool ocean current
- ⋯ Prevailing wind

▲ **Climate patterns** become apparent when viewed at the global level. A band of tropical wet climate hugs the Equator, and continental climates are present only in the Northern Hemisphere. Tundra and ice caps are found in the high latitudes near both Poles.

Continental

Warm Summer — Des Moines, Iowa, U.S.A.
Cool Summer — Minsk, Belarus
Subarctic — Fairbanks, Alaska, U.S.A.

Polar

Tundra — Resolute, Nunavut, Canada
Ice Cap — McMurdo, Antarctica

High Elevations

Highlands — Lhasa, China
Uplands — Kampala, Uganda

19

CLIMATE CONTROLS

The patterns of climate vary widely. Some climates, such as those near the Equator and the Poles, are nearly constant year-round. Others experience great seasonal variations, such as the wet and dry patterns of the tropical dry zone and the monthly average temperature extremes of the subarctic.

Climate patterns are not random. They are the result of complex interactions of basic climate controls: **latitude, elevation, prevailing winds, ocean currents, landforms,** and **location.**

These controls combine in various ways to create the bands of climate that can be seen on the world climate map on pages 18–19 and on the climate maps in the individual continent sections of this atlas. At the local level, however, special conditions may create microclimates that differ from those that are more typical of the region.

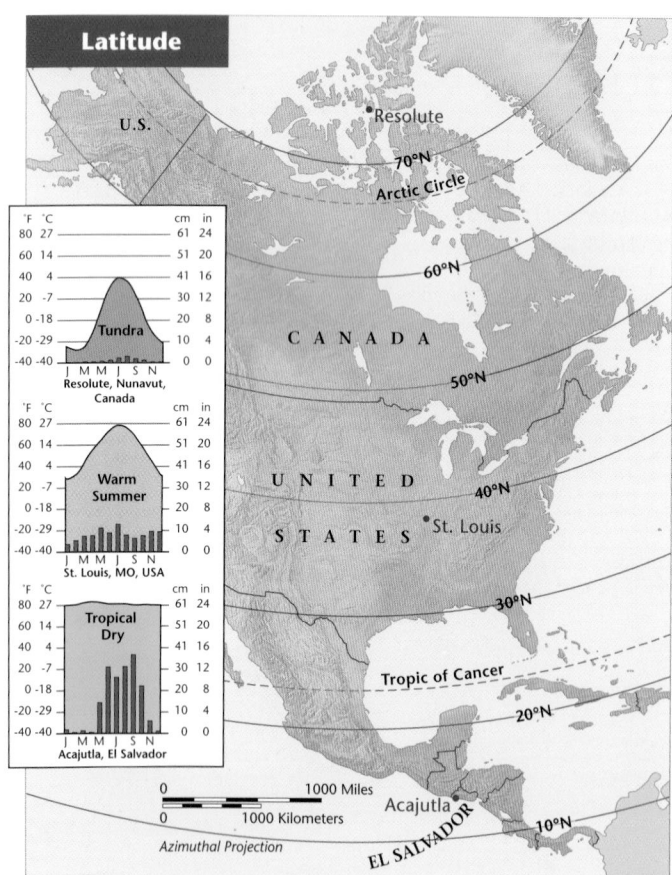

▲ **Latitude.** Energy from the sun strikes the Equator at a right angle. As latitude (distance north or south of the Equator) increases, the angle becomes increasingly oblique, or slanted. Less energy is received from the sun, and annual average temperatures fall. Therefore, the annual average temperature decreases as latitude increases from Acajutla, El Salvador, to St. Louis, Missouri, to Resolute, Canada.

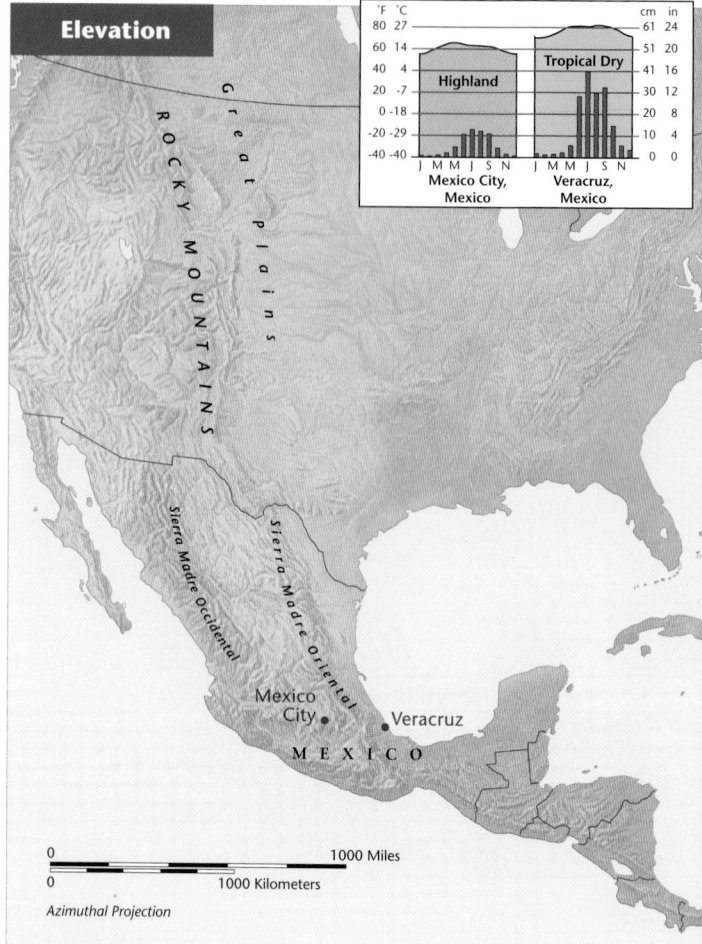

▲ **Elevation.** Not all locations at the same latitude experience similar climates. Air at higher elevations is cooler and holds less moisture than air at lower elevations. This explains why the climate at Veracruz, Mexico, which is near sea level, is warm and wet, and the climate at Mexico City, which is more than 7,000 feet (11,000 m) above sea level, is cooler and drier.

▶ **Landforms.** Air carried by prevailing winds blowing off the ocean is full of moisture. If that air encounters a mountain when it reaches land, it is forced to rise. It becomes cooler, causing precipitation on the windward side of the mountain (see Portland graph). When air descends on the side away from the wind—the leeward side— the air warms and absorbs available moisture. This creates a dry condition known as rain shadow (see Wallowa graph).

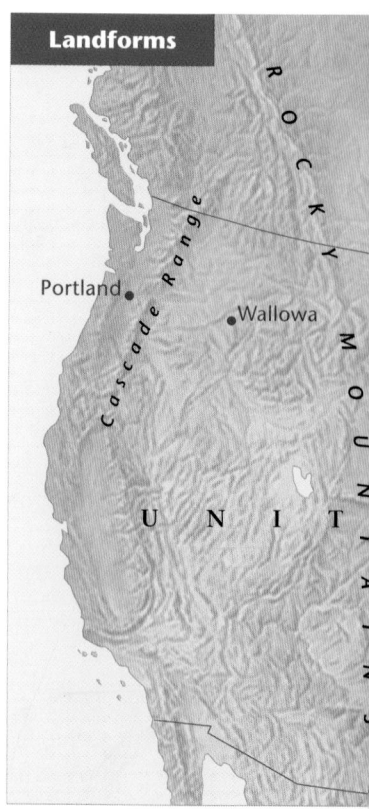

▶ Prevailing Winds and Ocean Currents. *Earth's rotation combined with heat energy from the sun creates patterns of movement in Earth's atmosphere called prevailing winds. In the oceans similar movements of water are called currents. Prevailing winds and ocean currents bring warm and cold temperatures to land areas. They also bring moisture or take it away. The Gulf Stream and the North Atlantic Drift, for example, are warm-water currents that influence average temperatures in eastern North America and northern Europe. Prevailing winds—trade winds, polar easterlies, and westerlies—also affect temperature and precipitation averages.*

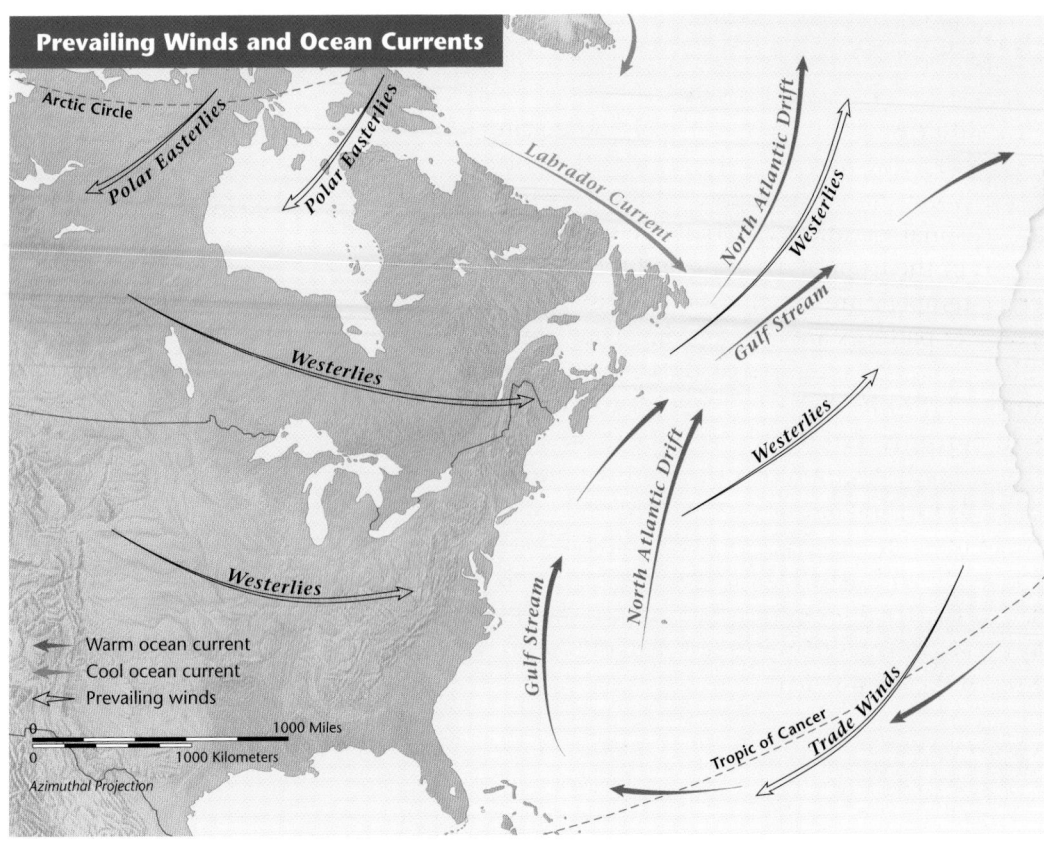

Prevailing Winds and Ocean Currents

→ Warm ocean current
→ Cool ocean current
⇐ Prevailing winds

0 — 1000 Miles
0 — 1000 Kilometers
Azimuthal Projection

▼ Location. *Marine locations—places near large bodies of water—have mild climates with little temperature variation because water gains and loses heat slowly (see San Francisco graph). Interior locations—places far from large water bodies—have much more extreme climates. There are great temperature variations because land gains and loses heat rapidly (see Wichita graph). Richmond, which is relatively near the Atlantic Ocean but which is also influenced by prevailing westerly winds blowing across the land, has moderate characteristics of both conditions.*

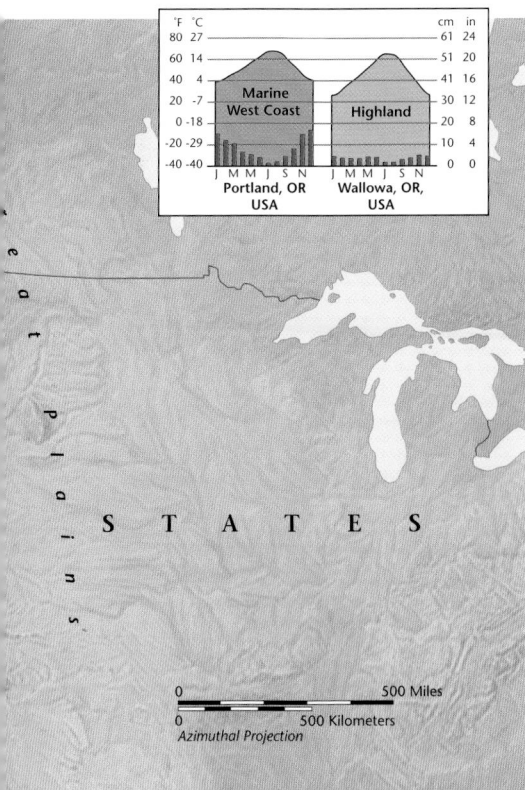

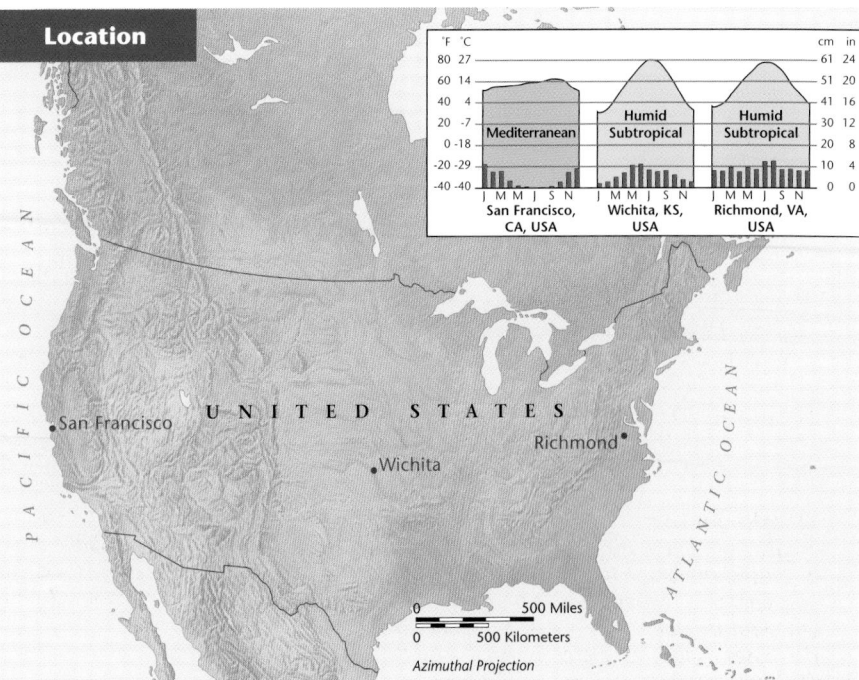

Location

EARTH'S NATURAL VEGETATION

Natural vegetation is the plant life that would be found in an area if it were undisturbed by human activity. Natural vegetation varies widely depending on climate and soil conditions. In the rain forest, trees tower as much as 200 feet (60 m) above the forest floor. In the tundra, dwarf species of shrubs and flowers are adaptations to harsh conditions at high latitudes and high elevations.

Vegetation is important to human life. It provides oxygen, food, fuel, products with economic value, even lifesaving medicines. Human activities, however, have greatly affected natural vegetation. Huge forests have been cut to provide fuel and lumber. Grasslands have yielded to the plow as people extend agricultural lands. As many as one in eight plants may become extinct as a result of human interference. Web Link

▼ **Types of Vegetation.** *Vegetation creates a mosaic of colors and textures across Earth's surface. Grasslands dominate in places where there is too little precipitation to support trees. In the wet conditions of the tropics, rain forests and mangroves flourish. Desert shrubs are adapted to dry climates, and tundra plants survive a short growing season. These photographs show some of the plants found in various vegetation regions. Each is keyed to the map by color and number.*

NORTH AMERICA

ATLANTIC

SOUTH AMERICA

PACIFIC OCEAN

60°N
30°N
TROPIC OF CANCER
EQUATOR
TROPIC OF CAPRICORN
30°S
60°S

150°W 120°W 90°W

| 0 | miles | 2000 |
| 0 | kilometers | 3000 |

Winkel Tripel Projection

▲ Tundra

▲ Northern coniferous forest

▲ Temperate broadleaf forest

▲ Desert shrub

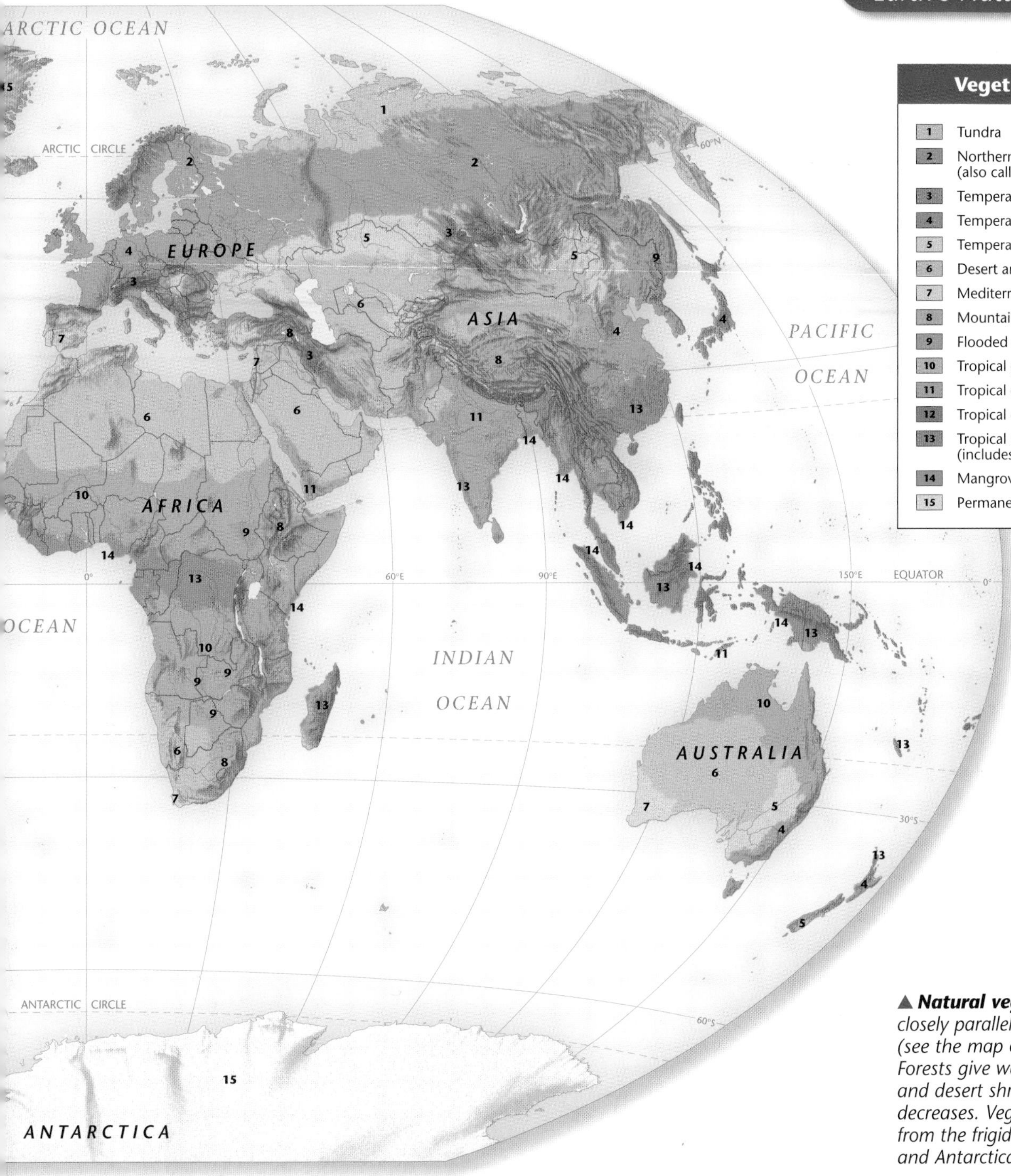

ARCTIC OCEAN

ARCTIC CIRCLE

EUROPE

ASIA

PACIFIC

OCEAN

AFRICA

INDIAN

OCEAN

OCEAN

AUSTRALIA

ANTARCTIC CIRCLE

ANTARCTICA

60°N

60°E

90°E

150°E

EQUATOR

0°

0°

30°S

60°S

Vegetation Zones

1	Tundra
2	Northern coniferous forest (also called boreal forest or taiga)
3	Temperate coniferous forest
4	Temperate broadleaf forest
5	Temperate grassland
6	Desert and dry shrub
7	Mediterranean shrub
8	Mountain grassland
9	Flooded grassland and savanna
10	Tropical grassland and savanna
11	Tropical dry forest
12	Tropical coniferous forest
13	Tropical moist broadleaf (includes rain forest)
14	Mangrove
15	Permanent ice cover

▲ **Natural vegetation** patterns closely parallel patterns of climate (see the map on pages 18–19). Forests give way to grasslands and desert shrubs as precipitation decreases. Vegetation is absent from the frigid ice caps of Greenland and Antarctica.

▲ **Temperate grassland**  ▲ **Tropical grassland**  ▲ **Tropical moist broadleaf**  ▲ **Mangrove**

Human Systems
THE POLITICAL WORLD

A map with the names and boundaries of countries shows the political world. Boundaries—some arrived at peacefully, others after years of conflict and war— carve up the land into 191 independent units, or countries, at the close of the 20th century. Boundaries are dynamic, meaning they change over time as political power shifts. For example, in 1990, West and East Germany became one country, removing a boundary that had separated them since 1949. In 1993 a new boundary divided Czechoslovakia into two separate countries, the Czech Republic and Slovakia.

Countries vary in size. Russia, the largest, stretches across northern Asia into Europe. Other countries are small enough to fit inside another country. For instance, the country of Lesotho, lies entirely within the country of South Africa. Web Link

▶ **The scale of this map** makes it impossible to name all 191 independent countries and their capital cities. For a complete listing, refer to pages 112–119 or use the place-name index and the political maps in each continent section.

▶ **View From the North Pole.** Ocean, not land, surrounds the area of the North Pole, so there are no political boundaries there. The Arctic Ocean, icebound much of the year, is part of the coastal waters of Earth's northernmost countries.

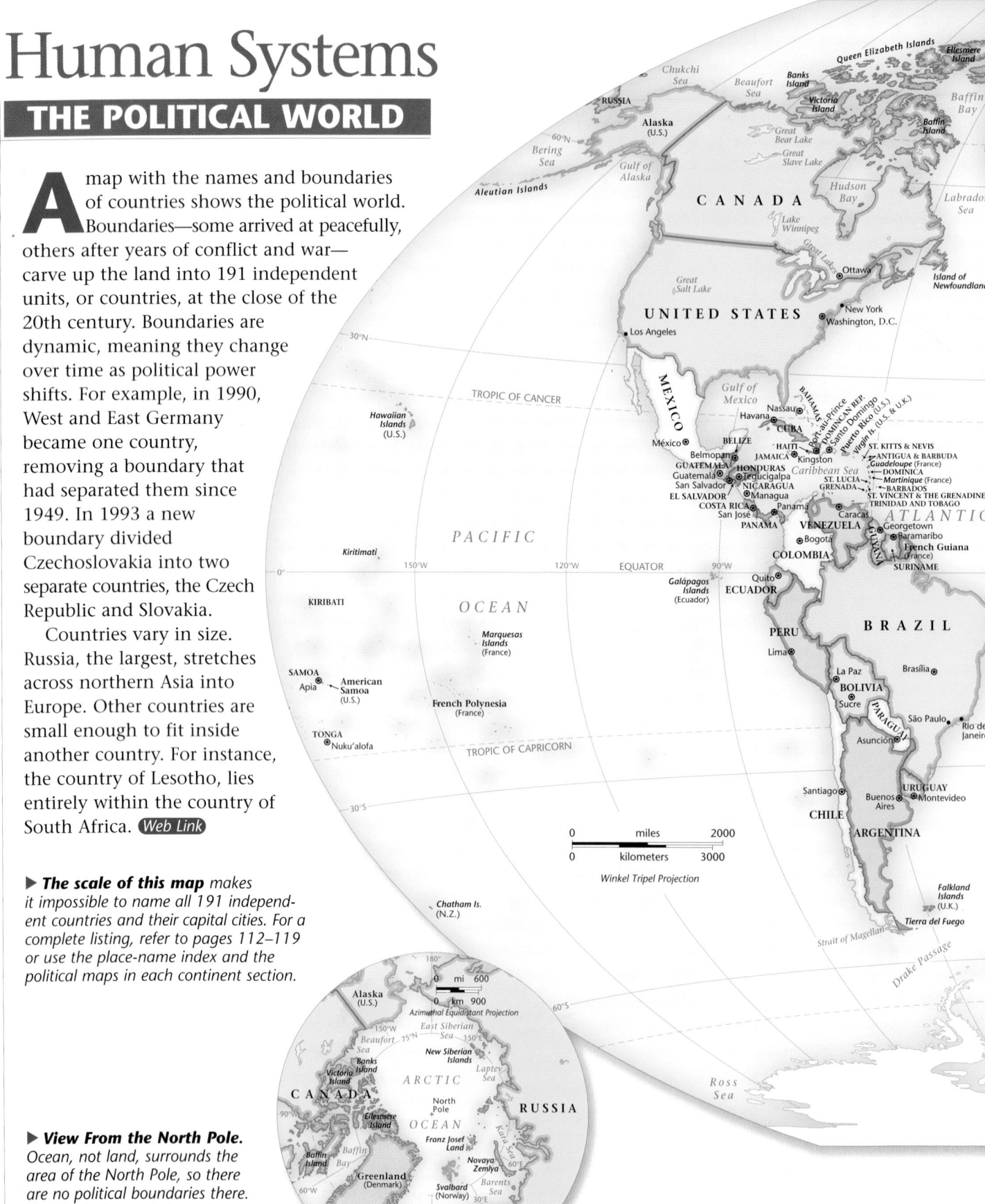

Cities

- ⊛ National capital
- • Urban area with more than 10 million people

The People's Republic of China claims Taiwan as its 23rd province.

▶ **View From the South Pole.** *Covered by ice, the continent of Antarctica has been set aside by treaty for scientific research. It has no permanent population and no political boundaries, although 7 countries claim territory there and 23 operate year-round research stations (see map page 111).*

25 ◀

WORLD POPULATION

Late in 1999 the United Nations announced that Earth's population had surpassed six billion. Although more than 80 million people are added each year, the rate, or annual percent, at which the population is growing is gradually decreasing. Earth's population has very uneven distribution, with huge clusters in Asia and in Europe. Population density, the number of people living in each square mile (or square kilometer) on average, is high in these regions. For example, there are more than 2,000 people per square mile (800 people per sq km)) in Bangladesh. Other areas, such as deserts and Arctic tundra, have less than 2 people per square mile (1 person per sq km). Web Link

▼ *Crowded streets, like this one in Shanghai, may become commonplace as Earth's population continues to increase and as more people move to urban areas.*

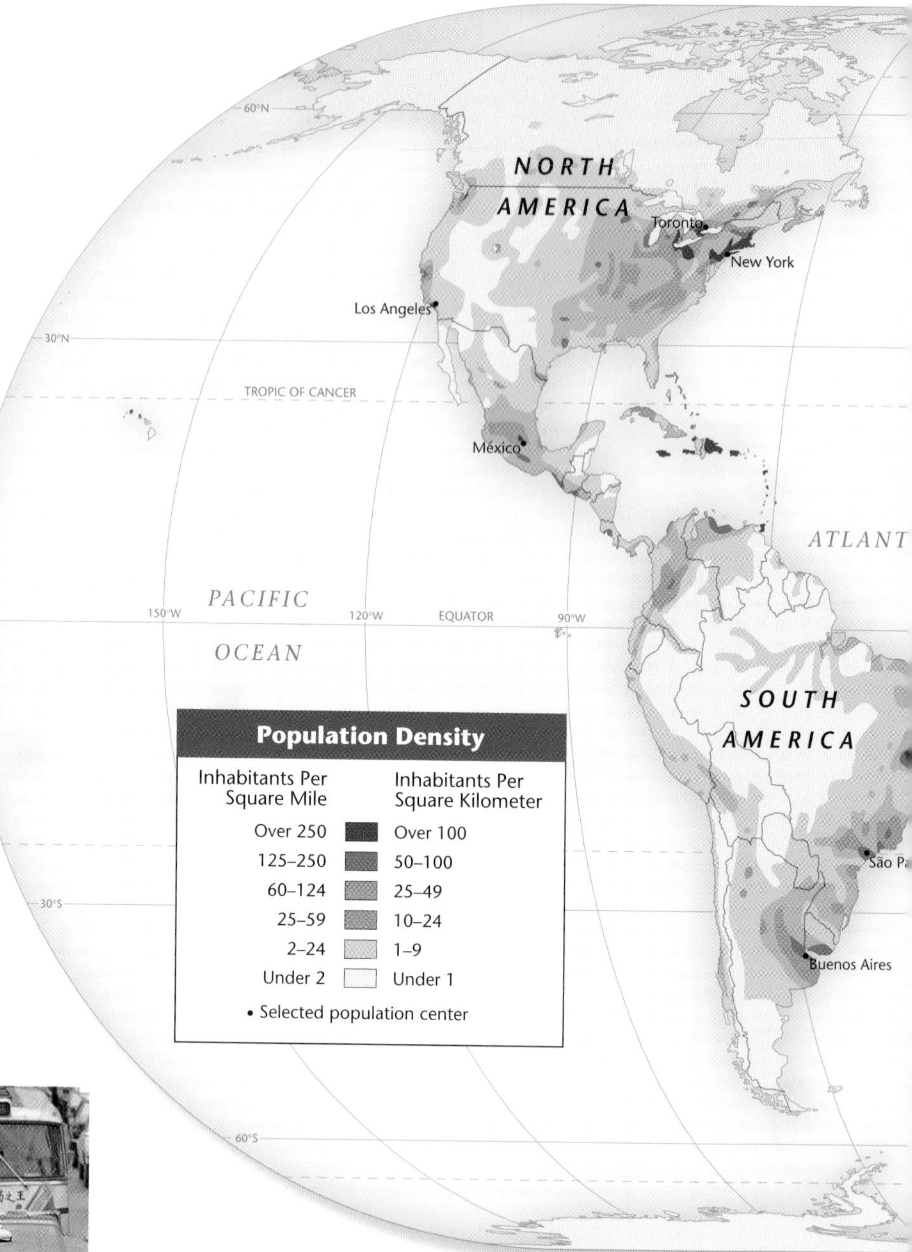

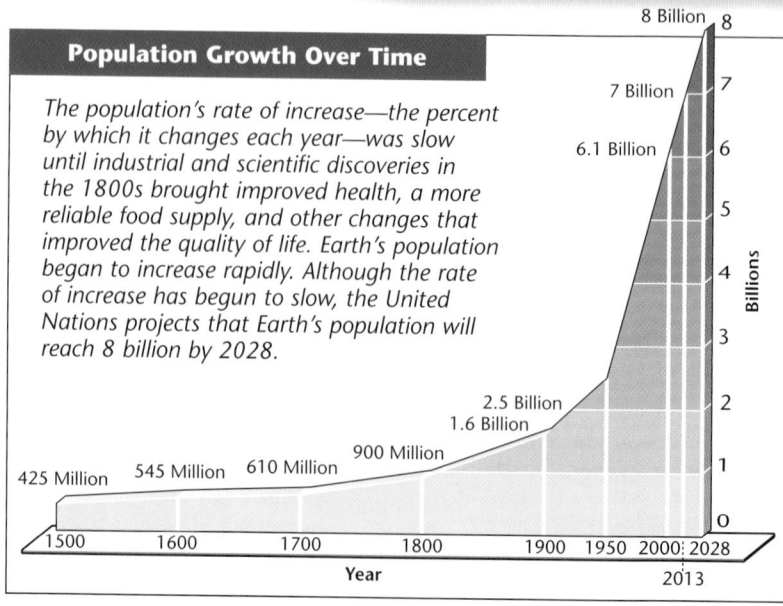

Population Density

Inhabitants Per Square Mile	Inhabitants Per Square Kilometer
Over 250	Over 100
125–250	50–100
60–124	25–49
25–59	10–24
2–24	1–9
Under 2	Under 1

• Selected population center

Population Growth Over Time

The population's rate of increase—the percent by which it changes each year—was slow until industrial and scientific discoveries in the 1800s brought improved health, a more reliable food supply, and other changes that improved the quality of life. Earth's population began to increase rapidly. Although the rate of increase has begun to slow, the United Nations projects that Earth's population will reach 8 billion by 2028.

8 Billion
7 Billion
6.1 Billion
2.5 Billion
1.6 Billion
900 Million
610 Million
545 Million
425 Million

Billions

1500 · 1600 · 1700 · 1800 · 1900 · 1950 · 2000 · 2028
2013

Year

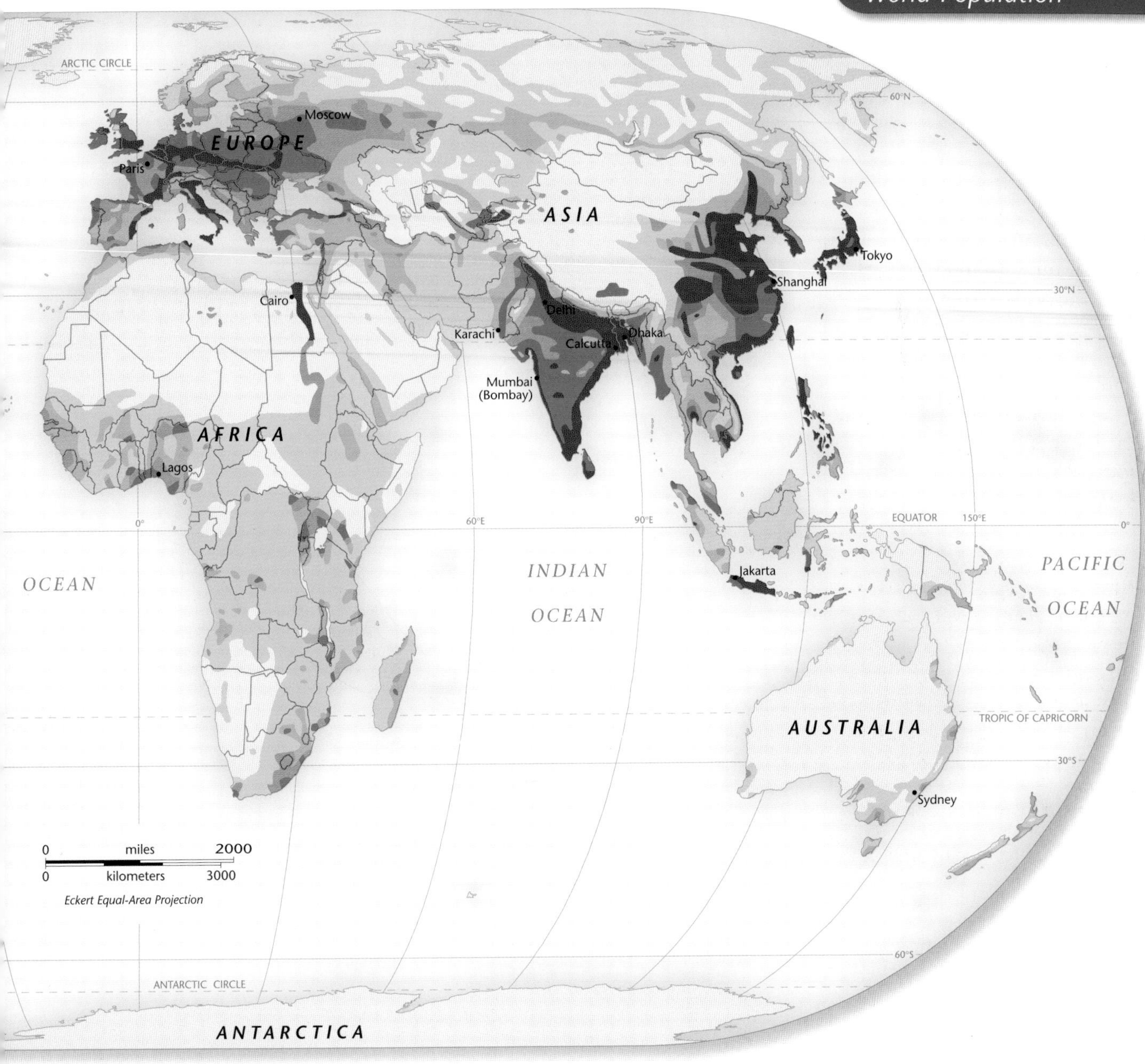

ARCTIC CIRCLE
Moscow
EUROPE
Paris
ASIA
Tokyo
Shanghai
60°N
30°N
Cairo
Karachi
Delhi
Dhaka
Calcutta
Mumbai (Bombay)
AFRICA
Lagos
0°
60°E
90°E
EQUATOR
150°E
OCEAN
INDIAN OCEAN
Jakarta
PACIFIC OCEAN
AUSTRALIA
TROPIC OF CAPRICORN
30°S
Sydney
0 miles 2000
0 kilometers 3000
Eckert Equal-Area Projection
60°S
ANTARCTIC CIRCLE
ANTARCTICA

Three Population Pyramids

A population pyramid is a special type of bar graph that shows the distribution of a country's population by sex and age. Italy has a very narrow pyramid, which shows that most people are in middle age. Its population is said to be aging, meaning the median age is increasing. The United States also has a narrow pyramid, but one that shows some growth due to a median age of about 35 years and a young immigrant population. By contrast, Côte d'Ivoire's pyramid has a broad base, showing it has a young population. Almost half its people are younger than 15 years.

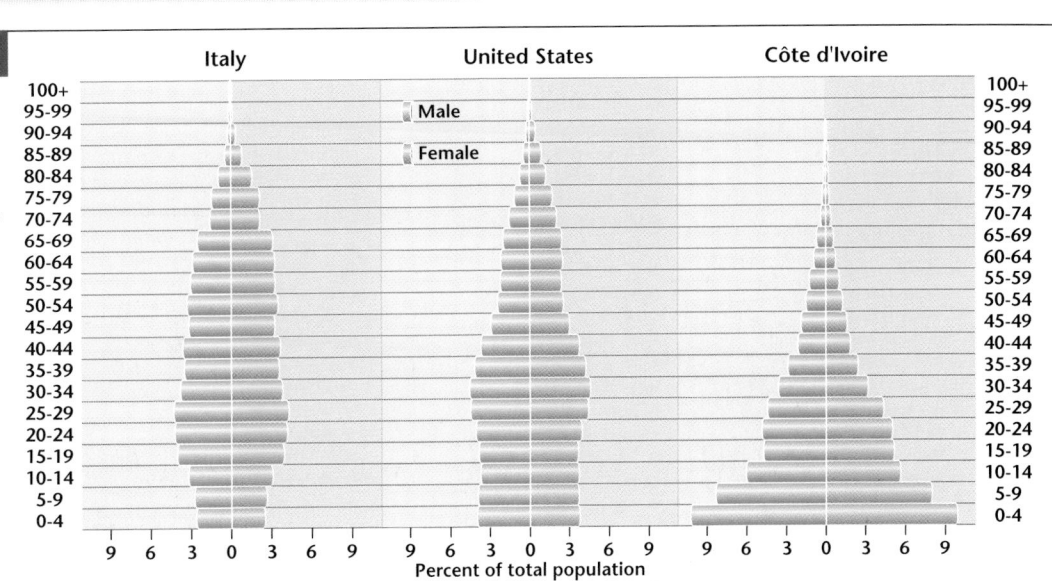

Italy
United States
Côte d'Ivoire
Male
Female
100+
95-99
90-94
85-89
80-84
75-79
70-74
65-69
60-64
55-59
50-54
45-49
40-44
35-39
30-34
25-29
20-24
15-19
10-14
5-9
0-4
9 6 3 0 3 6 9
Percent of total population

WORLD CITIES

Throughout most of history, people have lived spread across the land, first as hunters and gatherers, later as farmers. But urban geographers—people who study cities—predict that sometime in the next decade more people will be living in urban areas than in rural areas. Urban areas include one or more cities and their surrounding suburbs. People living there are employed primarily in industry or in service-related jobs. Large urban areas are sometimes called metropolitan areas. In some countries, such as Belgium, almost all the population lives in cities. But throughout much of Africa south of the Sahara, less than one-third of the people live in urban areas. Even so, the world's fastest growing urban areas are in Africa and Asia, as shown in the graph below.

Web Link

Most Populous Urban Areas

In 1950 New York topped a list of only 8 cities with populations of 5 million or greater. Just 50 years later, New York ranked fifth in a list of 41 cities with populations exceeding 5 million. By 2015, the list is projected to include 59 cities.

Cities with populations greater than five million for the years:

- 1950
- 2000
- 2015

North America 1, 4, 6
South America 1, 6, 7
Europe 4, 5, 5
Africa 0, 3, 6
Asia 2, 23, 35
Australia/Oceania 0, 0, 0

NORTH AMERICA

Toronto
Chicago
New York
Los Angeles

TROPIC OF CANCER

México
Guatemala City

ATLANTIC

Bogotá

PACIFIC OCEAN

EQUATOR

SOUTH AMERICA

Lima

Belo Horizonte
Rio de Janeiro
São Paulo

Santiago
Buenos Aires

| 0 | miles | 2000 |
| 0 | kilometers | 3000 |

Winkel Tripel Projection

Urban and Rural Populations

These graphs show the percentages of people living in urban and rural areas in various world regions. Only Asia and Africa are predominantly rural, although both are experiencing rapid urban growth. Asia, which had only 2 cities of five million or more people in 1950, now has 23.

United States & Canada

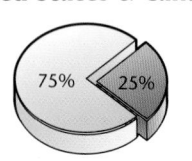

75% / 25%

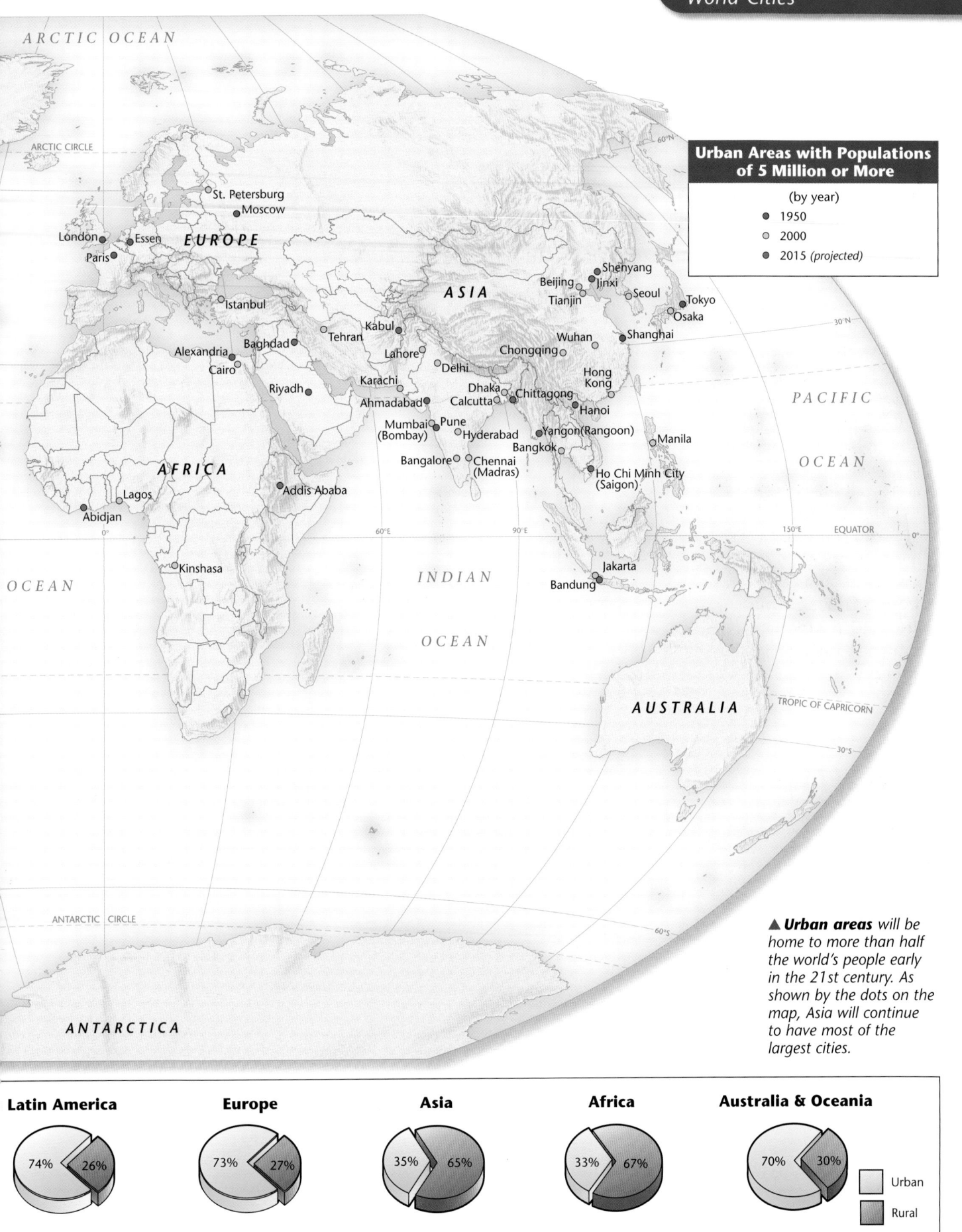

Urban Areas with Populations of 5 Million or More

(by year)
- 1950
- 2000
- 2015 (projected)

ARCTIC OCEAN

ARCTIC CIRCLE

St. Petersburg
Moscow
London
Essen
Paris
EUROPE
Istanbul
Kabul
Tehran
Baghdad
Alexandria
Cairo
Riyadh
Karachi
Ahmadabad
Lahore
Delhi
Mumbai (Bombay)
Pune
Hyderabad
Bangalore
Chennai (Madras)
Dhaka
Calcutta
Chittagong
ASIA
Shenyang
Beijing
Jinxi
Tianjin
Seoul
Tokyo
Osaka
Wuhan
Shanghai
Chongqing
Hong Kong
Hanoi
Yangon (Rangoon)
Bangkok
Ho Chi Minh City (Saigon)
Manila
Lagos
Abidjan
AFRICA
Addis Ababa
Kinshasa
OCEAN
INDIAN
OCEAN
Jakarta
Bandung
PACIFIC
OCEAN
60°N
30°N
150°E
EQUATOR
0°
60°E
90°E
0°E
AUSTRALIA
TROPIC OF CAPRICORN
30°S
60°S
ANTARCTIC CIRCLE
ANTARCTICA

▲ **Urban areas** will be home to more than half the world's people early in the 21st century. As shown by the dots on the map, Asia will continue to have most of the largest cities.

Latin America	Europe	Asia	Africa	Australia & Oceania
74% / 26%	73% / 27%	35% / 65%	33% / 67%	70% / 30%

Urban
Rural

WORLD CULTURES

Culture is all the shared things that define the way a people live—customs and symbols, food and clothing preferences, housing styles, systems of government, music and art forms, language and belief systems. Tracing the diffusion, or movement, of culture traits, or characteristics, is one way that geographers understand how places are connected.

For example, English originated in western Europe, but its widespread use today reflects the far-reaching effects of 19th-century colonial empires. About 6,000 languages are spoken in the world today, many of which will probably become extinct as global trade, communications, and travel blur distinctions among cultures.

Some religions also have spread far from their areas of origin—Islam and Christianity from southwestern Asia and Buddhism from southern Asia.

Web Link

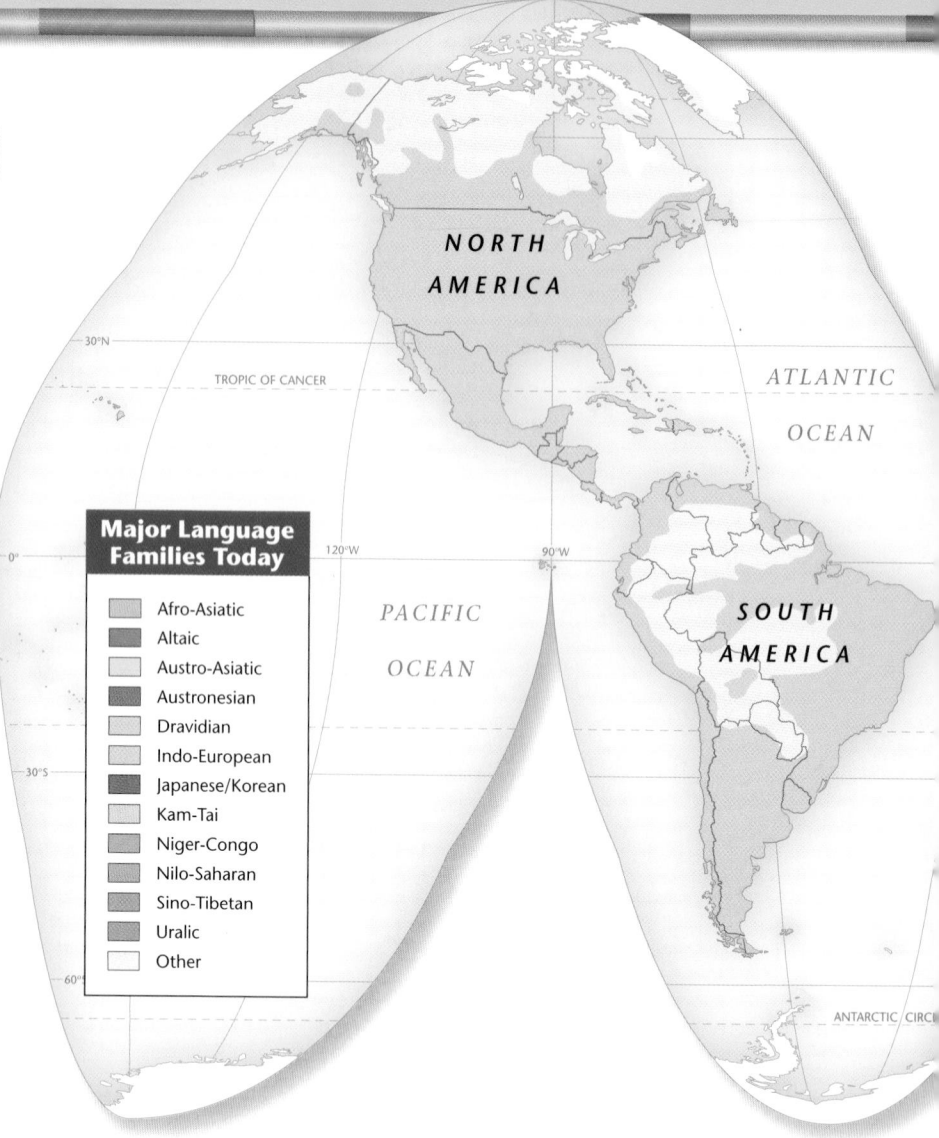

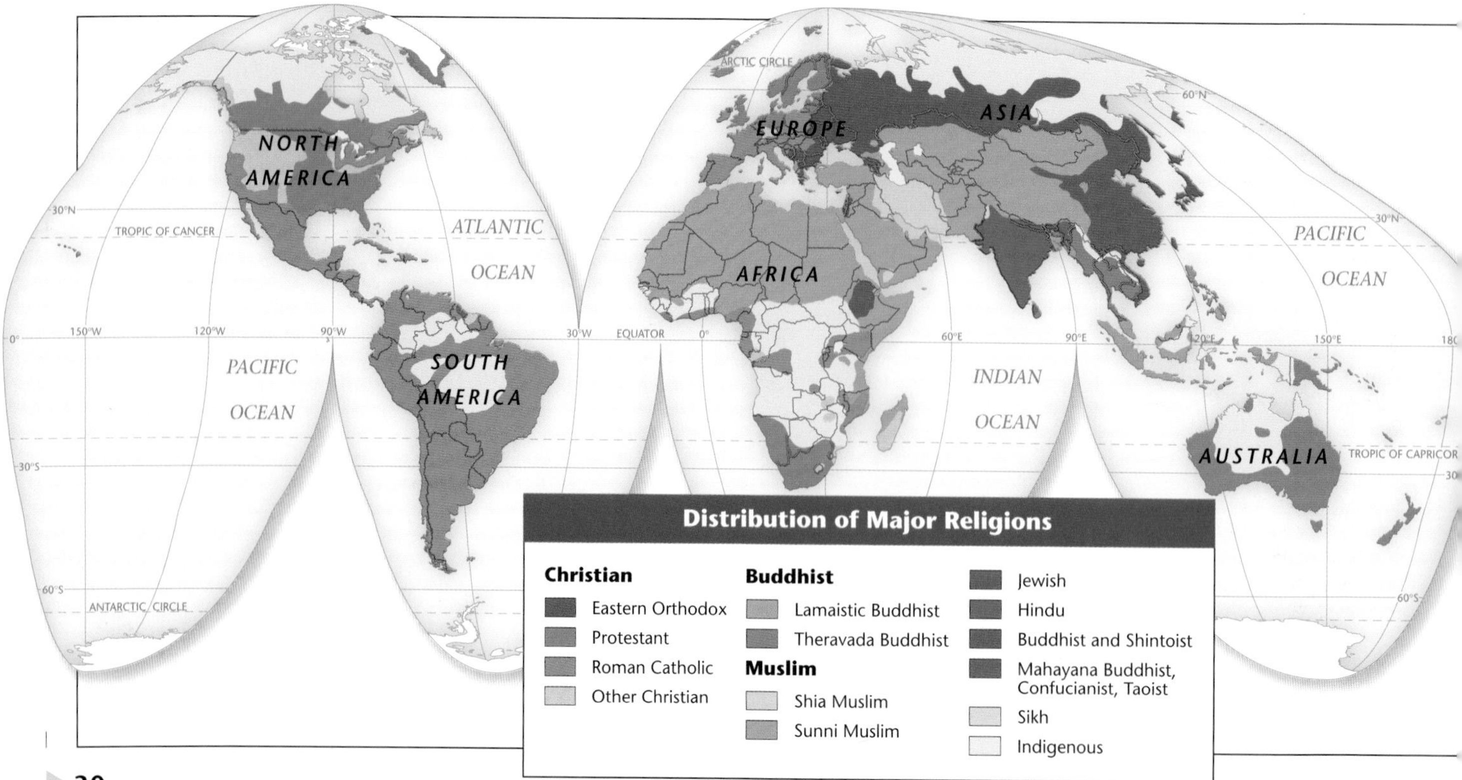

Major Language Families Today
Afro-Asiatic
Altaic
Austro-Asiatic
Austronesian
Dravidian
Indo-European
Japanese/Korean
Kam-Tai
Niger-Congo
Nilo-Saharan
Sino-Tibetan
Uralic
Other
NORTH AMERICA
SOUTH AMERICA
ATLANTIC OCEAN
PACIFIC OCEAN
TROPIC OF CANCER
ANTARCTIC CIRCLE
30°N
0°
30°S
60°
120°W
90°W

Distribution of Major Religions
Christian
Eastern Orthodox
Protestant
Roman Catholic
Other Christian
Buddhist
Lamaistic Buddhist
Theravada Buddhist
Muslim
Shia Muslim
Sunni Muslim
Jewish
Hindu
Buddhist and Shintoist
Mahayana Buddhist, Confucianist, Taoist
Sikh
Indigenous
NORTH AMERICA
SOUTH AMERICA
EUROPE
ASIA
AFRICA
AUSTRALIA
ATLANTIC OCEAN
PACIFIC OCEAN
INDIAN OCEAN
ARCTIC CIRCLE
TROPIC OF CANCER
TROPIC OF CAPRICORN
ANTARCTIC CIRCLE
EQUATOR
30°N
0°
30°S
60°S
60°N
150°W
120°W
90°W
30°W
60°E
90°E
120°E
150°E

ASIA

EUROPE

AFRICA

PACIFIC OCEAN

INDIAN OCEAN

AUSTRALIA

ANTARCTICA

ARCTIC CIRCLE

60°N

30°N

60°E · 90°E · 150°E · EQUATOR · 180°

TROPIC OF CAPRICORN

30°S

60°S

0 miles 2000
0 kilometers 3000
Goode Homolosine Projection

Most Commonly Spoken Languages

Of the most commonly spoken languages, only Mandarin and Japanese don't belong to the Indo-European language family.

Population (in millions)

Language	Population
Chinese (Mandarin)	885
English	322
Spanish	266
Hindi	189
Portuguese	182
Russian	170
Bengali	170
Japanese	125
German	98

Languages

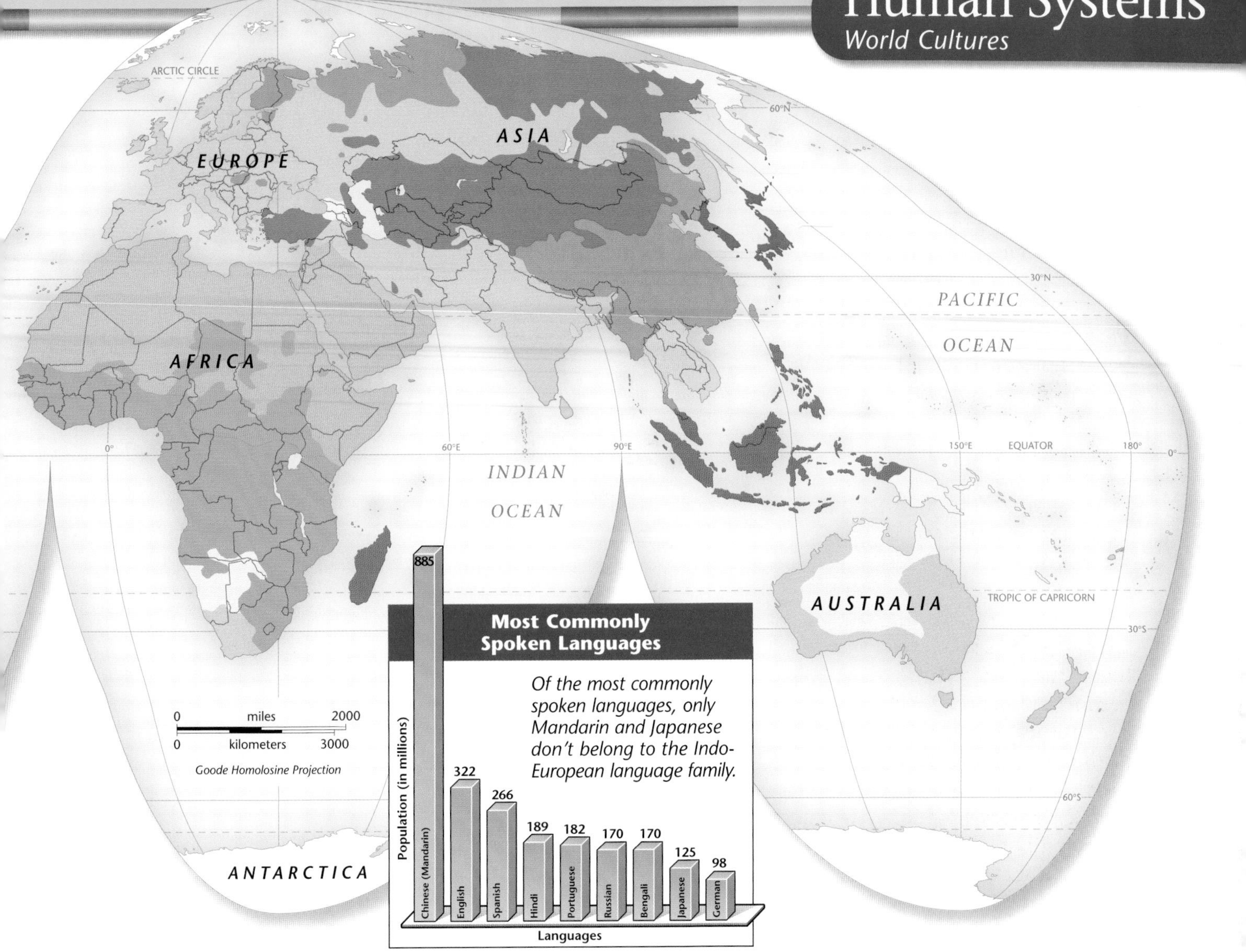

▶ **Distinct cultures** emerged in isolation thousands of years ago in different parts of the world. Places where unique cultures evolved, such as Mesopotamia in southwestern Asia and Mesoamerica in present-day Mexico and Guatemala, are called culture hearths. As populations grew and people traveled farther afield, culture traits were spread and shared. Revolutions in transportation and communication have greatly accelerated this process.

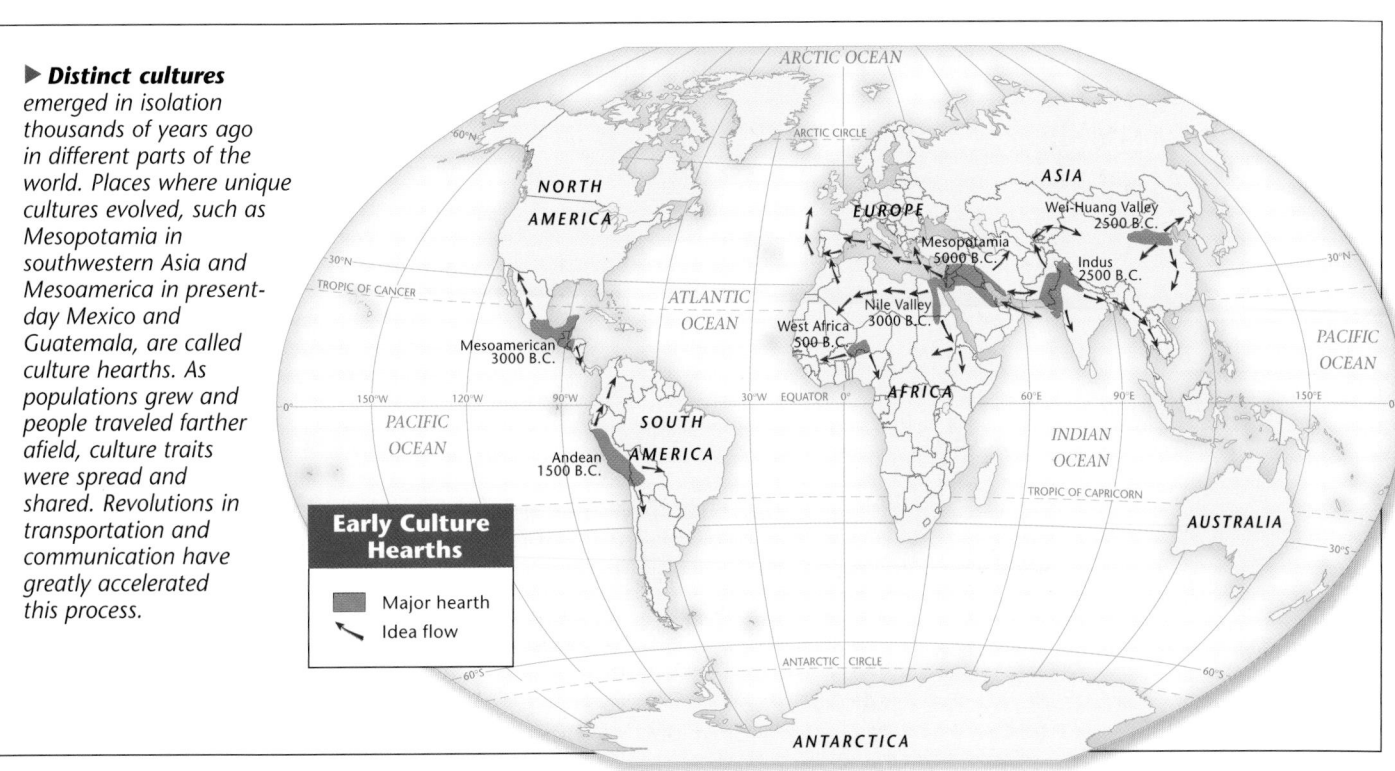

ARCTIC OCEAN

ARCTIC CIRCLE

NORTH AMERICA

EUROPE

ASIA

Wel-Huang Valley 2500 B.C.

Mesopotamia 5000 B.C.

Indus 2500 B.C.

Nile Valley 3000 B.C.

West Africa 500 B.C.

Mesoamerican 3000 B.C.

Andean 1500 B.C.

SOUTH AMERICA

AFRICA

ATLANTIC OCEAN

PACIFIC OCEAN

INDIAN OCEAN

PACIFIC OCEAN

AUSTRALIA

60°N · 30°N · TROPIC OF CANCER · EQUATOR · TROPIC OF CAPRICORN · 30°S · 60°S

150°W · 120°W · 90°W · 30°W · 0° · 60°E · 90°E · 150°E

ANTARCTIC CIRCLE

ANTARCTICA

Early Culture Hearths

- ■ Major hearth
- ↖ Idea flow

PREDOMINANT WORLD ECONOMIES

Economic activities are the many different ways that people create products and generate income to meet their needs and wants. Long ago most people lived by hunting and gathering. Today, most engage in a variety of other activities that are commonly grouped into the following categories. Primary activities: agriculture, fishing, forestry; secondary activities: manufacturing and processing industries; tertiary activities: services, such as finance, medicine, education; and quaternary activities: information exchange and e-commerce—buying and selling over the Internet. The more developed economies of the world have shifted from secondary activities toward tertiary and quaternary activities. Less developed economies continue to rely on primary activities. *Web Link*

Predominant Economy

- Selected population center
- Agriculture
- Agriculture and forestry
- Fishing
- Forestry (lumber and pulpwood)
- Hunting, fishing and forestry
- Subsistence agriculture
- Little or no economic activity
- Manufacturing
- Nomadic herding
- Stock raising on ranges

▲ **Subsistence Agriculture.** *Many people in developing countries, such as these farmers in Peru, use traditional methods to grow crops for their daily food requirements rather than for commercial sale.*

▶ **Fishing.** *Tuna is one of the chief commercial fishes as well as a favorite among big game fishermen. Japan is the world's leading harvester of tuna. Albacore, shown here, is one of the top commercial varieties.*

◀ **Logging.** *Workers ready logs to float down the Columbia River in Washington State. Processing plants will turn the logs into paper products or cut them into lumber for the construction industry.*

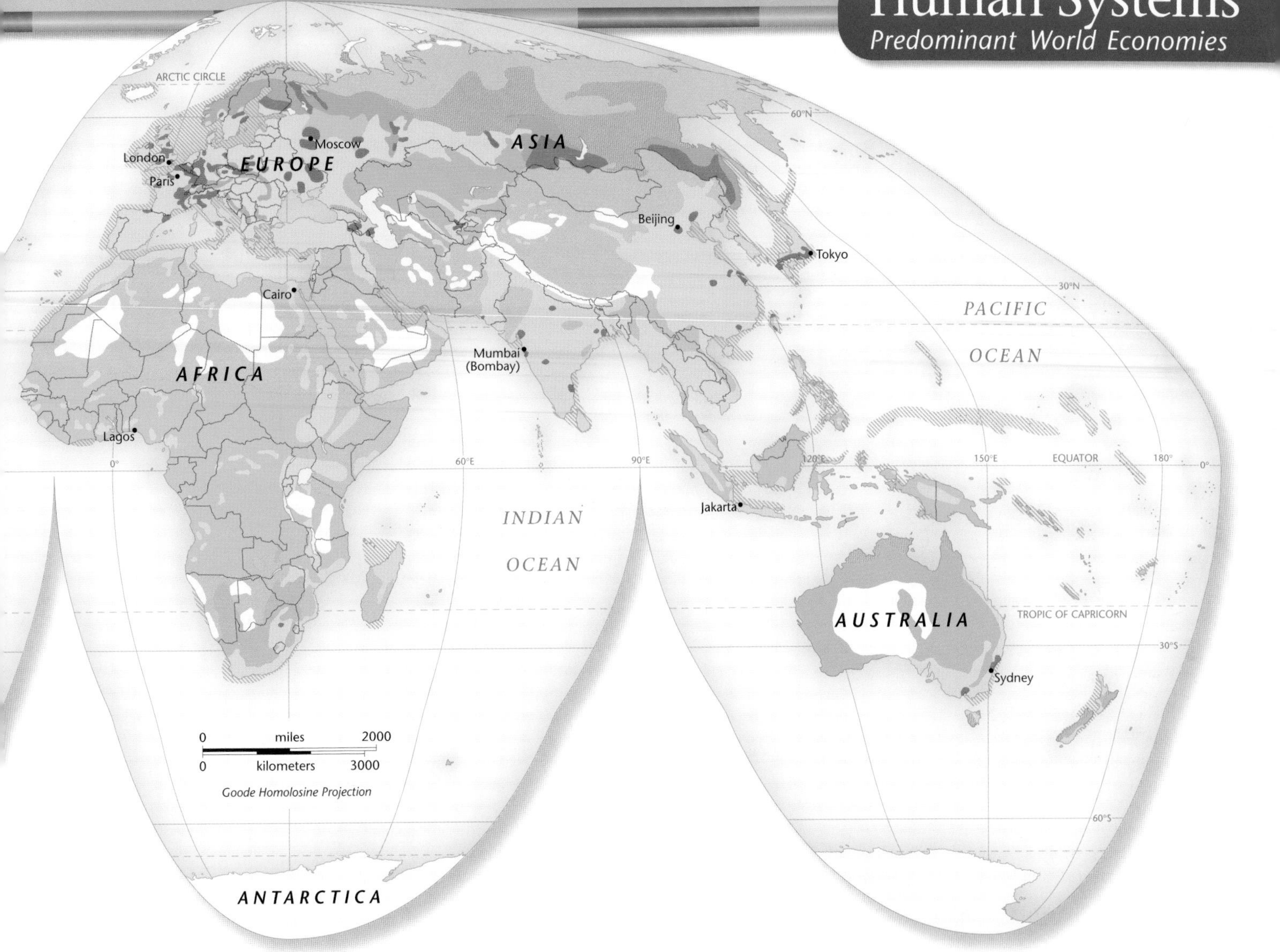

ARCTIC CIRCLE
60°N
London
Paris
Moscow
EUROPE
ASIA
Beijing
Tokyo
Cairo
30°N
PACIFIC
OCEAN
Mumbai
(Bombay)
AFRICA
Lagos
0°
60°E
90°E
120°E
150°E
EQUATOR
180°
Jakarta
INDIAN
OCEAN
AUSTRALIA
TROPIC OF CAPRICORN
30°S
Sydney
0 miles 2000
0 kilometers 3000
Goode Homolosine Projection
60°S
ANTARCTICA

▶ ***Education and Communications.*** *These services combine to allow students to interact with scientists working in the field. Here students explore the underwater ecology of California's Monterey Bay as part of renowned ocean explorer Robert Ballard's JASON Project.*

NATIONAL GEOGRAPHIC SOCIETY

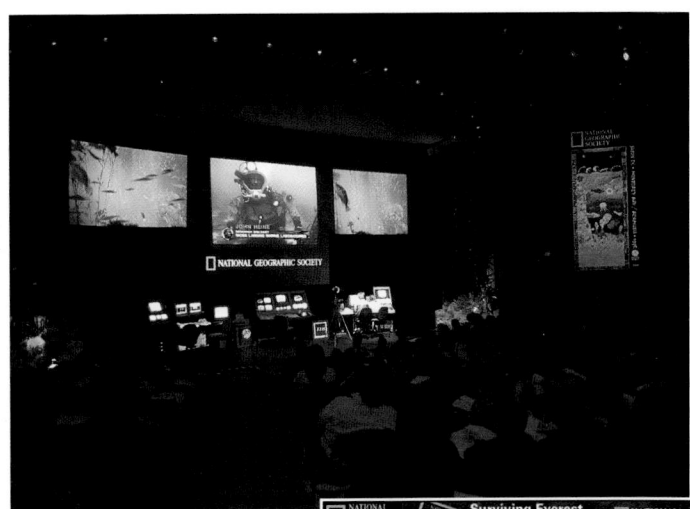

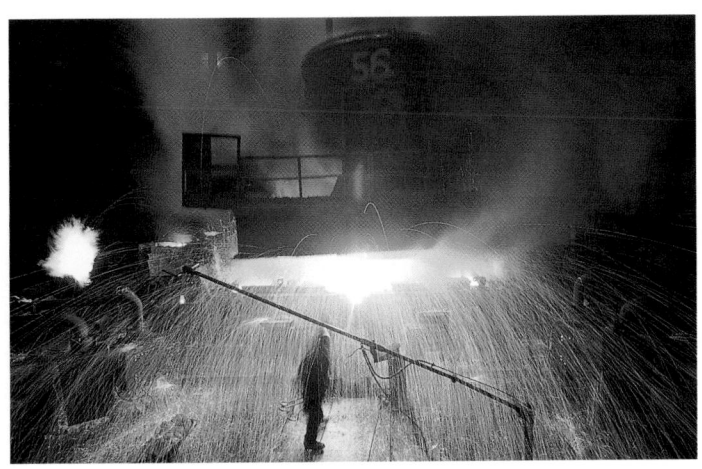

▲ ***Manufacturing.*** *This mill in Slovakia processes raw materials—coal and iron ore—to make steel, which in turn is used by other industries to produce cars, machinery, and other kinds of manufactured goods.*

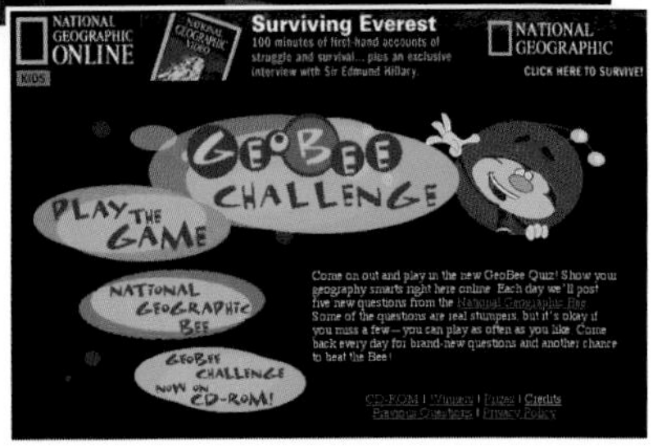

NATIONAL GEOGRAPHIC ONLINE
Surviving Everest
NATIONAL GEOGRAPHIC
CLICK HERE TO SURVIVE!
GEOBEE CHALLENGE
PLAY THE GAME

▶ ***The Internet.*** *This has opened a whole new way of exchanging information. E-mail connects people in places near and far, while e-commerce allows them to buy and sell products without ever leaving home.*

WORLD FOOD

As the 20th century drew to a close, the world's population surpassed six billion—six billion hungry mouths to feed. Productive cropland, though, like other natural resources, is unevenly distributed. In addition, access to modern farming methods and technology varies from country to country. Some countries produce large surpluses; others struggle to feed their populations. Grains such as rice, corn, and wheat provide 80 percent of the world's food energy supply.

Web Link

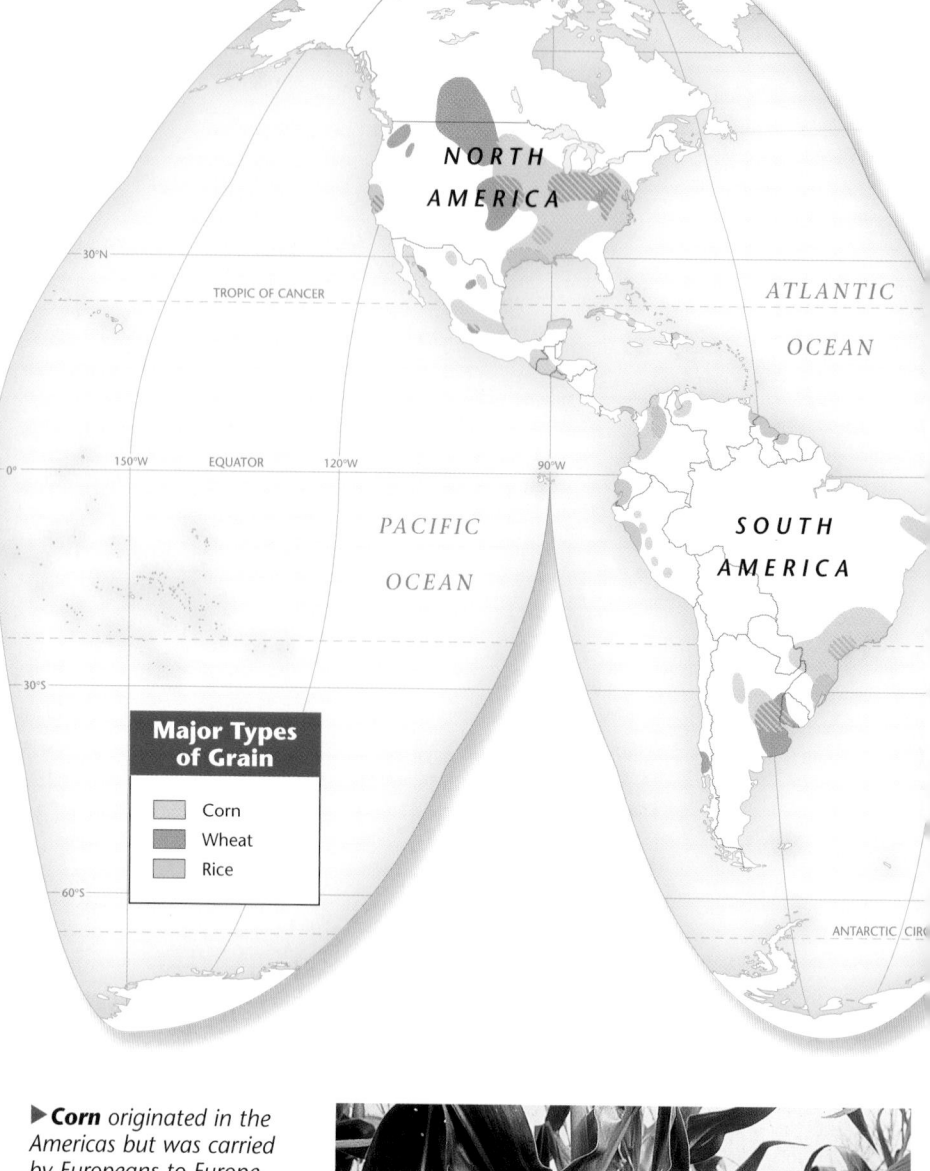

NORTH AMERICA

ATLANTIC OCEAN

TROPIC OF CANCER

30°N

150°W   EQUATOR   120°W   90°W

0°

PACIFIC OCEAN

SOUTH AMERICA

30°S

60°S

ANTARCTIC CIRC

Major Types of Grain

- Corn
- Wheat
- Rice

▶ **Corn** originated in the Americas but was carried by Europeans to Europe, Asia, and Africa. Corn is an important food grain for both people and livestock.

▲ **Rice** is an important staple food crop, especially in eastern and southern Asia. Although China produces about one-third of the world's rice, it is also a major importer of rice to feed its population of more than a billion people.

◀ **Wheat** is the world's leading export grain. It is a main ingredient in bread and pasta and is grown on every inhabited continent. Each year trade in this grain exceeds 100 million tons.

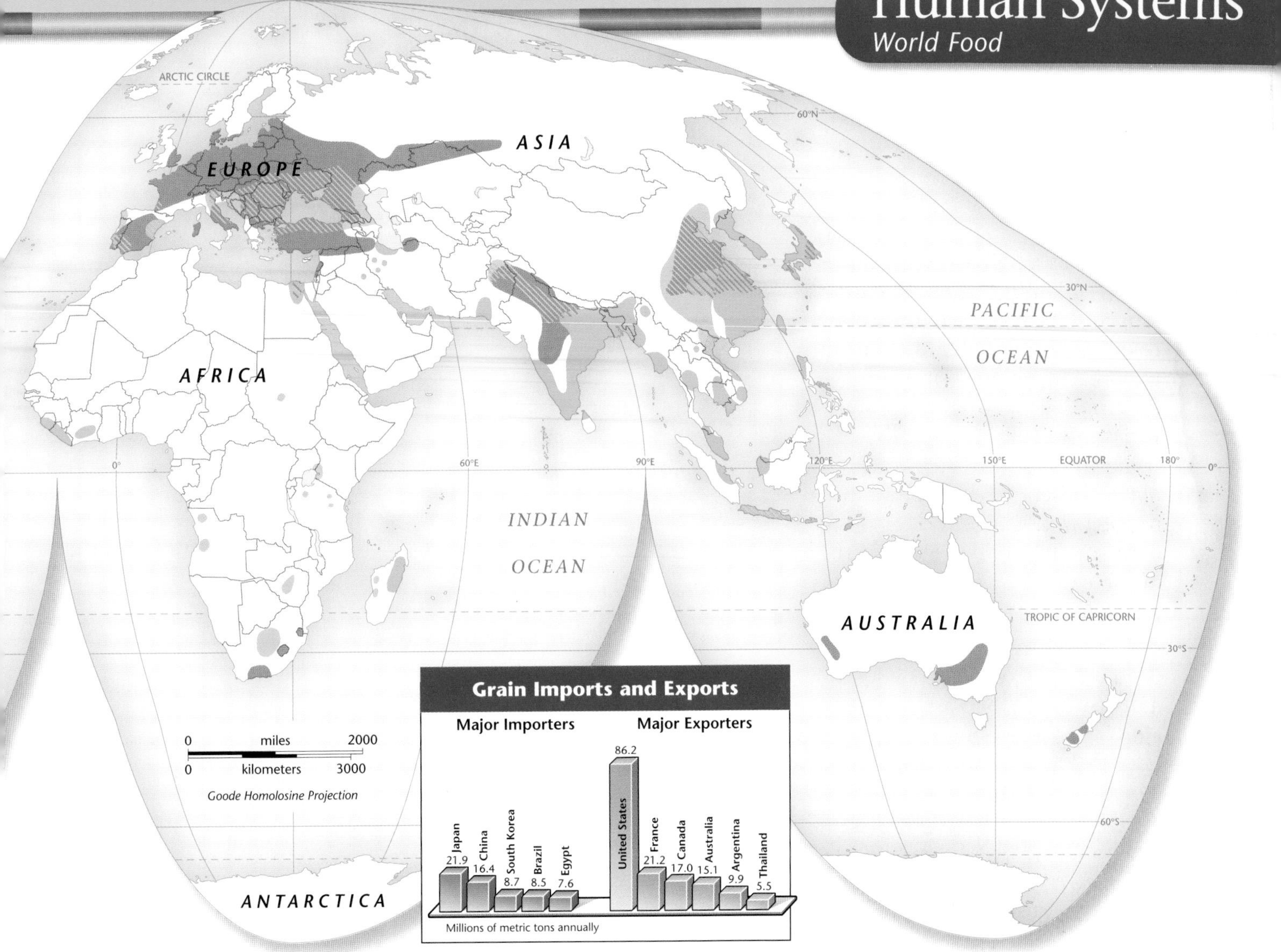

ASIA

EUROPE

AFRICA

60°N

PACIFIC

OCEAN

30°N

0°

60°E

90°E

120°E

150°E

EQUATOR

180°

0°

INDIAN

OCEAN

AUSTRALIA

TROPIC OF CAPRICORN

30°S

0   miles   2000

0   kilometers   3000

Goode Homolosine Projection

ANTARCTICA

60°S

Grain Imports and Exports

Major Importers   **Major Exporters**

86.2

Japan 21.9
China 16.4
South Korea 8.7
Brazil 8.5
Egypt 7.6

United States 86.2
France 21.2
Canada 17.0
Australia 15.1
Argentina 9.9
Thailand 5.5

Millions of metric tons annually

▶ **The demand for food**
becomes greater as the world's population increases. Farmers apply fertilizers to cropland to increase yields so they can meet the demand.

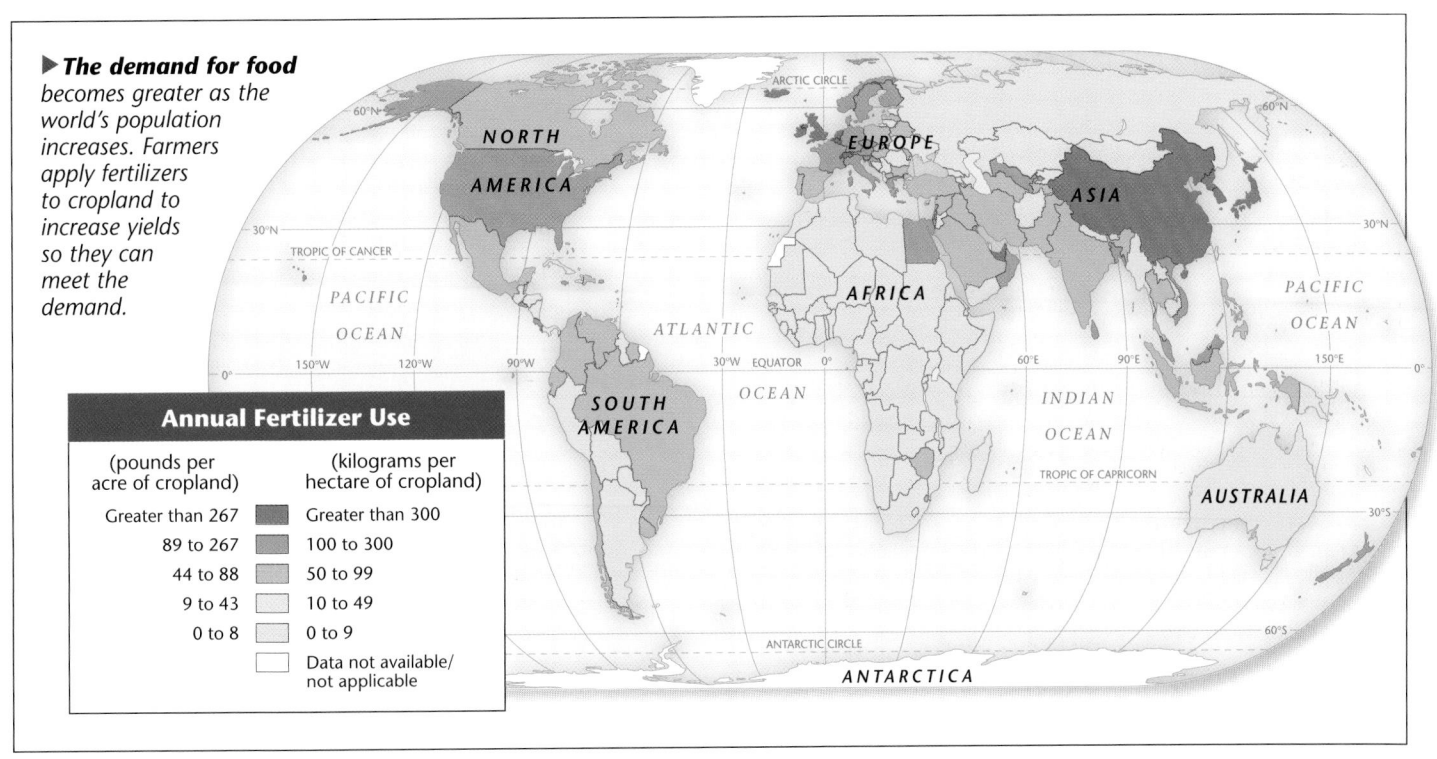

ARCTIC CIRCLE

60°N

60°N

NORTH
AMERICA

EUROPE

ASIA

30°N

TROPIC OF CANCER

AFRICA

PACIFIC
OCEAN

ATLANTIC

PACIFIC
OCEAN

150°W

120°W

90°W

OCEAN

30°W

EQUATOR

0°

60°E

90°E

150°E

0°

SOUTH
AMERICA

INDIAN
OCEAN

TROPIC OF CAPRICORN

AUSTRALIA

30°S

Annual Fertilizer Use

(pounds per acre of cropland)	(kilograms per hectare of cropland)
Greater than 267	Greater than 300
89 to 267	100 to 300
44 to 88	50 to 99
9 to 43	10 to 49
0 to 8	0 to 9
	Data not available/ not applicable

ANTARCTIC CIRCLE

60°S

ANTARCTICA

WORLD WATER

Water is essential for life and is one of Earth's most valuable natural resources. It is even more important than food. More than 70 percent of Earth's surface is covered with water, but most of it—about 97 percent—is salty. Without treatment it is not usable for drinking or growing crops. The remaining 3 percent is fresh, but most of this is either trapped in glaciers or ice caps or lies too deep underground to be tapped economically.

Water is a renewable resource. We can use it over and over because the hydrologic, or water, cycle purifies water as it moves through the processes of evaporation, condensation, precipitation, runoff, and infiltration. But careless use can diminish the supply of usable fresh water. Water may become polluted as a result of runoff from industries, cultivated fields, and urban areas. In addition, water, like other natural resources, is unevenly distributed on Earth. Some countries have an abundance of water while others face serious water shortages, especially in parts of Asia and Africa. Web Link

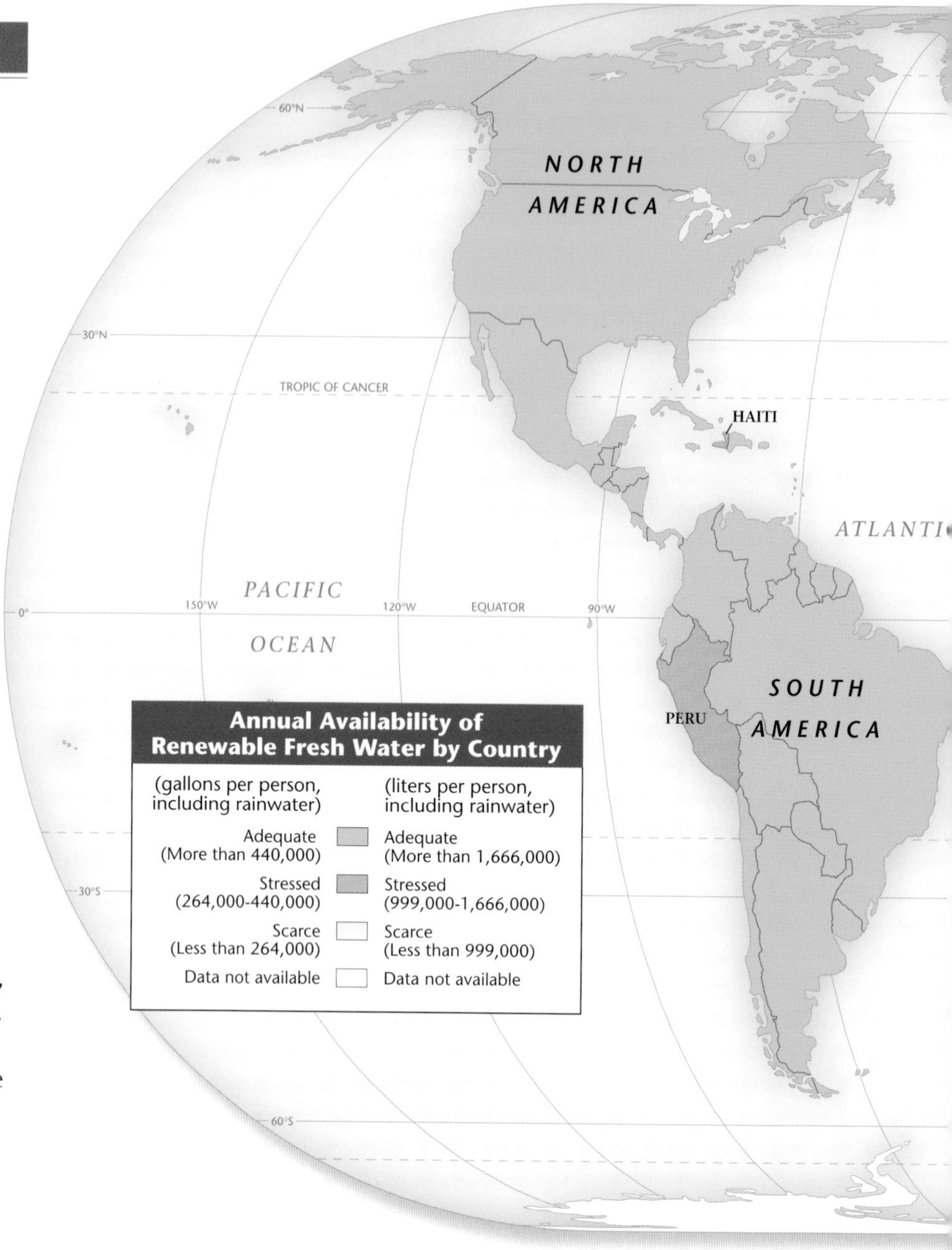

NORTH AMERICA
SOUTH AMERICA
HAITI
PERU
PACIFIC OCEAN
ATLANTI
60°N
30°N
TROPIC OF CANCER
0°
150°W
120°W
EQUATOR
90°W
30°S
60°S
Annual Availability of Renewable Fresh Water by Country
(gallons per person, including rainwater)
(liters per person, including rainwater)
Adequate (More than 440,000)
Adequate (More than 1,666,000)
Stressed (264,000-440,000)
Stressed (999,000-1,666,000)
Scarce (Less than 264,000)
Scarce (Less than 999,000)
Data not available
Data not available

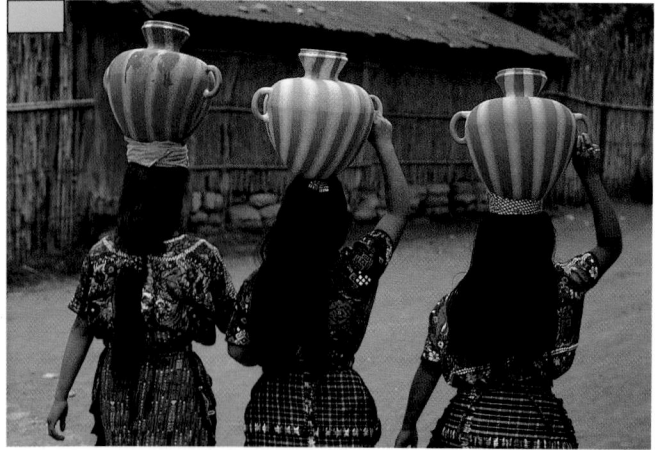

▲ ***Domestic Water Use.*** *In much of the less developed world, people haul water daily for household use, as in this village in Central America.*

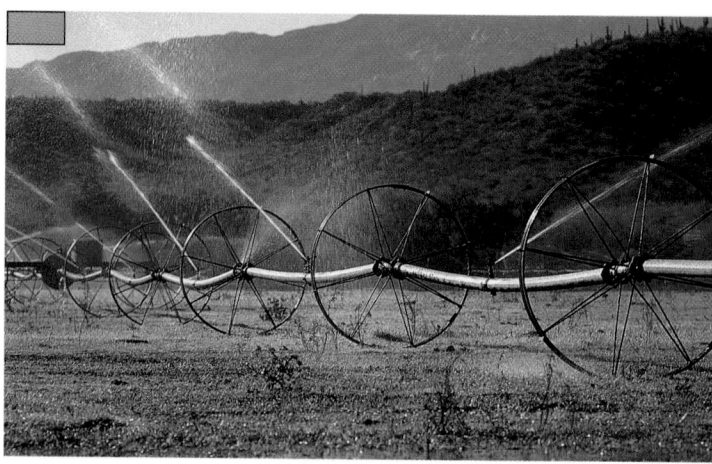

▲ ***Agricultural Water Use.*** *Irrigation has made agriculture possible in dry areas such as the San Pedro Valley in Arizona, shown here.*

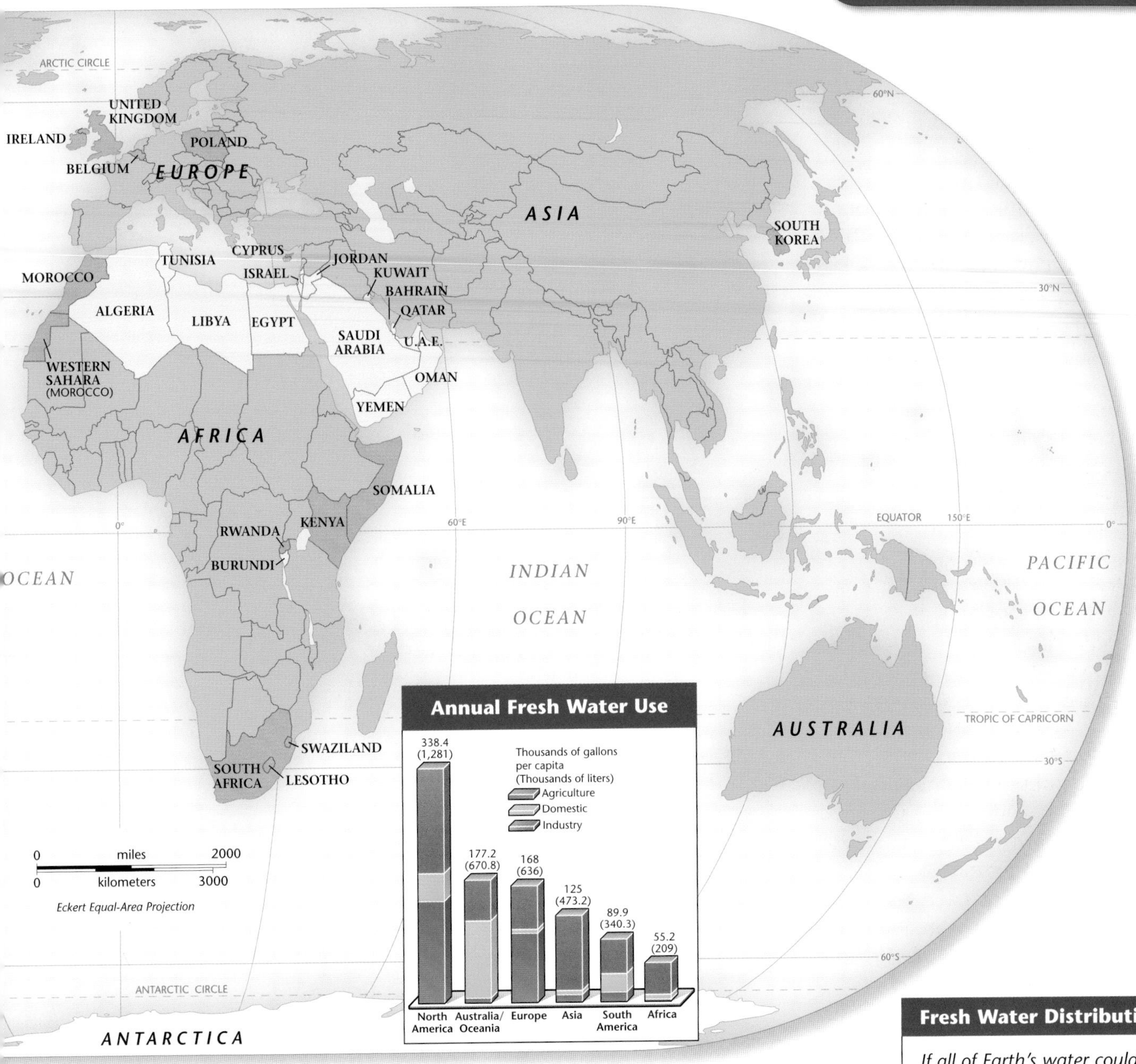

Map labels:

ARCTIC CIRCLE

IRELAND
UNITED KINGDOM
BELGIUM
POLAND
EUROPE
60°N

ASIA

SOUTH KOREA

MOROCCO
TUNISIA
CYPRUS
ISRAEL
JORDAN
KUWAIT
BAHRAIN
QATAR
ALGERIA
LIBYA
EGYPT
SAUDI ARABIA
U.A.E.
OMAN
YEMEN
30°N

WESTERN SAHARA (MOROCCO)

AFRICA

SOMALIA

RWANDA
KENYA
BURUNDI

0°
60°E
90°E
EQUATOR
150°E
0°

INDIAN OCEAN

PACIFIC OCEAN

OCEAN

SWAZILAND
SOUTH AFRICA
LESOTHO

AUSTRALIA

TROPIC OF CAPRICORN
30°S

0 miles 2000
0 kilometers 3000

Eckert Equal-Area Projection

ANTARCTIC CIRCLE

60°S

ANTARCTICA

Annual Fresh Water Use

Thousands of gallons per capita
(Thousands of liters)
■ Agriculture
■ Domestic
■ Industry

North America	338.4 (1,281)
Australia/Oceania	177.2 (670.8)
Europe	168 (636)
Asia	125 (473.2)
South America	89.9 (340.3)
Africa	55.2 (209)

Fresh Water Distribution

If all of Earth's water could fit into a gallon (4.5 liter) jug, only slightly more than a tablespoon of it would be available fresh water. This graph shows the sources of Earth's fresh water.

1% Rivers/lakes/swamps
30% Groundwater
69% Glaciers/ice caps

▲ **Industrial Water Use.** Hydroelectric projects, such as South America's Itaipú Dam, harness running water to generate electricity that powers industry.

▲ **Water Stress.** By using groundwater faster than it is renewed, agriculture in dry areas puts stress on limited water supplies.

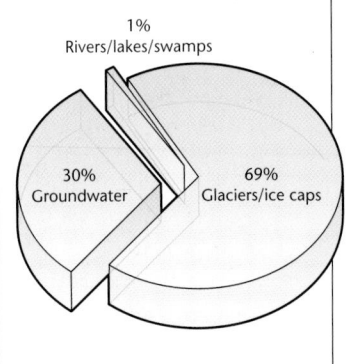

WORLD ENERGY & MINERAL RESOURCES

Beginning in the 19th century, as the Industrial Revolution spread across Europe and around the world, the demand for energy and mineral resources skyrocketed. Fossil fuels—first coal, then oil—provided the energy that kept the wheels of industry turning. Minerals such as iron ore, which is essential for the production of steel, and copper, which is used for electrical wiring, became increasingly important.

Energy and minerals, like all non-renewable resources, are in limited supply and are unevenly distributed. Countries with major deposits play an important role in the global economy. For example, the Organization of Petroleum Exporting Countries (OPEC) influences the world supply of oil and, therefore, fuel prices. *Web Link*

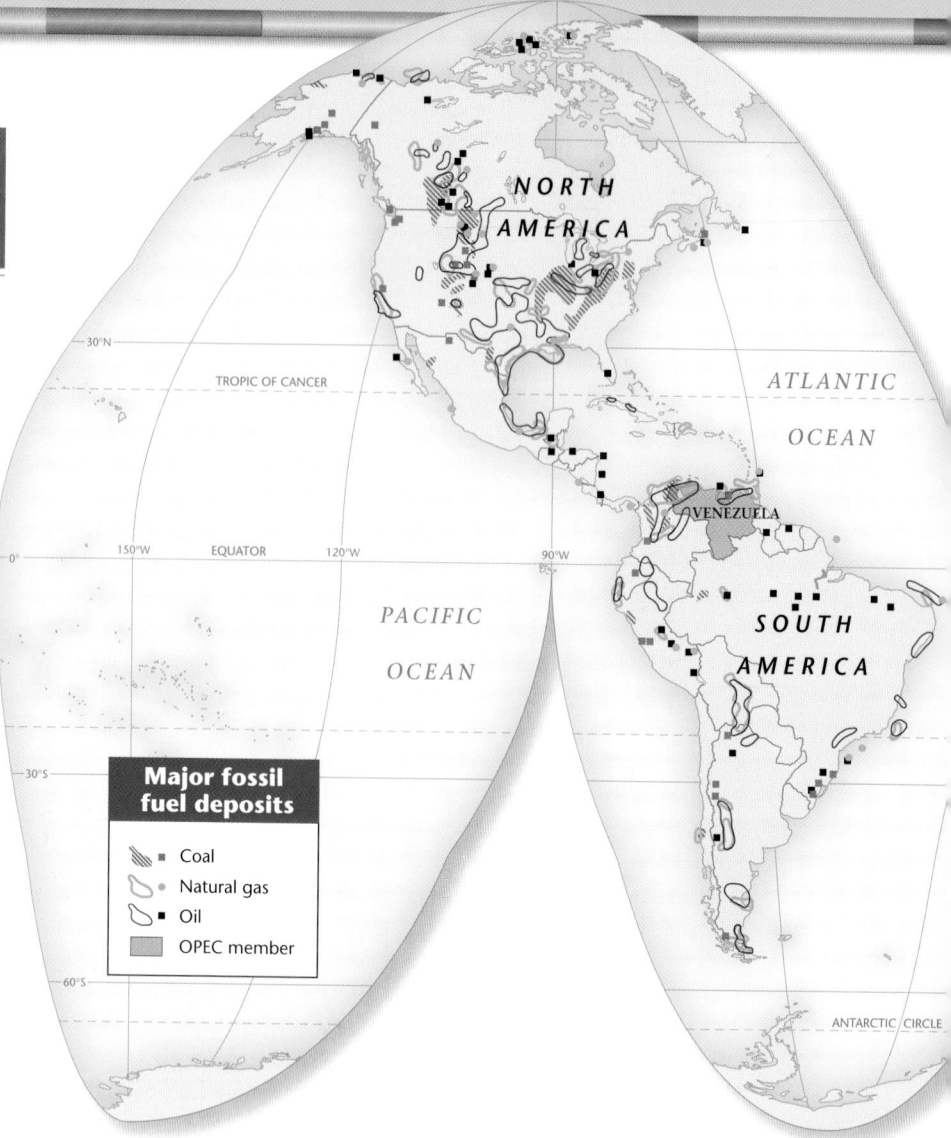

Major fossil fuel deposits

- Coal
- Natural gas
- Oil
- OPEC member

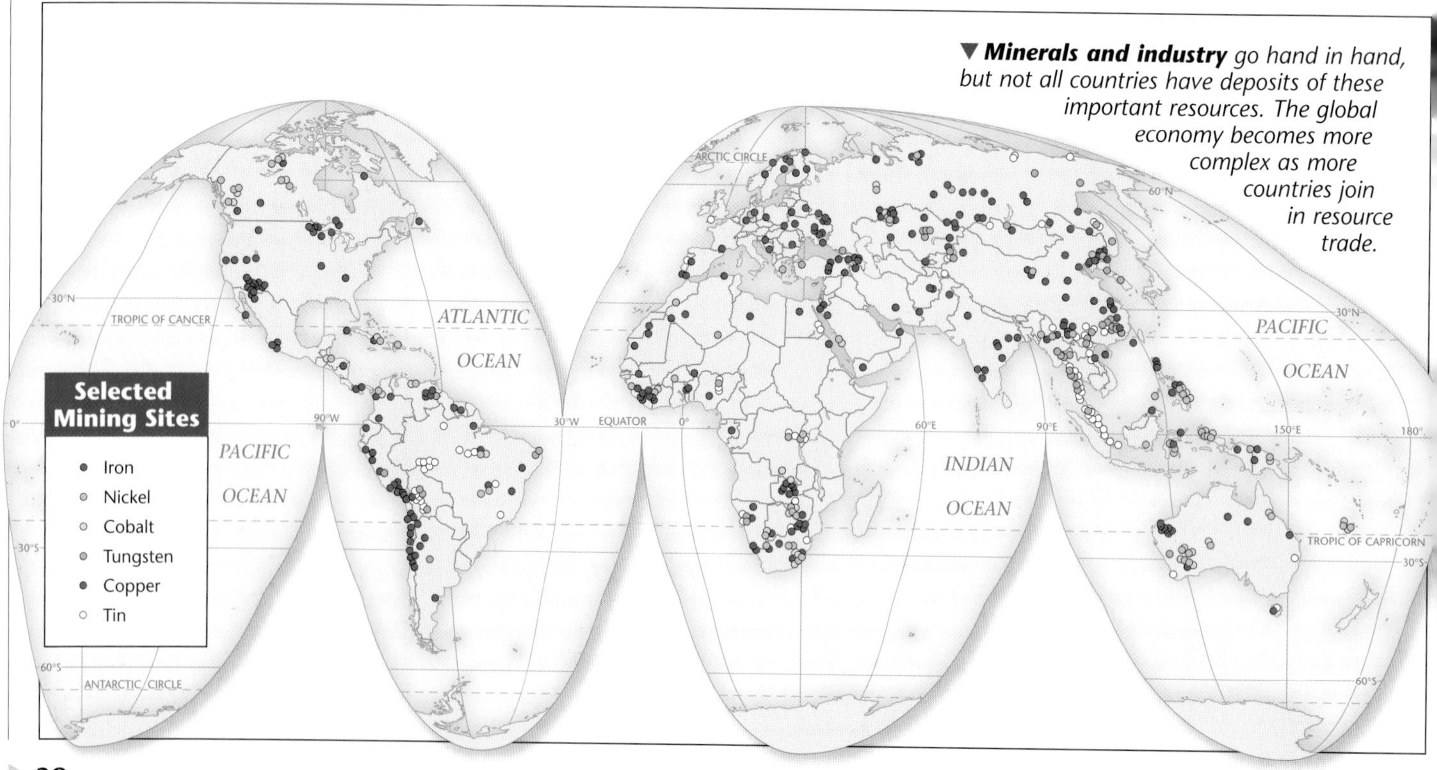

▼ *Minerals and industry* go hand in hand, but not all countries have deposits of these important resources. The global economy becomes more complex as more countries join in resource trade.

Selected Mining Sites

- Iron
- Nickel
- Cobalt
- Tungsten
- Copper
- Tin

Top Oil Producers & Consumers

Production
Millions of barrels daily

Saudi Arabia	United States	Russia	Iran	Mexico
9.2	8.0	6.2	3.8	3.5

Consumption
Millions of barrels daily

United States	Japan	China	Germany	Russia
17.8	5.6	4.1	2.9	2.5

Goode Homolosine Projection

| 0 | miles | 2000 |
| 0 | kilometers | 3000 |

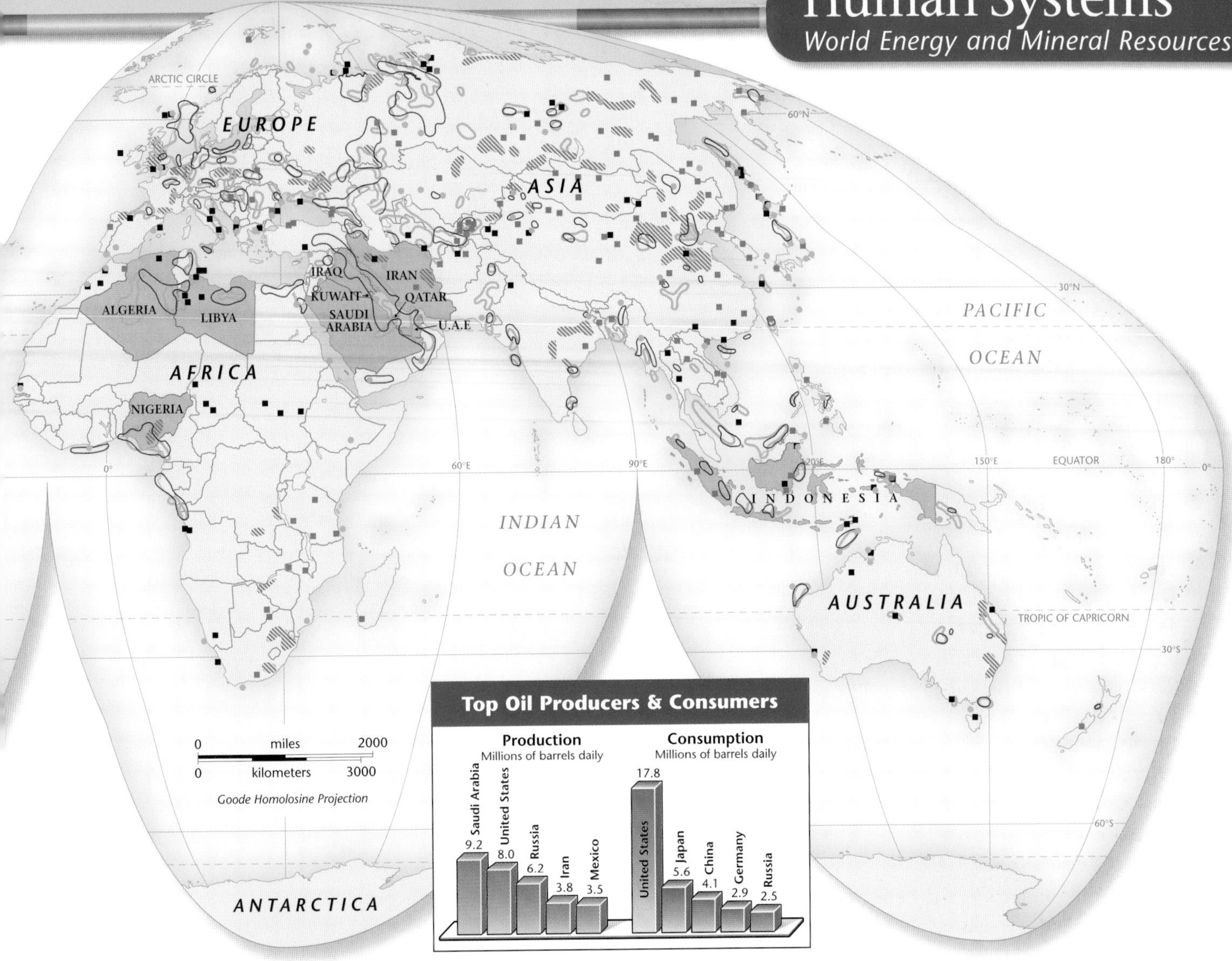

▶ **Reactors** *near Sacramento, California, produce nuclear energy, and solar panels capture energy from the sun. These two sources of energy are important alternatives to nonrenewable fossil fuels.*

▲ **A wind energy farm** *near Tehachapi, California, uses windmills to capture the energy of winds blowing off the Pacific Ocean.*

◀ **A geothermal power plant,** *fueled by heat from deep within Earth, produces energy to heat homes in Iceland. Runoff creates a warm pool for bathers.*

▼ **Dependence on oil** *for motor vehicles, industries, and domestic power and heating makes the United States the world's leading consumer of this energy resource.*

North America

Viewed from high above, North America stretches from the frozen expanses of the Arctic Ocean and Greenland to the lush green of Panama's tropical forests. Hudson Bay and the Great Lakes, fingerprints of long-departed glaciers, dominate the continent's east, while the brown landscapes of the west and southwest tell of dry lands where water is scarce.

Facts & Figures

▶ **Land area:** 9,449,500 sq mi (24,474,000 sq km)

▶ **Population:** 479,326,000

▶ **Highest point:** Mount McKinley (Denali), Alaska: 20,320 ft (6,194 m)

▶ **Lowest point:** Death Valley, California: 282 ft (86 m) below sea level

▶ **Longest river:** Mississippi-Missouri, United States: 3,710 mi (5,971 km)

▶ **Largest lake:** Lake Superior, U.S.-Canada: 31,701 sq mi (82,100 sq km)

▶ **Number of Independent countries:** 23

▶ **Largest country:** Canada: 3,849,670 sq mi (9,970,610 sq km)

▶ **Smallest country:** St. Kitts and Nevis: 101 sq mi (261 sq km)

▶ **Most populous country:** United States: Pop. 275,600,000

▶ **Least populous country:** St. Kitts and Nevis: Pop. 43,000

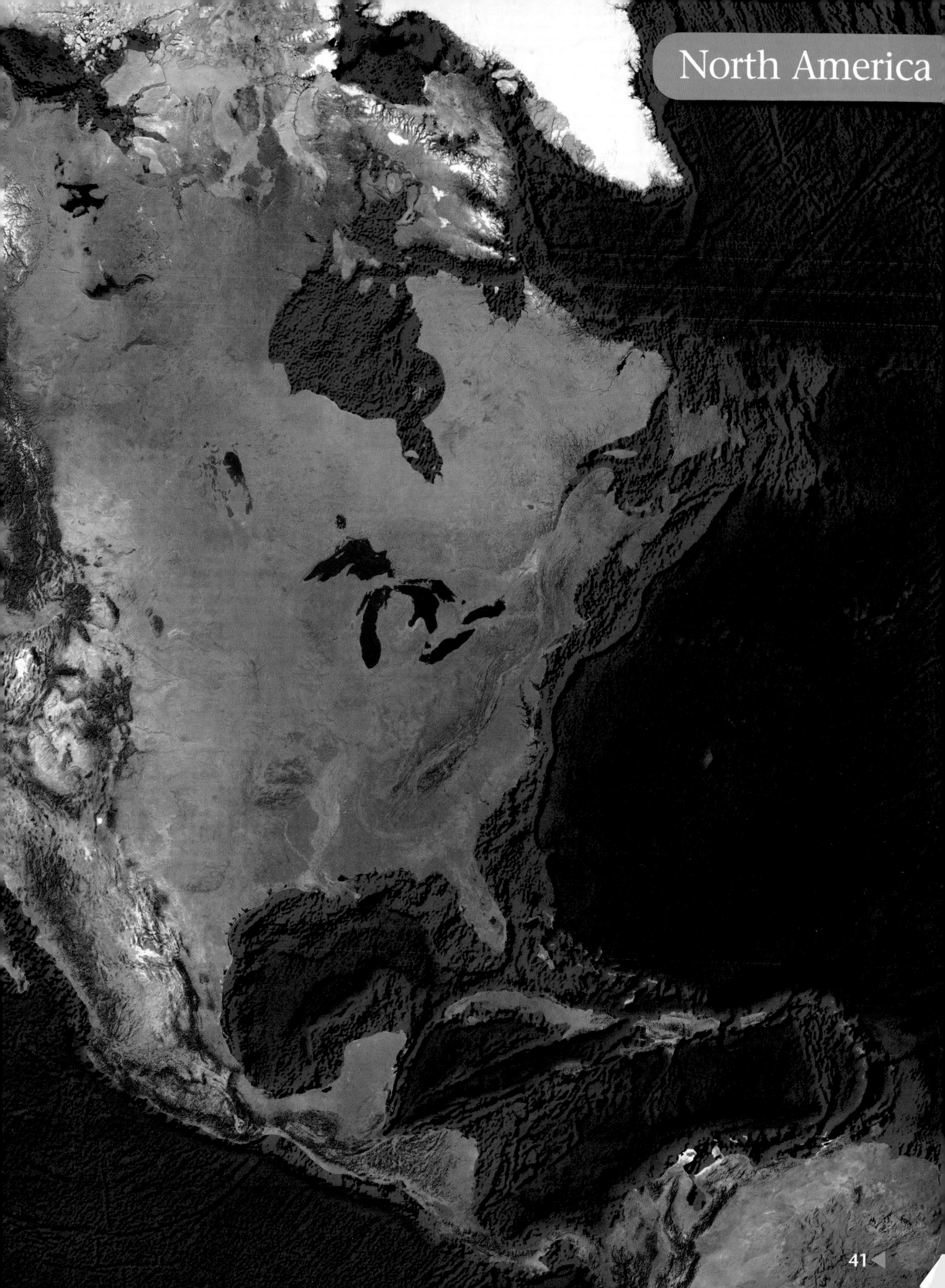

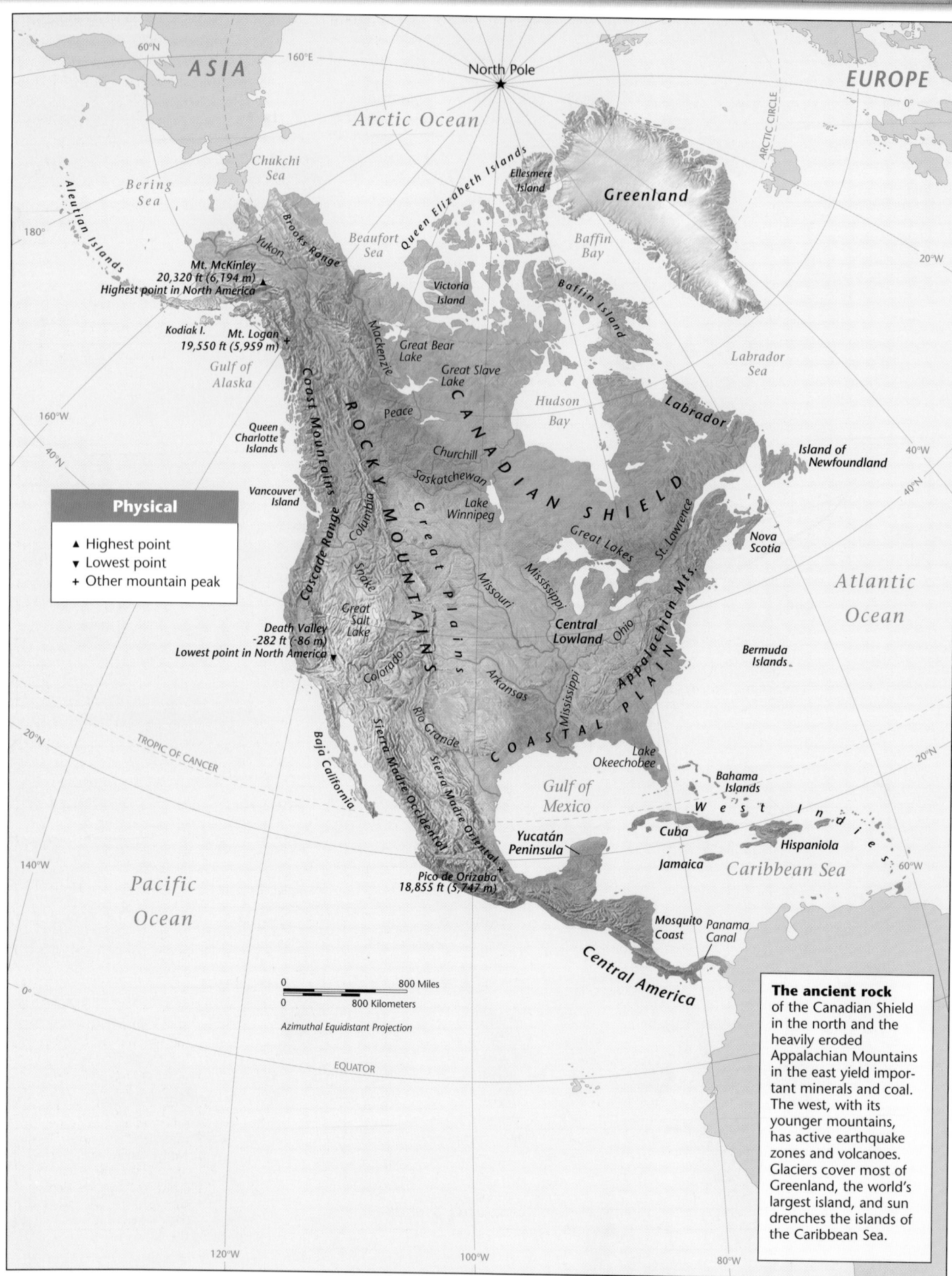

Physical Map of North America

ASIA

EUROPE

North Pole

Arctic Ocean

Chukchi Sea

Bering Sea

Aleutian Islands

Brooks Range

Yukon

Mt. McKinley
20,320 ft (6,194 m)
Highest point in North America

Kodiak I.

Mt. Logan
19,550 ft (5,959 m)

Gulf of Alaska

Queen Charlotte Islands

Vancouver Island

Coast Mountains

Cascade Range

Columbia

Snake

Great Salt Lake

Death Valley
-282 ft (-86 m)
Lowest point in North America

Colorado

Baja California

Sierra Madre Occidental

ROCKY MOUNTAINS

Great Plains

Missouri

Arkansas

Rio Grande

Sierra Madre Oriental

Pico de Orizaba
18,855 ft (5,747 m)

Yucatán Peninsula

Central America

Beaufort Sea

Queen Elizabeth Islands

Ellesmere Island

Greenland

Baffin Bay

Victoria Island

Baffin Island

Mackenzie

Peace

Great Bear Lake

Great Slave Lake

CANADIAN SHIELD

Hudson Bay

Labrador

Labrador Sea

Churchill

Saskatchewan

Lake Winnipeg

Great Lakes

St. Lawrence

Island of Newfoundland

Nova Scotia

Mississippi

Central Lowland

Ohio

Appalachian Mts.

COASTAL PLAIN

Bermuda Islands

Atlantic Ocean

Mississippi

Lake Okeechobee

Gulf of Mexico

Bahama Islands

West Indies

Cuba

Hispaniola

Jamaica

Caribbean Sea

Mosquito Coast

Panama Canal

Pacific Ocean

ARCTIC CIRCLE

TROPIC OF CANCER

EQUATOR

60°N   160°E   0°

180°   20°W

160°W   40°W

40°N   40°N

20°N   20°N

140°W   60°W

120°W   100°W   80°W

0°

Physical

▲ Highest point
▼ Lowest point
+ Other mountain peak

0   800 Miles
0   800 Kilometers

Azimuthal Equidistant Projection

The ancient rock of the Canadian Shield in the north and the heavily eroded Appalachian Mountains in the east yield important minerals and coal. The west, with its younger mountains, has active earthquake zones and volcanoes. Glaciers cover most of Greenland, the world's largest island, and sun drenches the islands of the Caribbean Sea.

North America

Political
⊛ National capital
• Other city

ASIA

EUROPE

Arctic Ocean

North Pole

Greenland
(Denmark)

ARCTIC CIRCLE

Alaska
(U.S.)

• Anchorage

C A N A D A

• Edmonton
• Calgary

Vancouver
Victoria
• Seattle
• Portland

Winnipeg • Thunder
Bay

Montréal
Ottawa
Toronto

Boston

Atlantic
Ocean

Minneapolis • St. Paul
Omaha • Chicago
Detroit
Cleveland
New York
Philadelphia
⊛ Washington, D.C.

Sacramento
San Francisco • San Jose
Fresno

Denver •
St. Louis
Indianapolis

U N I T E D   S T A T E S
Nashville

Pacific
Ocean

Los Angeles
San Diego
Tijuana

Las Vegas
• Phoenix

Oklahoma
City
Tulsa
Memphis
Birmingham
Atlanta

Charlotte

El Paso
Fort
Worth
Dallas
Austin

New
Orleans
Jacksonville

Ciudad
Juárez
San Antonio

Houston
Tampa

TROPIC OF CANCER

Chihuahua

Monterrey

M E X I C O

San Luis Potosí

Miami
Nassau
BAHAMAS
W e s t   I n d i e s

Gulf of
Mexico
Havana
⊛ CUBA

Guadalajara

México ⊛
Veracruz

Acapulco

BELIZE
Belmopan
Guatemala

Caribbean Sea

AREA ENLARGED

GUATEMALA
San Salvador
EL SALVADOR

HONDURAS
Tegucigalpa

NICARAGUA
⊛ Managua

San José ⊛
COSTA RICA   PANAMA

• Panamá

SOUTH AMERICA

Central America

800 Miles
800 Kilometers
Azimuthal Equidistant Projection

Two countries— Canada and the United States—dominate the political map of North America. But more than two dozen other countries and territories make up that part of North America referred to as Middle America, which includes Mexico, Central America, and the many islands of the West Indies.

CUBA

Cayman
Islands
(U.K.)

HAITI
Port-au-
Prince

JAMAICA   Kingston

DOMINICAN
REPUBLIC

Santo
Domingo
Puerto Rico
(U.S.)

San Juan

Virgin Islands
(U.S.)   (U.K.)

ST. KITTS
& NEVIS

Basseterre

St. John's

ANTIGUA & BARBUDA

DOMINICA
Roseau

EQUATOR

Caribbean Sea

ST. LUCIA
Kingstown

Castries

BARBADOS
Bridgetown

400 Miles
400 Kilometers

Aruba
(Neth.)

Curaçao
(Neth.)

Bonaire
(Neth.)

ST. VINCENT &
THE GRENADINES

GRENADA   St. George's

TRINIDAD & TOBAGO
Port-of-
Spain

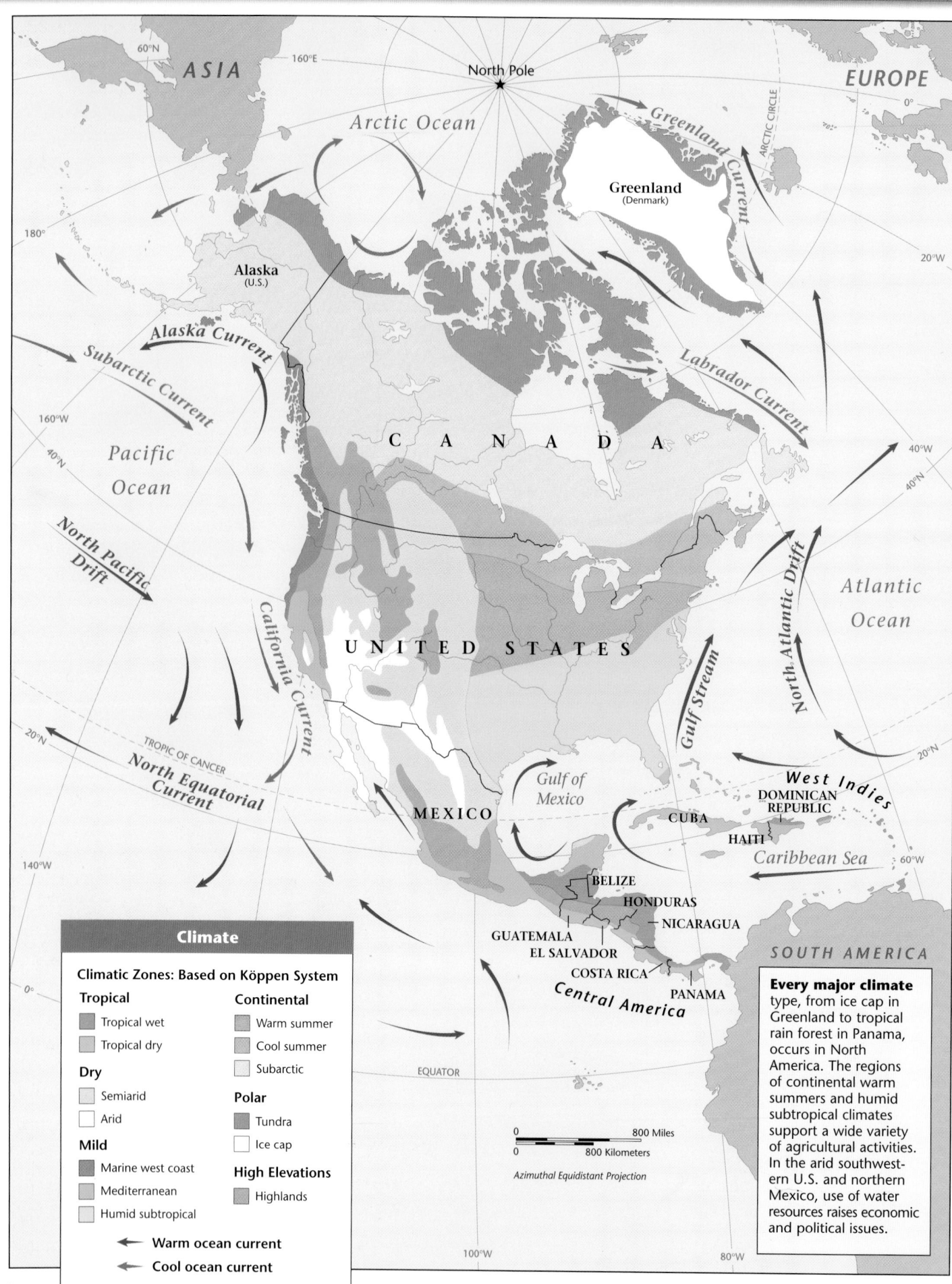

ASIA

160°E

North Pole

EUROPE

0°

Arctic Ocean

Greenland Current

ARCTIC CIRCLE

Greenland
(Denmark)

180°

20°W

Alaska
(U.S.)

Alaska Current

160°W

Subarctic Current

40°N

Pacific Ocean

North Pacific Drift

Labrador Current

C A N A D A

40°W

40°N

California Current

U N I T E D   S T A T E S

Atlantic Ocean

Gulf Stream

North Atlantic Drift

20°N

TROPIC OF CANCER

North Equatorial Current

140°W

60°W

20°N

West Indies

DOMINICAN
REPUBLIC

CUBA

HAITI

Gulf of Mexico

M E X I C O

Caribbean Sea

BELIZE

HONDURAS

NICARAGUA

GUATEMALA

EL SALVADOR

COSTA RICA

PANAMA

Central America

SOUTH AMERICA

EQUATOR

0°

Climate

Climatic Zones: Based on Köppen System

Tropical
- Tropical wet
- Tropical dry

Dry
- Semiarid
- Arid

Mild
- Marine west coast
- Mediterranean
- Humid subtropical

Continental
- Warm summer
- Cool summer
- Subarctic

Polar
- Tundra
- Ice cap

High Elevations
- Highlands

← Warm ocean current
← Cool ocean current

0   800 Miles
0   800 Kilometers

Azimuthal Equidistant Projection

Every major climate type, from ice cap in Greenland to tropical rain forest in Panama, occurs in North America. The regions of continental warm summers and humid subtropical climates support a wide variety of agricultural activities. In the arid southwestern U.S. and northern Mexico, use of water resources raises economic and political issues.

100°W

80°W

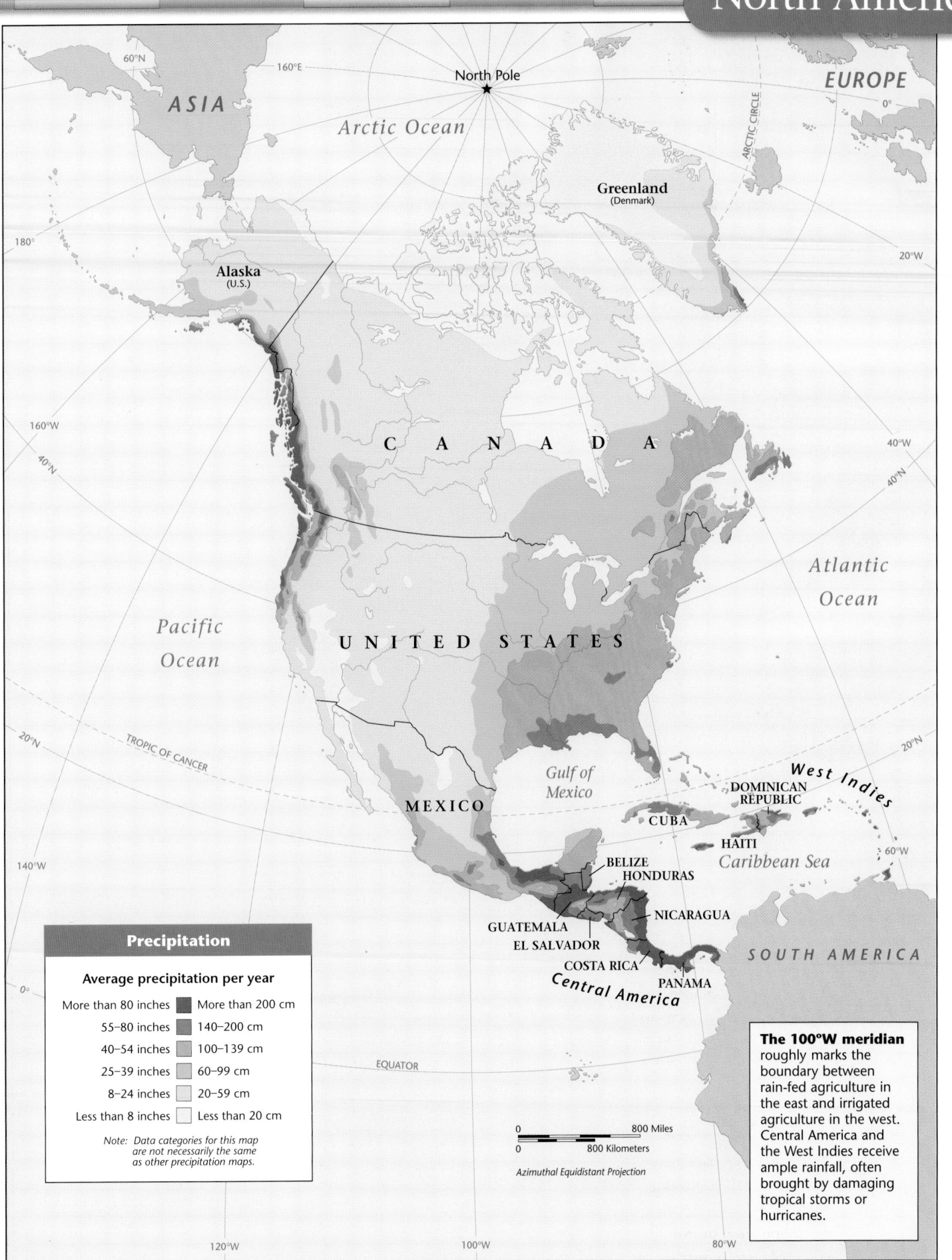

ASIA

North Pole

Arctic Ocean

Greenland
(Denmark)

EUROPE

Alaska
(U.S.)

C A N A D A

*Pacific
Ocean*

*Atlantic
Ocean*

U N I T E D   S T A T E S

TROPIC OF CANCER

MEXICO

*Gulf of
Mexico*

West Indies

DOMINICAN
REPUBLIC

CUBA

HAITI

Caribbean Sea

BELIZE
HONDURAS

NICARAGUA

GUATEMALA
EL SALVADOR

SOUTH AMERICA

COSTA RICA
PANAMA

Central America

EQUATOR

Precipitation

Average precipitation per year

More than 80 inches	▓	More than 200 cm
55–80 inches	▓	140–200 cm
40–54 inches	▒	100–139 cm
25–39 inches	░	60–99 cm
8–24 inches	░	20–59 cm
Less than 8 inches	□	Less than 20 cm

*Note: Data categories for this map
are not necessarily the same
as other precipitation maps.*

0   800 Miles
0   800 Kilometers

Azimuthal Equidistant Projection

The 100°W meridian
roughly marks the
boundary between
rain-fed agriculture in
the east and irrigated
agriculture in the west.
Central America and
the West Indies receive
ample rainfall, often
brought by damaging
tropical storms or
hurricanes.

45

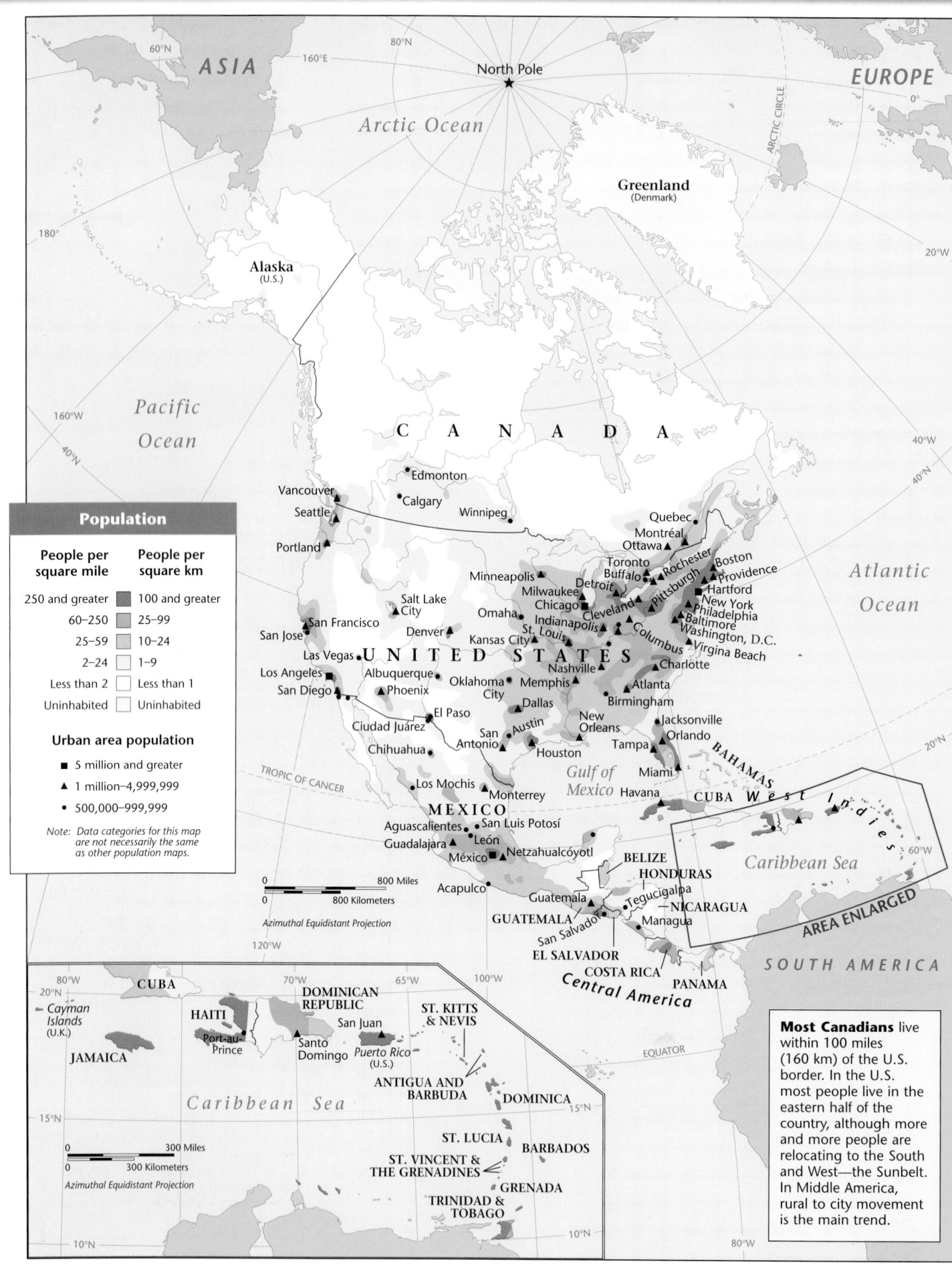

Population

People per square mile		People per square km
250 and greater		100 and greater
60–250		25–99
25–59		10–24
2–24		1–9
Less than 2		Less than 1
Uninhabited		Uninhabited

Urban area population

- ■ 5 million and greater
- ▲ 1 million–4,999,999
- • 500,000–999,999

Note: Data categories for this map are not necessarily the same as other population maps.

0   800 Miles
0   800 Kilometers
Azimuthal Equidistant Projection

0   300 Miles
0   300 Kilometers
Azimuthal Equidistant Projection

Most Canadians live within 100 miles (160 km) of the U.S. border. In the U.S. most people live in the eastern half of the country, although more and more people are relocating to the South and West—the Sunbelt. In Middle America, rural to city movement is the main trend.

North America

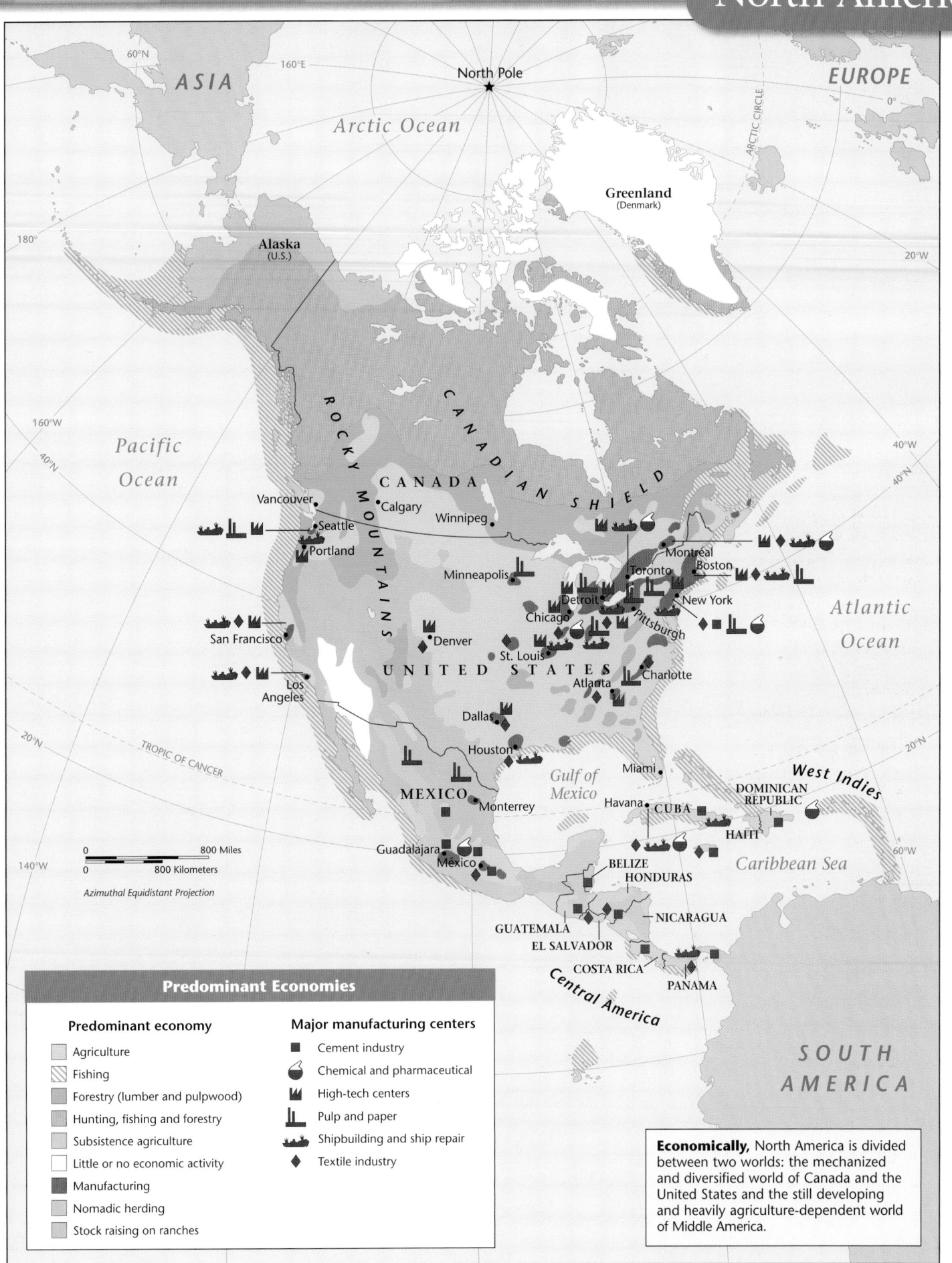

Predominant Economies

Predominant economy
- Agriculture
- Fishing
- Forestry (lumber and pulpwood)
- Hunting, fishing and forestry
- Subsistence agriculture
- Little or no economic activity
- Manufacturing
- Nomadic herding
- Stock raising on ranches

Major manufacturing centers
- Cement industry
- Chemical and pharmaceutical
- High-tech centers
- Pulp and paper
- Shipbuilding and ship repair
- Textile industry

Economically, North America is divided between two worlds: the mechanized and diversified world of Canada and the United States and the still developing and heavily agriculture-dependent world of Middle America.

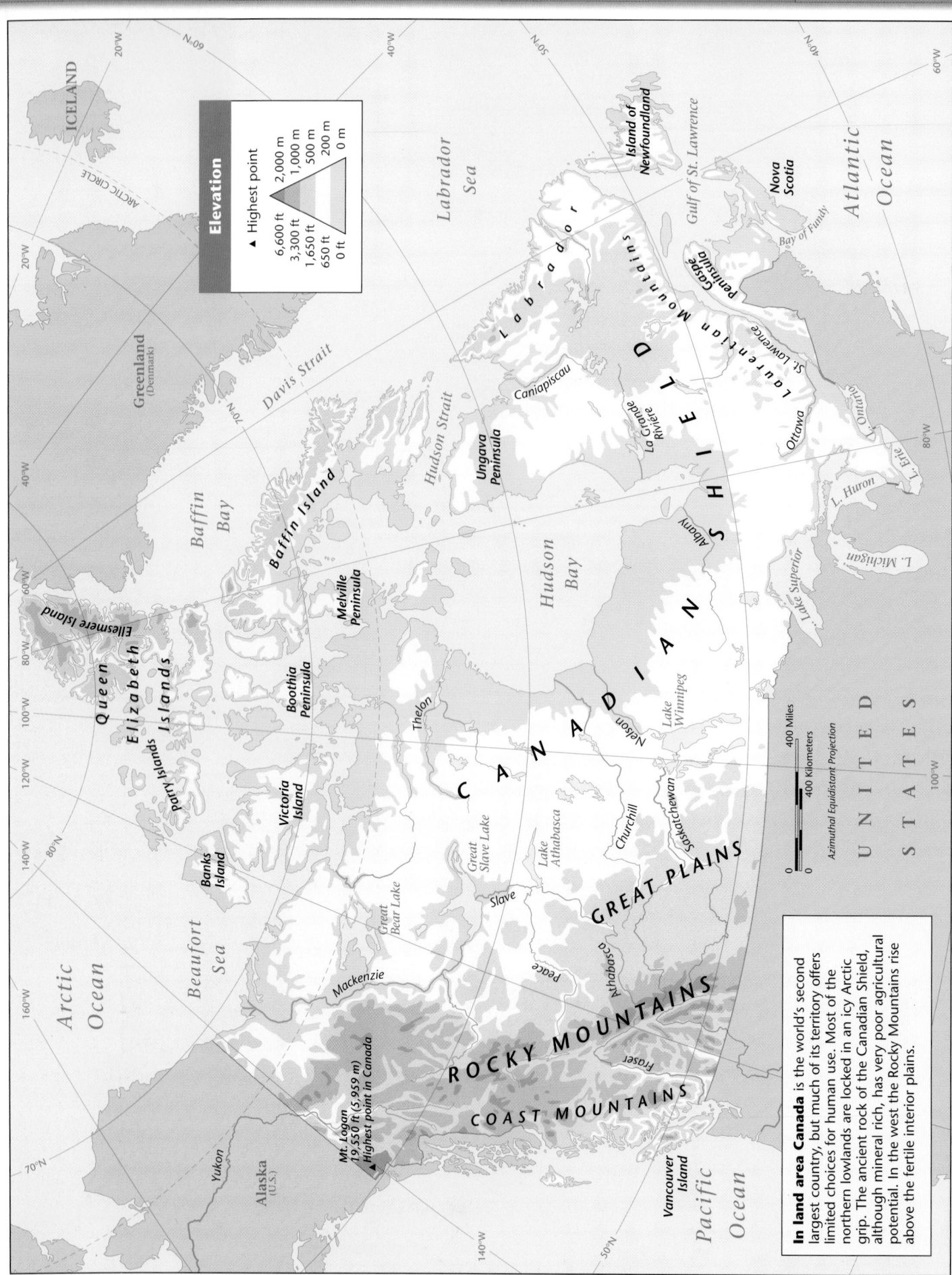

Elevation

▲ Highest point

2,000 m
1,000 m
500 m
200 m
0 m

6,600 ft
3,300 ft
1,650 ft
650 ft
0 ft

ICELAND

ARCTIC CIRCLE

Greenland
(Denmark)

Labrador
Sea

Island of
Newfoundland

Gulf of St. Lawrence

Nova
Scotia

Atlantic
Ocean

Bay of Fundy

Gaspé
Peninsula

St. Lawrence

Laurentian Mountains

Labrador

Ottawa

Caniapiscau

La Grande
Rivière

L. Ontario

L. Erie

Davis Strait

Baffin
Bay

Baffin Island

Hudson Strait

Ungava
Peninsula

Hudson
Bay

Albany

C A N A D I A N   S H I E L D

Lake Superior

L. Huron

L. Michigan

Ellesmere Island

Queen
Elizabeth
Islands

Parry Islands

Melville
Peninsula

Boothia
Peninsula

Thelon

Nelson

Lake
Winnipeg

Victoria
Island

Great
Slave Lake

Lake
Athabasca

Saskatchewan

Churchill

GREAT PLAINS

Banks
Island

Great
Bear Lake

Slave

U N I T E D
S T A T E S

Beaufort
Sea

Arctic
Ocean

Mackenzie

Peace

Athabasca

ROCKY MOUNTAINS

Fraser

Yukon

Alaska
(U.S.)

Mt. Logan
19,550 ft (5,959 m)
▲ Highest point in Canada

COAST MOUNTAINS

Vancouver
Island

Pacific
Ocean

400 Miles

400 Kilometers

Azimuthal Equidistant Projection

In land area Canada is the world's second largest country, but much of its territory offers limited choices for human use. Most of the northern lowlands are locked in an icy Arctic grip. The ancient rock of the Canadian Shield, although mineral rich, has very poor agricultural potential. In the west the Rocky Mountains rise above the fertile interior plains.

North America
Canada

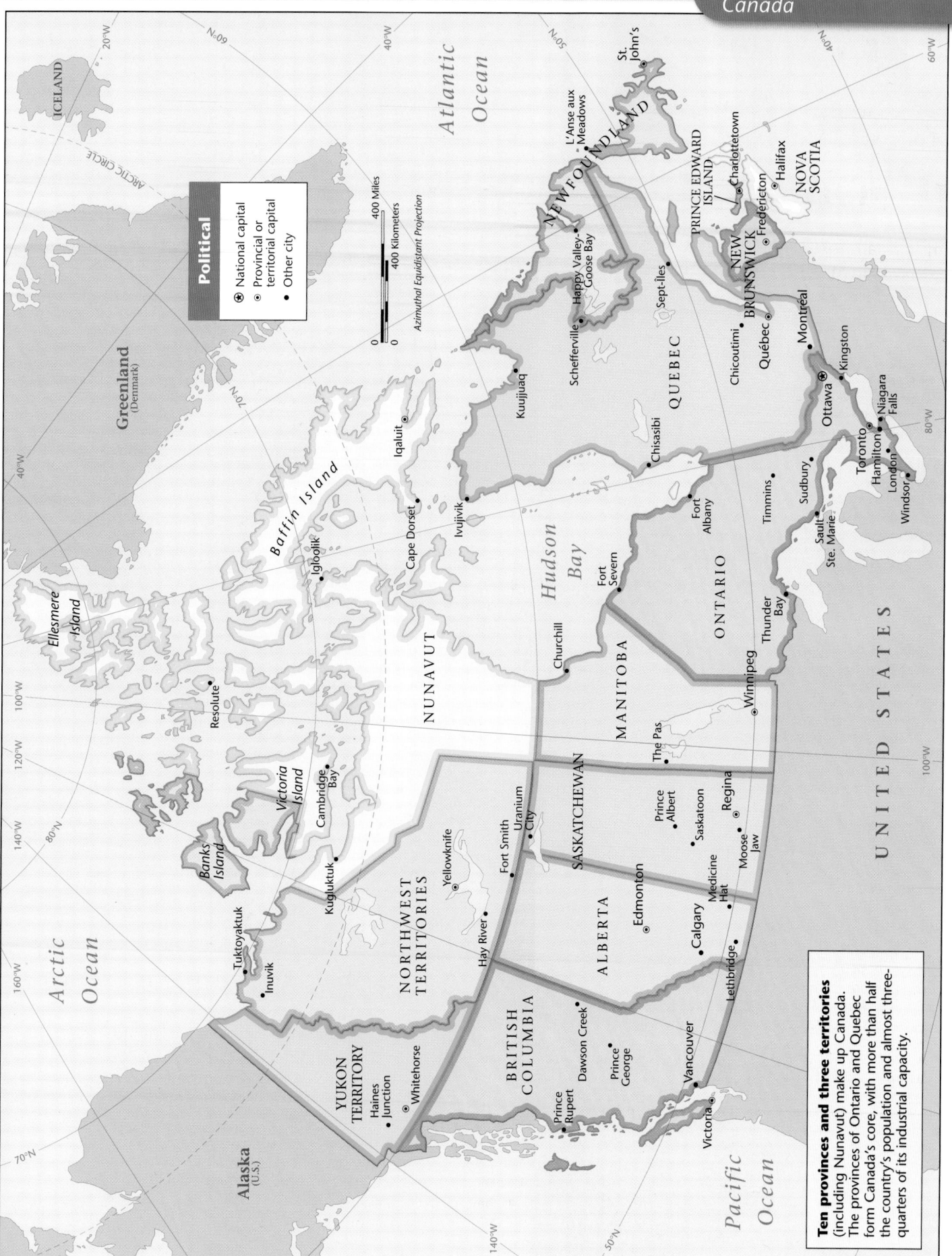

Political
- ⊛ National capital
- ⊙ Provincial or territorial capital
- • Other city

400 Miles
400 Kilometers
Azimuthal Equidistant Projection
0
0

ICELAND

Greenland
(Denmark)

ARCTIC CIRCLE

Ellesmere
Island

Baffin Island

Banks
Island

Victoria
Island

Resolute •

Cambridge
Bay

Igloolik •

Iqaluit ⊙

Cape Dorset •

Ivujivik •

Kuujjuaq •

NUNAVUT

Hudson
Bay

Churchill •

Fort
Severn •

Fort
Albany •

Atlantic
Ocean

St.
John's •

L'Anse aux
Meadows •

NEWFOUNDLAND

Happy Valley-
Goose Bay •

Sept-Îles •

Schefferville •

Chisasibi •

QUEBEC

PRINCE EDWARD
ISLAND

Charlottetown •

Halifax •
NOVA
SCOTIA
Fredericton ⊙

NEW
BRUNSWICK

Chicoutimi •
Québec ⊙
Montréal •

Kingston •
Ottawa ⊛

Sudbury •
Timmins •

Niagara
Falls •
Toronto ⊙
Hamilton •
London •
Windsor •

Sault
Ste. Marie •

ONTARIO

Thunder
Bay •

Winnipeg ⊙

MANITOBA

The Pas •

UNITED STATES

Tuktoyaktuk •

Inuvik •

Kugluktuk •

NORTHWEST
TERRITORIES

Yellowknife ⊙

Hay River •

Fort Smith •

Uranium
City •

SASKATCHEWAN

Prince
Albert •
Saskatoon •

Regina ⊙
Moose
Jaw •

ALBERTA

Edmonton ⊙

Calgary •

Medicine
Hat •

Lethbridge •

Arctic
Ocean

Alaska
(U.S.)

YUKON
TERRITORY

Haines
Junction •
Whitehorse ⊙

BRITISH
COLUMBIA

Dawson Creek •

Prince
George •

Prince
Rupert •

Vancouver •

Victoria ⊙

Pacific
Ocean

Ten provinces and three territories
(including Nunavut) make up Canada.
The provinces of Ontario and Quebec
form Canada's core, with more than half
the country's population and almost three-
quarters of its industrial capacity.

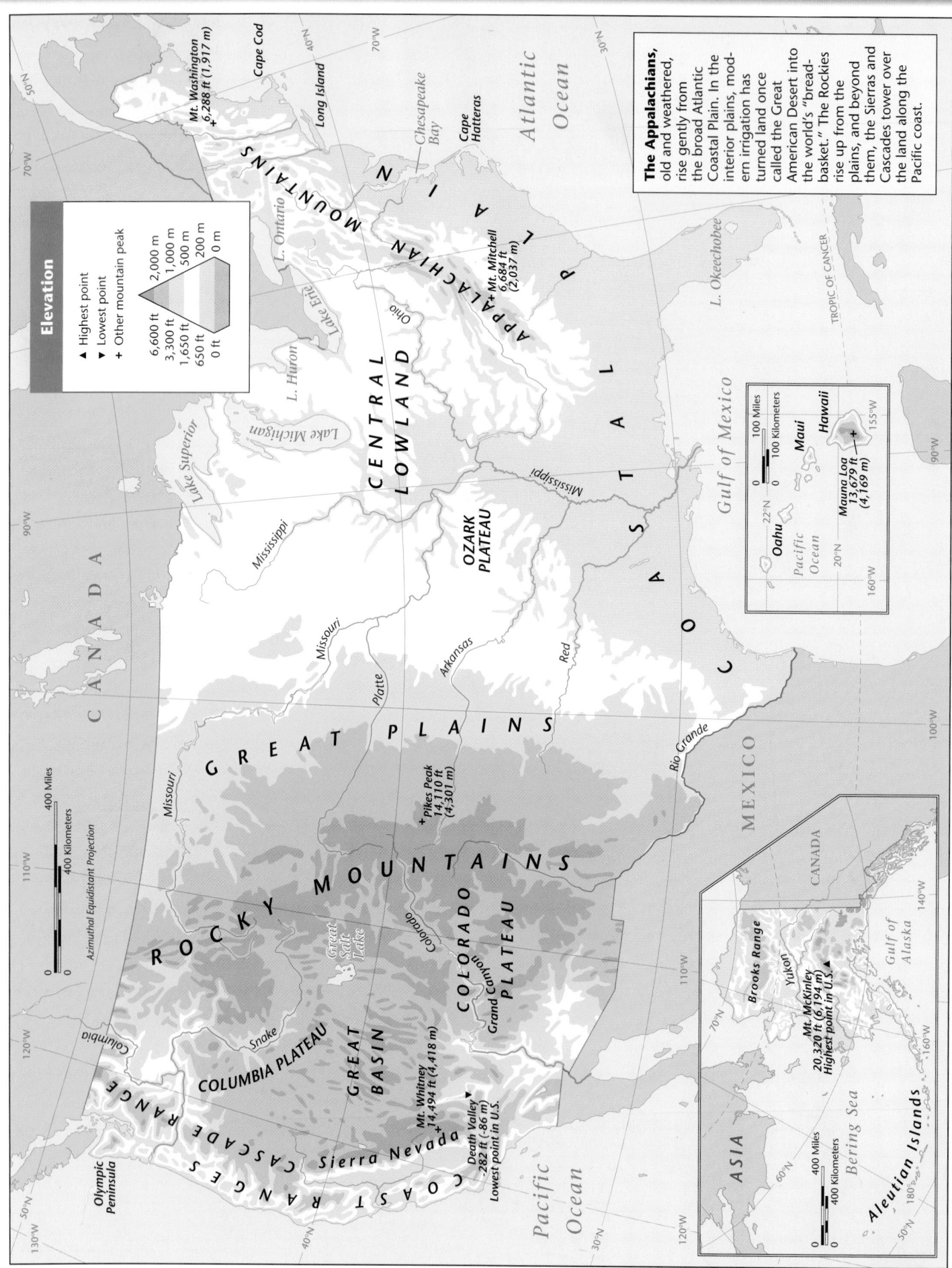

Elevation

▲ Highest point
▼ Lowest point
+ Other mountain peak

6,600 ft	2,000 m
3,300 ft	1,000 m
1,650 ft	500 m
650 ft	200 m
0 ft	0 m

The Appalachians, old and weathered, rise gently from the broad Atlantic Coastal Plain. In the interior plains, modern irrigation has turned land once called the Great American Desert into the world's "breadbasket." The Rockies rise up from the plains, and beyond them, the Sierras and Cascades tower over the land along the Pacific coast.

Mt. Washington 6,288 ft (1,917 m)
Cape Cod
Long Island
Chesapeake Bay
Cape Hatteras
Atlantic Ocean

APPALACHIAN MOUNTAINS
+ Mt. Mitchell 6,684 ft (2,037 m)

L. Ontario
Lake Erie
L. Huron
Lake Superior
Lake Michigan
Ohio

CENTRAL LOWLAND

OZARK PLATEAU

Mississippi
Missouri
Platte
Arkansas
Red
Rio Grande
Mississippi

CANADA

GREAT PLAINS

+ Pikes Peak 14,110 ft (4,301 m)

ROCKY MOUNTAINS

Great Salt Lake
Colorado
COLORADO PLATEAU
Grand Canyon

GREAT BASIN
COLUMBIA PLATEAU
Snake
Columbia

Mt. Whitney 14,494 ft (4,418 m)
Death Valley -282 ft (-86 m) Lowest point in U.S.

Sierra Nevada
COAST RANGES
CASCADE RANGE
Olympic Peninsula

Pacific Ocean

L. Okeechobee
TROPIC OF CANCER
Gulf of Mexico

COASTAL

MEXICO

400 Miles
400 Kilometers
Azimuthal Equidistant Projection

Hawaii
100 Miles
100 Kilometers
Maui
Oahu
Pacific Ocean
Mauna Loa 13,679 ft (4,169 m)

Alaska inset:
Brooks Range
Yukon
Mt. McKinley 20,320 ft (6,194 m) Highest point in U.S. ▲
Gulf of Alaska
CANADA
ASIA
Bering Sea
Aleutian Islands
400 Miles
400 Kilometers

North America
United States

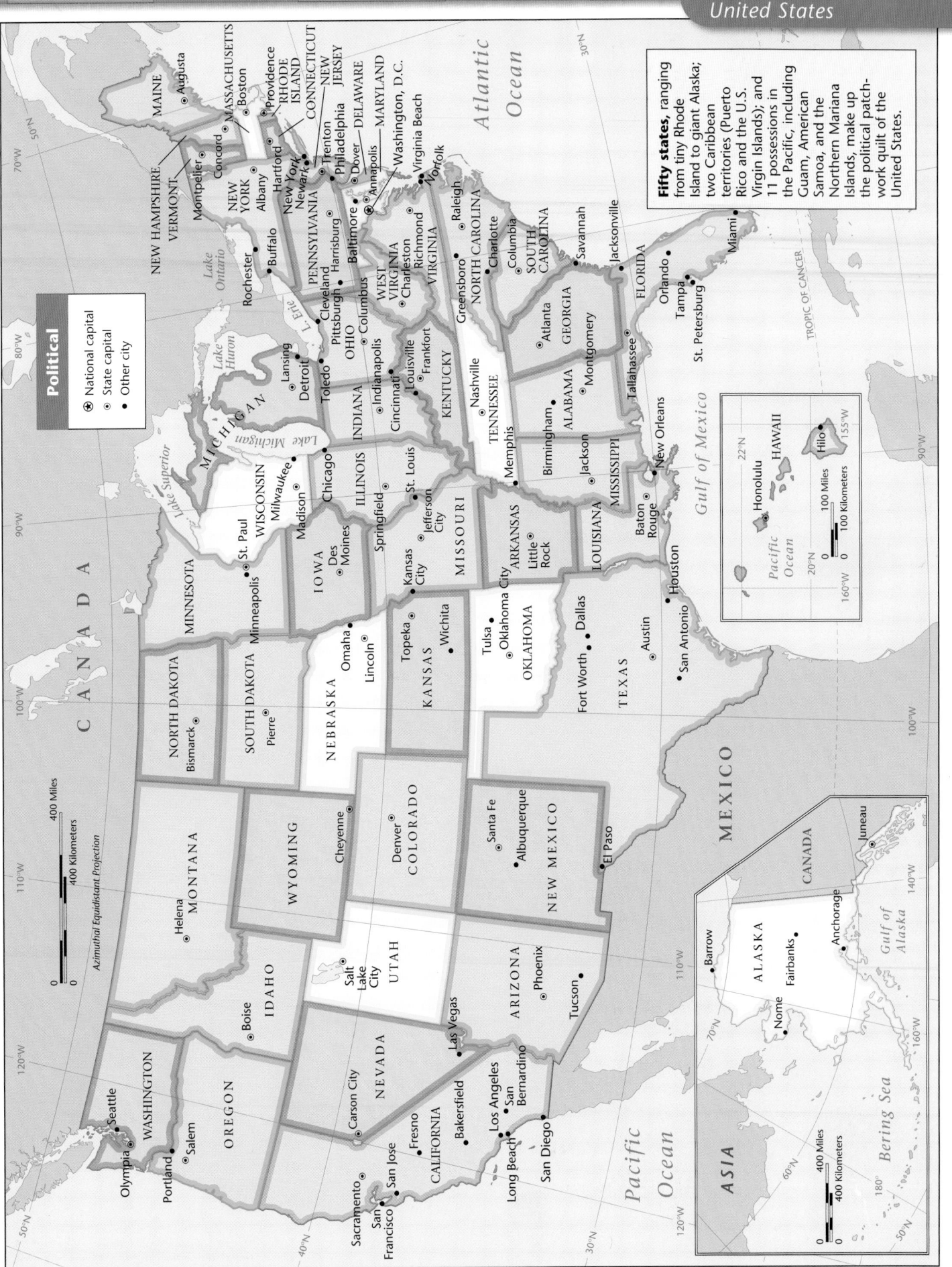

Political

⊛ National capital
⊙ State capital
● Other city

Selected labels

MAINE · Augusta
MASSACHUSETTS · Boston
RHODE ISLAND · Providence
CONNECTICUT
NEW JERSEY
DELAWARE
MARYLAND
Washington, D.C.
NEW HAMPSHIRE · Concord
VERMONT · Montpelier
NEW YORK · Albany
Hartford
Newark
New York
Trenton
Philadelphia
Dover
Annapolis
Virginia Beach
Norfolk
Rochester
Buffalo
PENNSYLVANIA
Harrisburg
Baltimore
WEST VIRGINIA
Charleston
Richmond
VIRGINIA
Raleigh
Greensboro
NORTH CAROLINA
Charlotte
Columbia
SOUTH CAROLINA
Savannah
Jacksonville
Cleveland
Pittsburgh
Columbus
OHIO
Louisville
Frankfort
KENTUCKY
Nashville
TENNESSEE
Atlanta
GEORGIA
Montgomery
Tallahassee
FLORIDA
Orlando
Tampa
St. Petersburg
Miami
Lansing
Detroit
Toledo
Indianapolis
Cincinnati
INDIANA
MICHIGAN
Lake Michigan
Lake Superior
Lake Huron
Lake Ontario
L. Erie
Chicago
ILLINOIS
Springfield
St. Louis
Jefferson City
MISSOURI
Memphis
Birmingham
ALABAMA
Jackson
MISSISSIPPI
Baton Rouge
New Orleans
Gulf of Mexico
WISCONSIN
Milwaukee
Madison
St. Paul
IOWA
Des Moines
Kansas City
ARKANSAS
Little Rock
LOUISIANA
Houston
MINNESOTA
Minneapolis
NORTH DAKOTA
Bismarck
SOUTH DAKOTA
Pierre
NEBRASKA
Omaha
Lincoln
Topeka
Wichita
KANSAS
Tulsa
Oklahoma City
OKLAHOMA
Dallas
Fort Worth
Austin
San Antonio
TEXAS
CANADA
MONTANA
Helena
WYOMING
Cheyenne
Denver
COLORADO
Santa Fe
Albuquerque
NEW MEXICO
El Paso
MEXICO
IDAHO
Boise
UTAH
Salt Lake City
ARIZONA
Phoenix
Tucson
Las Vegas
NEVADA
Carson City
WASHINGTON
Seattle
Olympia
Portland
Salem
OREGON
Sacramento
San Francisco
San Jose
Fresno
Bakersfield
CALIFORNIA
Los Angeles
San Bernardino
Long Beach
San Diego
Pacific Ocean
Atlantic Ocean

400 Miles
400 Kilometers
Azimuthal Equidistant Projection

Inset (Hawaii):
HAWAII
Honolulu
Hilo
Pacific Ocean
Gulf of Mexico
TROPIC OF CANCER
100 Miles
100 Kilometers

Inset (Alaska):
ALASKA
Barrow
Nome
Fairbanks
Anchorage
Juneau
Gulf of Alaska
Bering Sea
CANADA
ASIA
400 Miles
400 Kilometers

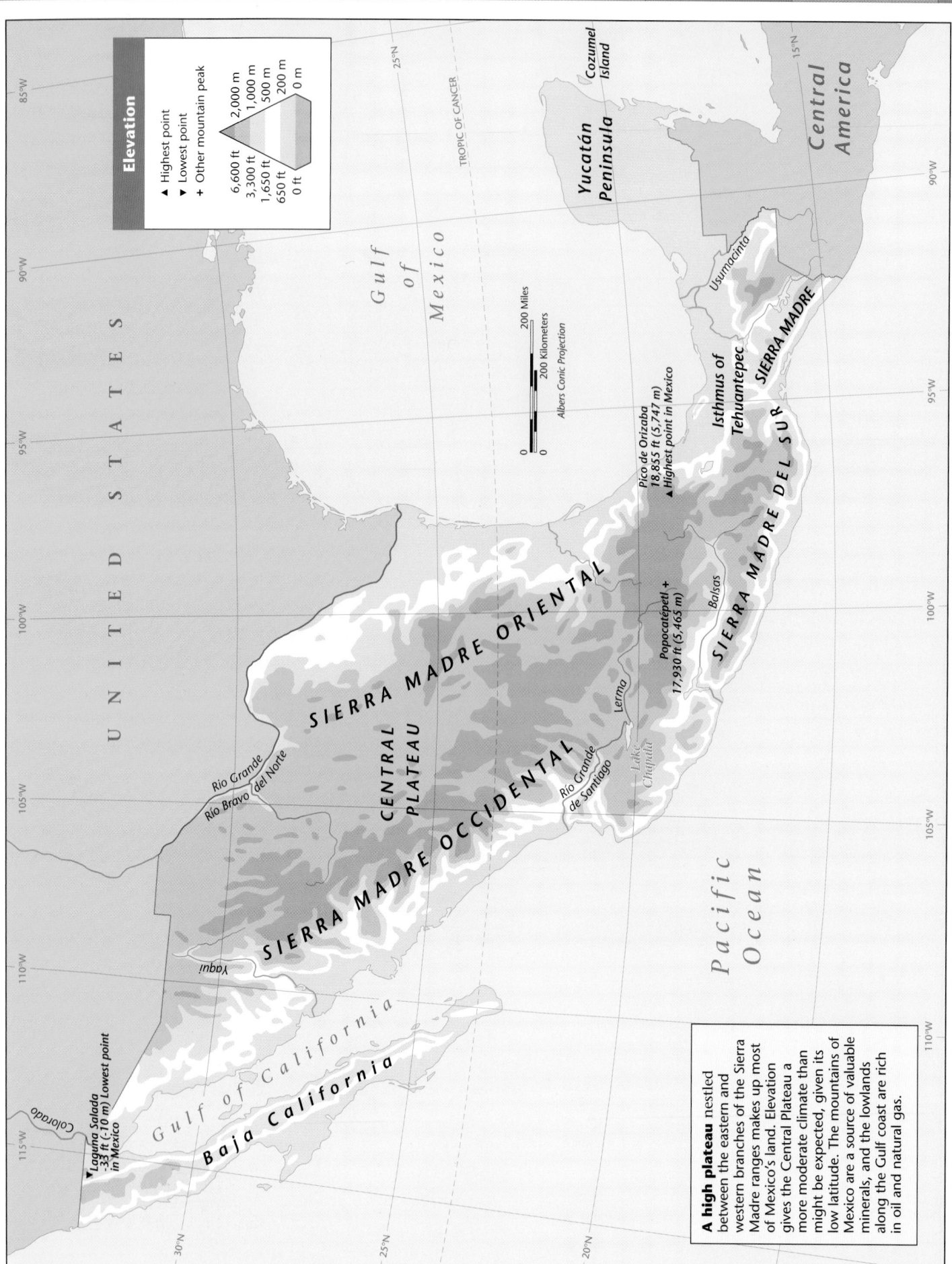

Elevation

▲ Highest point
▼ Lowest point
+ Other mountain peak

2,000 m — 6,600 ft
1,000 m — 3,300 ft
500 m — 1,650 ft
200 m — 650 ft
0 m — 0 ft

UNITED STATES

Gulf of Mexico

TROPIC OF CANCER

Cozumel Island

Yucatán Peninsula

Central America

Usumacinta

SIERRA MADRE

Isthmus of Tehuantepec

200 Miles
200 Kilometers
Albers Conic Projection

Pico de Orizaba
18,855 ft (5,747 m)
▲ Highest point in Mexico

SIERRA MADRE ORIENTAL

CENTRAL PLATEAU

Balsas

Popocatépetl +
17,930 ft (5,465 m)

SIERRA MADRE DEL SUR

Lerma

Rio Grande de Santiago

Lake Chapala

Rio Grande
Río Bravo del Norte

SIERRA MADRE OCCIDENTAL

Yaqui

Gulf of California

Baja California

Pacific Ocean

Colorado

▼ Laguna Salada
-33 ft (-10 m) Lowest point
in Mexico

A high plateau nestled between the eastern and western branches of the Sierra Madre ranges makes up most of Mexico's land. Elevation gives the Central Plateau a more moderate climate than might be expected, given its low latitude. The mountains of Mexico are a source of valuable minerals, and the lowlands along the Gulf coast are rich in oil and natural gas.

North America
Mexico

Political
- ⊛ National capital
- ⊙ State capital
- • Other city

UNITED STATES

Gulf of Mexico

Pacific Ocean

Gulf of California

200 Miles
200 Kilometers
Albers Conic Projection

TROPIC OF CANCER

BELIZE
HONDURAS
GUATEMALA
EL SALVADOR

QUINTANA ROO
Chetumal
YUCATÁN
Mérida
CAMPECHE
Campeche
CHIAPAS
Tuxtla Gutiérrez
TABASCO
Villahermosa
VERACRUZ
Veracruz
Xalapa
OAXACA
Oaxaca
Poza Rica
TLAXCALA
Tlaxcala
Puebla
PUEBLA
Cuernavaca
MÉXICO
MORELOS
Pachuca
HIDALGO
México
FEDERAL DISTRICT
Toluca
GUERRERO
Chilpancingo
Acapulco
QUERÉTARO
Querétaro
Guanajuato
GUANAJUATO
León
MICHOACÁN
Morelia
Colima
COLIMA
JALISCO
Guadalajara
Puerto Vallarta
NAYARIT
Tepic
Tampico
Ciudad Victoria
TAMAULIPAS
Matamoros
Reynosa
SAN LUIS POTOSÍ
San Luis Potosí
AGUASCALIENTES
Aguascalientes
ZACATECAS
Zacatecas
Nuevo Laredo
NUEVO LEÓN
Monterrey
COAHUILA
Saltillo
Torreón
DURANGO
Durango
SINALOA
Culiacán
Mazatlán
CHIHUAHUA
Chihuahua
Ciudad Juárez
SONORA
Hermosillo
Nogáles
BAJA CALIFORNIA
Mexicali
Tijuana
BAJA CALIFORNIA SUR
La Paz

Mexico is divided into 31 states and the Federal District of Mexico City. With more than 100 million people, it is the largest Spanish-speaking country in the world. Modern Mexico is the product of a rich cultural tradition rooted first in the Maya and Aztec Empires, and later in the Spanish colonial empire. Most Mexicans are mestizos, people of mixed Indian and Spanish ancestry.

FOCUS ON

Natural Hazards

The forces of nature inspire awe. They can also bring damage and destruction, especially when people locate homes and businesses in places that are at risk of experiencing violent storms, earthquakes, volcanoes, floods, wildfires, or other natural hazards.

Tornadoes, violent, swirling storms with winds that can exceed 200 miles (300 km) per hour, strike the U.S. more than 800 times each year. Hurricanes, massive low-pressure storms that form over warm ocean waters, bring destructive winds and rain primarily to the Gulf of Mexico and the southeastern mainland. Melting spring snows and heavy rains trigger flooding; periods of drought make other regions vulnerable to wildfires. These and other hazards of nature are not limited to this continent. Natural hazards pose serious threats to lives and property wherever people live.

▲ **Volcanoes.** From deep inside Earth, molten rock, called magma, rises and breaks through the surface, sometimes quietly, but more often violently, shooting billowing ash clouds as shown here at Mount St. Helens, in Washington State.

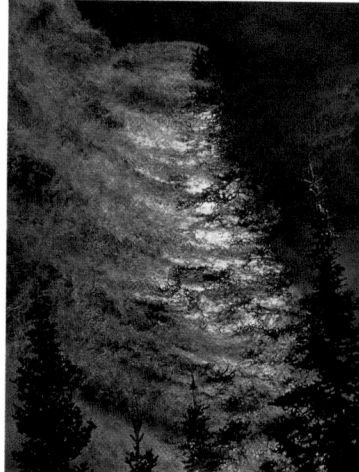

▼ **Wildfires.** Putting lives and property at great risk, wildfires destroy millions of acres of forest each year. At the same time, fires help renew ecosystems by removing debris and encouraging seedling growth.

▶ **Floods.** Towns and farmland that occupy fertile plains along rivers are always in danger from floods. In 1993 the great Mississippi River floods devastated millions of people in the midwestern United States.

Web Link for information on natural hazards: www.cindi.usgs.gov

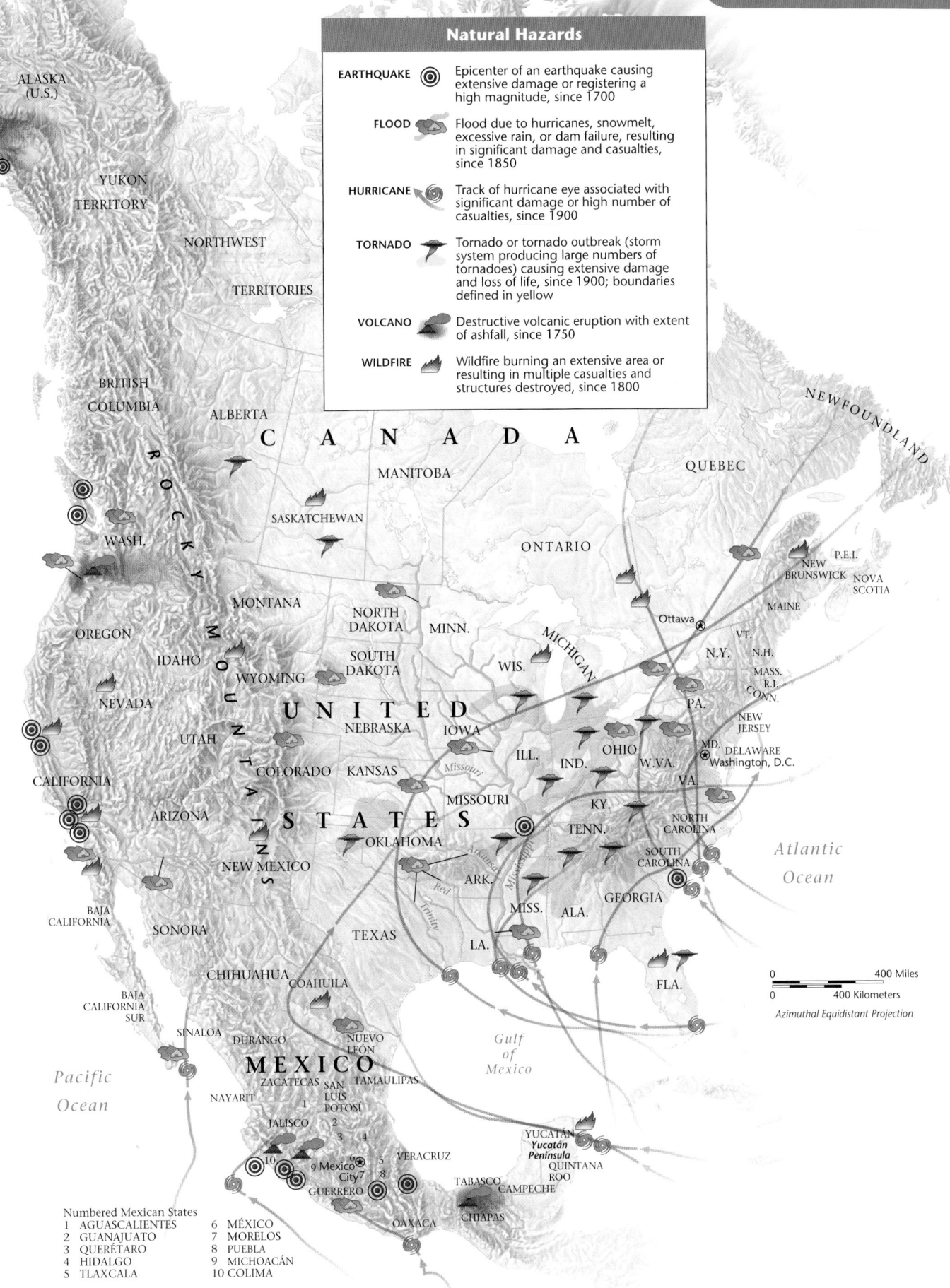

North America
Natural Hazards

Natural Hazards

EARTHQUAKE — Epicenter of an earthquake causing extensive damage or registering a high magnitude, since 1700

FLOOD — Flood due to hurricanes, snowmelt, excessive rain, or dam failure, resulting in significant damage and casualties, since 1850

HURRICANE — Track of hurricane eye associated with significant damage or high number of casualties, since 1900

TORNADO — Tornado or tornado outbreak (storm system producing large numbers of tornadoes) causing extensive damage and loss of life, since 1900; boundaries defined in yellow

VOLCANO — Destructive volcanic eruption with extent of ashfall, since 1750

WILDFIRE — Wildfire burning an extensive area or resulting in multiple casualties and structures destroyed, since 1800

ALASKA (U.S.)

YUKON TERRITORY

NORTHWEST TERRITORIES

BRITISH COLUMBIA

ALBERTA

CANADA

MANITOBA

SASKATCHEWAN

ONTARIO

QUEBEC

NEWFOUNDLAND

P.E.I.

NEW BRUNSWICK

NOVA SCOTIA

MAINE

Ottawa

WASH.

OREGON

MONTANA

NORTH DAKOTA

MINN.

MICHIGAN

WIS.

VT.

N.H.

N.Y.

MASS.

R.I.

CONN.

IDAHO

WYOMING

SOUTH DAKOTA

IOWA

PA.

NEW JERSEY

NEVADA

UNITED

NEBRASKA

ILL.

IND.

OHIO

W.VA.

MD.

DELAWARE

Washington, D.C.

CALIFORNIA

UTAH

COLORADO

KANSAS

Missouri

MISSOURI

KY.

VA.

ARIZONA

STATES

OKLAHOMA

TENN.

NORTH CAROLINA

NEW MEXICO

Arkansas

ARK.

Red

Mississippi

SOUTH CAROLINA

Atlantic Ocean

BAJA CALIFORNIA

SONORA

TEXAS

Trinity

MISS.

ALA.

GEORGIA

LA.

FLA.

BAJA CALIFORNIA SUR

CHIHUAHUA

COAHUILA

Gulf of Mexico

SINALOA

DURANGO

NUEVO LEÓN

MEXICO

TAMAULIPAS

Pacific Ocean

NAYARIT

ZACATECAS

SAN LUIS POTOSÍ

1

JALISCO

2

3

4

YUCATÁN

Yucatán Peninsula

QUINTANA ROO

10

9 Mexico City 7

6

5

8

VERACRUZ

TABASCO

CAMPECHE

GUERRERO

OAXACA

CHIAPAS

0 — 400 Miles
0 — 400 Kilometers

Azimuthal Equidistant Projection

Numbered Mexican States
1 AGUASCALIENTES
2 GUANAJUATO
3 QUERÉTARO
4 HIDALGO
5 TLAXCALA
6 MÉXICO
7 MORELOS
8 PUEBLA
9 MICHOACÁN
10 COLIMA

South America

From the towering, snow-capped Andes in the west to the steamy rain forest of the Amazon Basin in the north, and from the fertile grasslands of the Pampas to the arid Atacama Desert along the Pacific coast, South America is a continent of extremes. North to south the continent extends from the tropical waters of the Caribbean Sea to the windblown islands of Tierra del Fuego. Its longest river, the Amazon, carries more water than any other river in the world.

Facts & Figures

- **Land area:** 6,880,500 sq mi (17,819,000 sq km)
- **Population:** 344,790,000
- **Highest point:** Aconcagua, Argentina: 22,834 ft (6,960 m)
- **Lowest point:** Valdés Peninsula, Argentina: 131 ft (40 m) below sea level
- **Longest river:** Amazon: 4,000 mi (6,437 km)
- **Largest lake:** Lake Titicaca, Bolivia-Peru: 3,200 sq mi (8,287 sq km)

- **Number of independent countries:** 12
- **Largest country:** Brazil: 3,286,488 sq mi (8,511,965 sq km)
- **Smallest country:** Suriname: 63,037 sq mi (163,265 sq km)
- **Most populous country:** Brazil: Pop. 170,115,000
- **Least populous country:** Suriname: Pop. 434,000

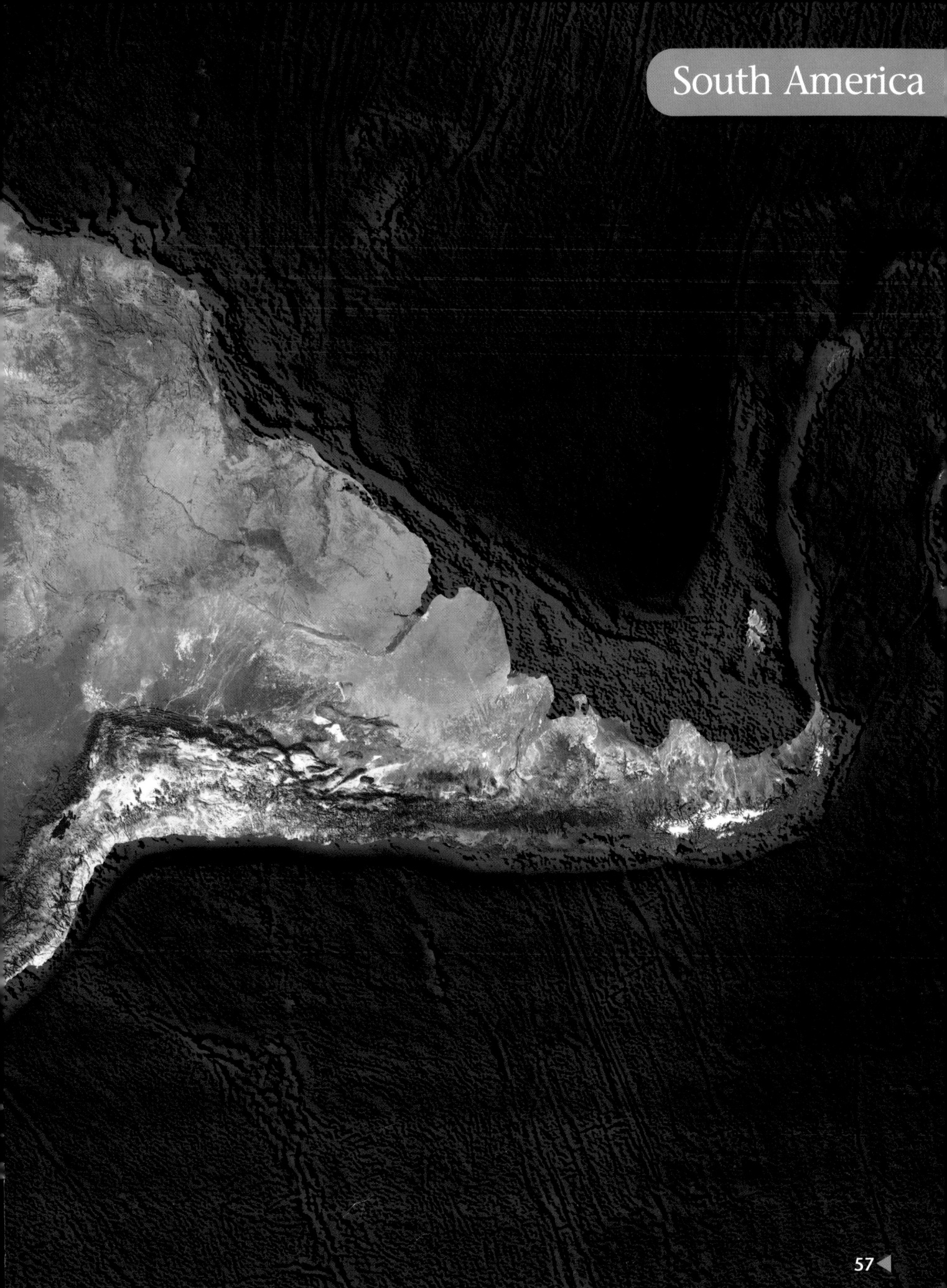

Two physical features dominate South America's landscape—the rugged Andes that stretch north to south from Colombia to Tierra del Fuego, and the Amazon Basin, the drainage area of the Amazon River and site of the world's largest tropical forest.

Caribbean Sea

Central America

Malpelo I.

Lake Maracaibo

Orinoco

Llanos

Angel Falls

GUIANA HIGHLANDS

Negro

A M A Z O N

Amazon

B A S I N

Purus

Madeira

Ucayali

Marajó I.

Amazon

EQUATOR

Tapajós

Xingu

Tocantins

São Francisco

Lake Titicaca

Mato Grosso Plateau

B R A Z I L I A N

H I G H L A N D S

San Félix I.   San Ambrosio I.

Atacama Desert

A N D E S

Gran Chaco

paraguay

Iguazú Falls

TROPIC OF CAPRICORN

Ojos del Salado 22,572 ft (6,880 m)

Atlantic Ocean

Cerro Aconcagua 22,834 ft (6,960 m) Highest point in South America

Juan Fernández Is.

P A M P A S

Paraná

Uruguay

Río de la Plata

Pacific Ocean

Colorado

Isla Grande de Chiloé

P A T A G O N I A

Valdés Peninsula -131 ft (-40 m) Lowest point in South America

Gulf of San Jorge

Physical
▲ Highest point
▼ Lowest point
+ Other mountain peak

Falkland Islands

Strait of Magellan

Tierra del Fuego

Cape Horn

South Georgia

0   600 Miles
0   600 Kilometers

Azimuthal Equidistant Projection

South America

Twelve countries and one French territory (French Guiana) make up South America. The continent was under mainly Spanish and Portuguese control from the 16th to the 19th century. Colonial influence is still evident in the use of Spanish and Portuguese languages and in the widespread presence of the Roman Catholic church.

Political

⊛ National capital

• Other city

Azimuthal Equidistant Projection

0 — 600 Miles
0 — 600 Kilometers

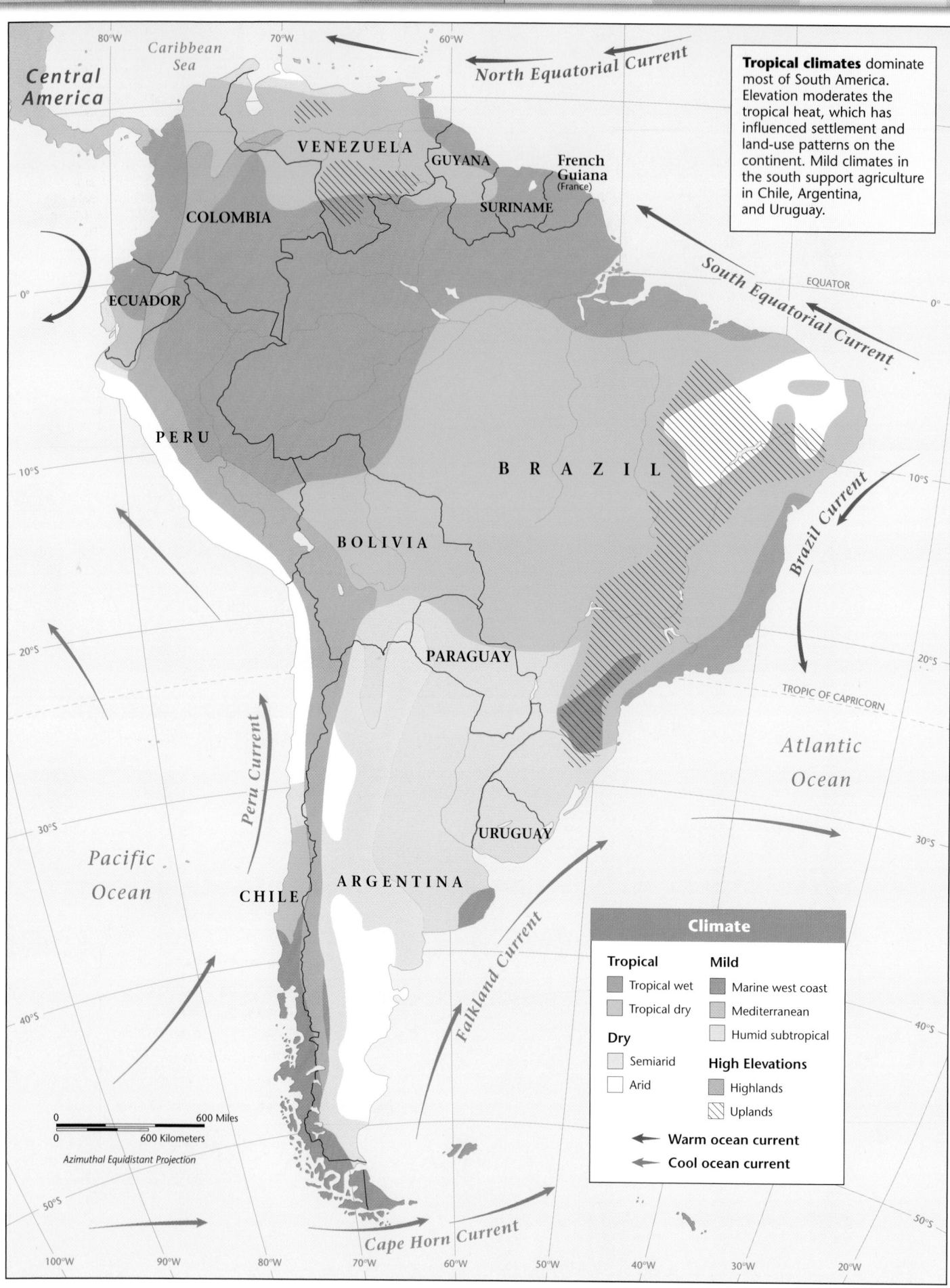

Tropical climates dominate most of South America. Elevation moderates the tropical heat, which has influenced settlement and land-use patterns on the continent. Mild climates in the south support agriculture in Chile, Argentina, and Uruguay.

Central America

Caribbean Sea

North Equatorial Current

VENEZUELA
GUYANA
French Guiana (France)
SURINAME
COLOMBIA
ECUADOR

South Equatorial Current

EQUATOR

PERU

B R A Z I L

Brazil Current

BOLIVIA

PARAGUAY

TROPIC OF CAPRICORN

Atlantic Ocean

Peru Current

Pacific Ocean

URUGUAY

CHILE   A R G E N T I N A

Falkland Current

Climate

Tropical
- Tropical wet
- Tropical dry

Dry
- Semiarid
- Arid

Mild
- Marine west coast
- Mediterranean
- Humid subtropical

High Elevations
- Highlands
- Uplands

← Warm ocean current
← Cool ocean current

0   600 Miles
0   600 Kilometers
Azimuthal Equidistant Projection

Cape Horn Current

South America

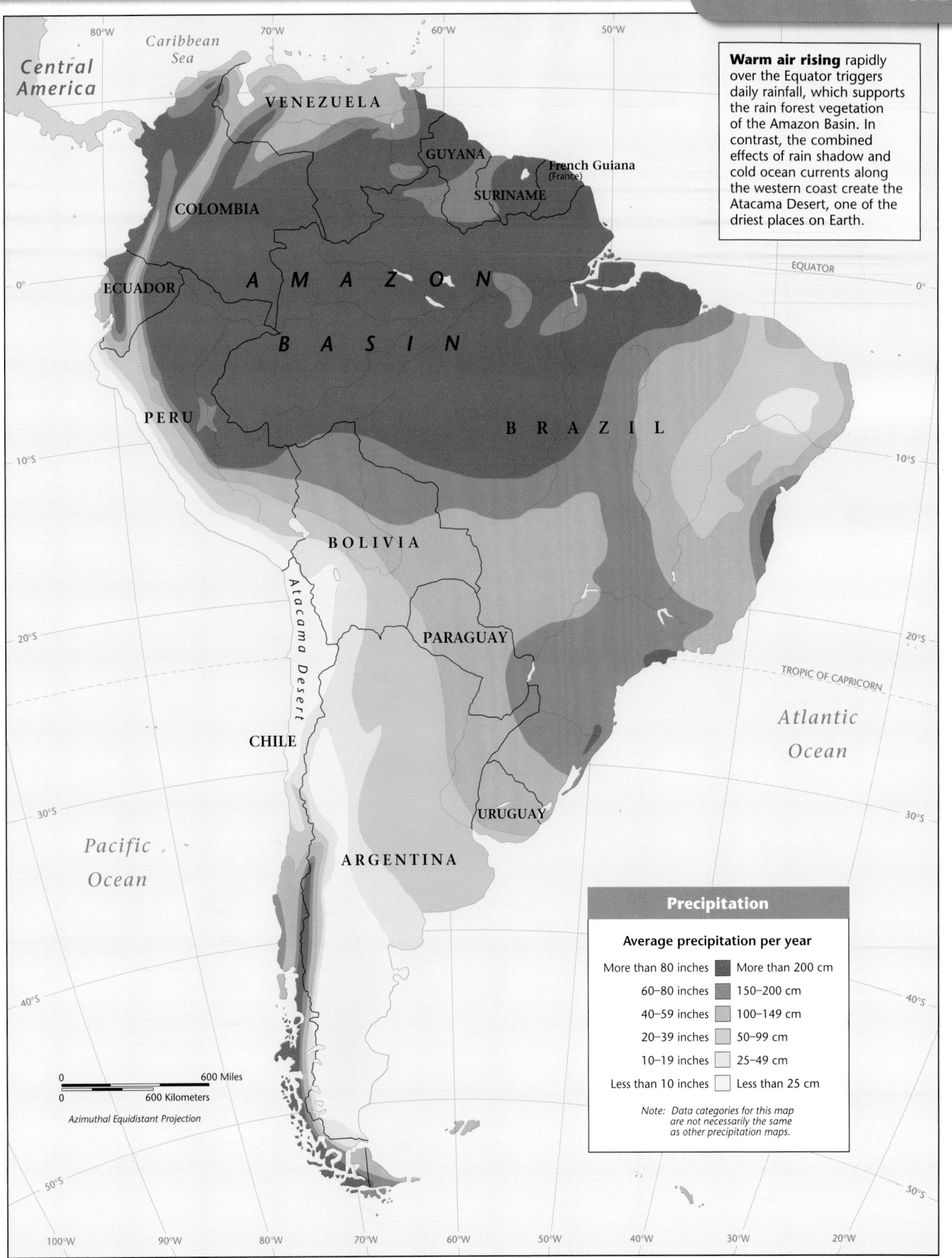

Warm air rising rapidly over the Equator triggers daily rainfall, which supports the rain forest vegetation of the Amazon Basin. In contrast, the combined effects of rain shadow and cold ocean currents along the western coast create the Atacama Desert, one of the driest places on Earth.

Central America

Caribbean Sea

VENEZUELA

GUYANA

French Guiana (France)

SURINAME

COLOMBIA

EQUATOR

ECUADOR

A M A Z O N

B A S I N

PERU

BRAZIL

Atacama Desert

BOLIVIA

PARAGUAY

TROPIC OF CAPRICORN

Atlantic Ocean

CHILE

URUGUAY

Pacific Ocean

ARGENTINA

0 — 600 Miles
0 — 600 Kilometers

Azimuthal Equidistant Projection

Precipitation

Average precipitation per year

More than 80 inches	More than 200 cm
60–80 inches	150–200 cm
40–59 inches	100–149 cm
20–39 inches	50–99 cm
10–19 inches	25–49 cm
Less than 10 inches	Less than 25 cm

Note: Data categories for this map are not necessarily the same as other precipitation maps.

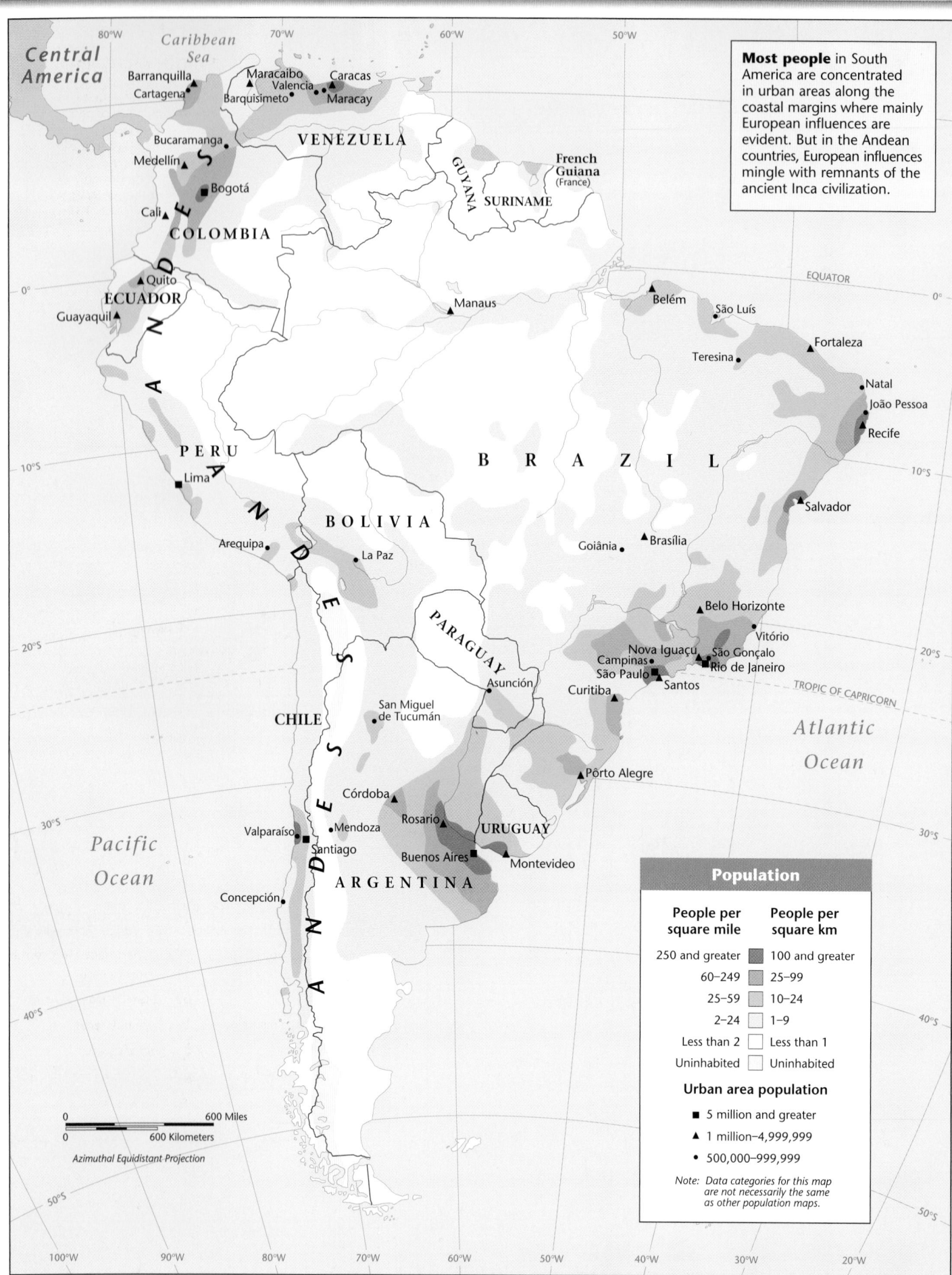

Most people in South America are concentrated in urban areas along the coastal margins where mainly European influences are evident. But in the Andean countries, European influences mingle with remnants of the ancient Inca civilization.

Central America

Caribbean Sea

80°W

70°W

60°W

50°W

Barranquilla
Cartagena
Maracaibo
Valencia
Caracas
Maracay
Barquisimeto
VENEZUELA
GUYANA
SURINAME
French Guiana (France)

Bucaramanga
Medellín
Bogotá
Cali
COLOMBIA

EQUATOR

Quito
ECUADOR
Guayaquil

0°

Belém
São Luís
Fortaleza
Manaus
Teresina
Natal
João Pessoa
Recife

PERU
Lima

B R A Z I L

10°S

Salvador

Arequipa
BOLIVIA
La Paz

Goiânia
Brasília

A N D E S

Belo Horizonte
Vitório

PARAGUAY
20°S

Nova Iguaçu
São Gonçalo
Campinas
Rio de Janeiro
São Paulo
Santos
Curitiba

Asunción

TROPIC OF CAPRICORN

Atlantic Ocean

San Miguel de Tucumán
CHILE

Pôrto Alegre

Pacific Ocean

Córdoba
Valparaíso
Mendoza
Santiago
Rosario
URUGUAY
Buenos Aires
Montevideo

30°S

Concepción
A R G E N T I N A

Población

0   600 Miles
0   600 Kilometers
Azimuthal Equidistant Projection

Population	
People per square mile	**People per square km**
250 and greater	100 and greater
60–249	25–99
25–59	10–24
2–24	1–9
Less than 2	Less than 1
Uninhabited	Uninhabited

Urban area population

■ 5 million and greater
▲ 1 million–4,999,999
• 500,000–999,999

Note: Data categories for this map are not necessarily the same as other population maps.

100°W   90°W   80°W   70°W   60°W   50°W   40°W   30°W   20°W

South America

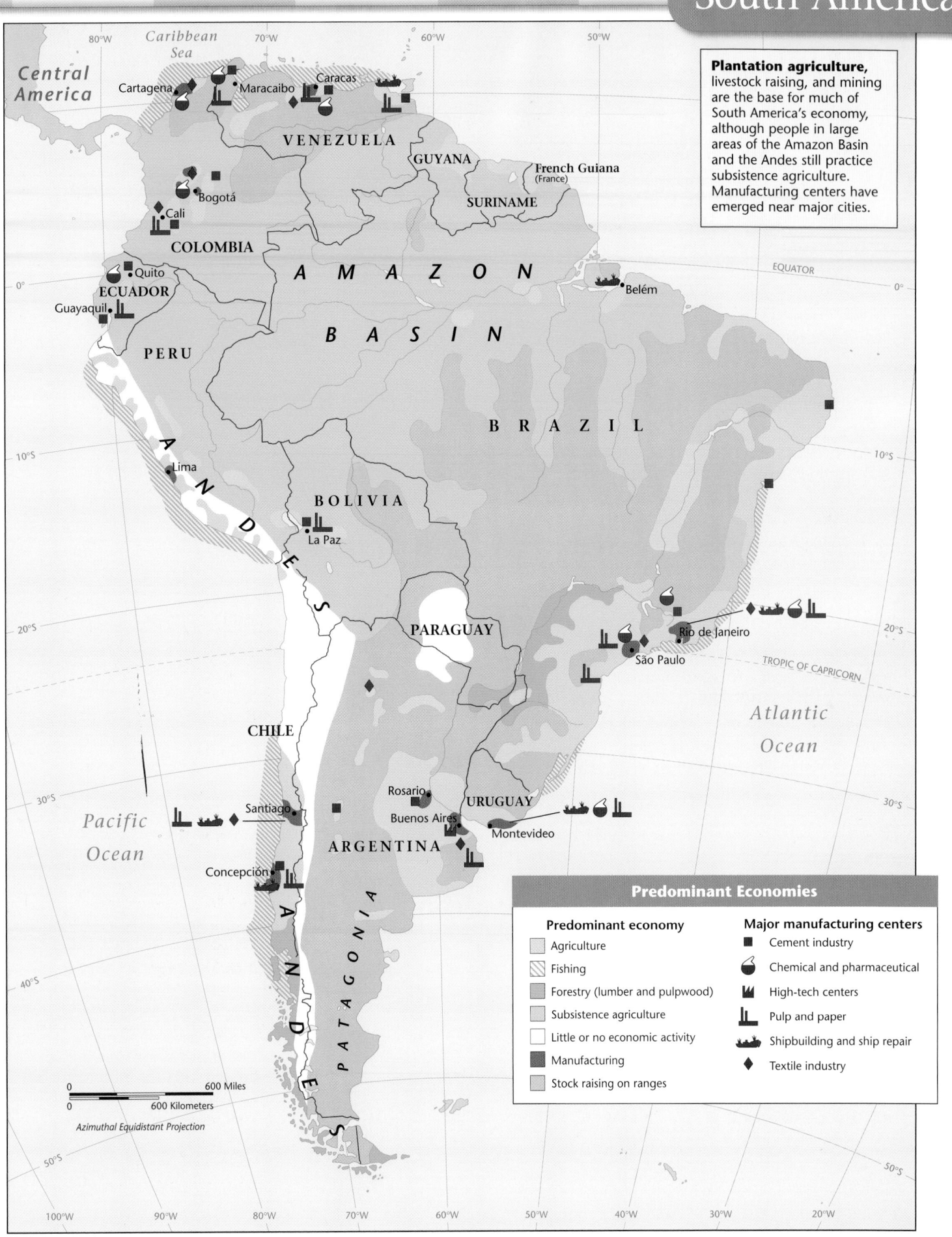

Plantation agriculture, livestock raising, and mining are the base for much of South America's economy, although people in large areas of the Amazon Basin and the Andes still practice subsistence agriculture. Manufacturing centers have emerged near major cities.

Predominant Economies

Predominant economy
- Agriculture
- Fishing
- Forestry (lumber and pulpwood)
- Subsistence agriculture
- Little or no economic activity
- Manufacturing
- Stock raising on ranges

Major manufacturing centers
- Cement industry
- Chemical and pharmaceutical
- High-tech centers
- Pulp and paper
- Shipbuilding and ship repair
- Textile industry

0 600 Miles
0 600 Kilometers
Azimuthal Equidistant Projection

Amazon Rain Forest

The Amazon rain forest, which covers approximately 2.7 million square miles (7 million sq km), is the world's largest tropical forest. Located mainly in Brazil, the Amazon rain forest accounts for more than 20 percent of all the world's tropical forests. Known in Brazil as the selva, the rain forest is a vast storehouse of biological diversity, filled with plants and animals both familiar and exotic. According to estimates, at least half of all species are found in tropical forests, but many of these species have not yet been identified.

Tropical forests contain many valuable resources, including cacao (chocolate), nuts, spices, rare hardwoods, and plant extracts used to make medicines. Some drugs used in treating cancer and heart disease come from plants found only in tropical forests. But human intervention—logging, mining, and clearing land for crops and grazing—has put tropical forests at great risk. In Brazil, roads cut into the rain forest have opened the way for settlers, who clear away the forest only to discover soil too poor in nutrients to sustain agriculture for more than a few years. Land usually is cleared by a method called slash-and-burn, which contributes to global warming by releasing great amounts of carbon dioxide into the atmosphere.

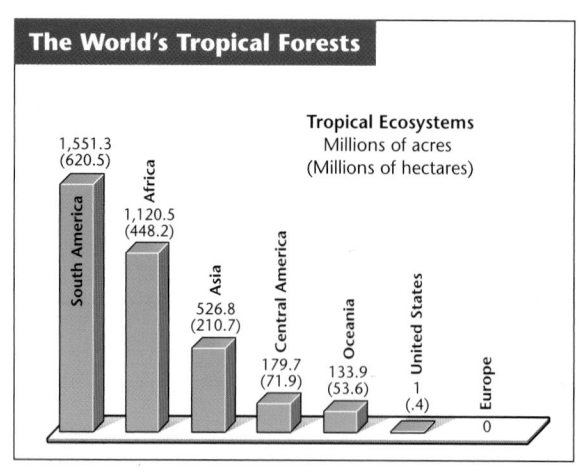

▶ **Tropical rain forests** grow in parts of every continent except Europe and Antarctica. Together, the tropical forests of South America and Africa make up three-quarters of the world's total. Brazil alone has more than 300 million acres (120 million hectares)—more than any other country.

The World's Tropical Forests

Tropical Ecosystems
Millions of acres
(Millions of hectares)

- South America: 1,551.3 (620.5)
- Africa: 1,120.5 (448.2)
- Asia: 526.8 (210.7)
- Central America: 179.7 (71.9)
- Oceania: 133.9 (53.6)
- United States: 1 (.4)
- Europe: 0

Price of Progress

CLEARING TREES to make way for expanding economic activities leads to widespread environmental destruction. Slash-and-burn agriculture exposes fragile soils to heat and torrential rains, and the runoff from mining operations pollutes streams and rivers. In an effort to reverse this trend, some countries and international organizations have set up national parks, reserves, and other protected areas.

Web Link for information on rain forests: www.wri.org

▶ **Dense canopy of the rain forest** stands in sharp contrast to the silt-laden waters of one of the Amazon's many tributaries. Although seemingly endless, the forest is rapidly decreasing in size at the rate of 200,000 acres (80,940 hectares) per day.

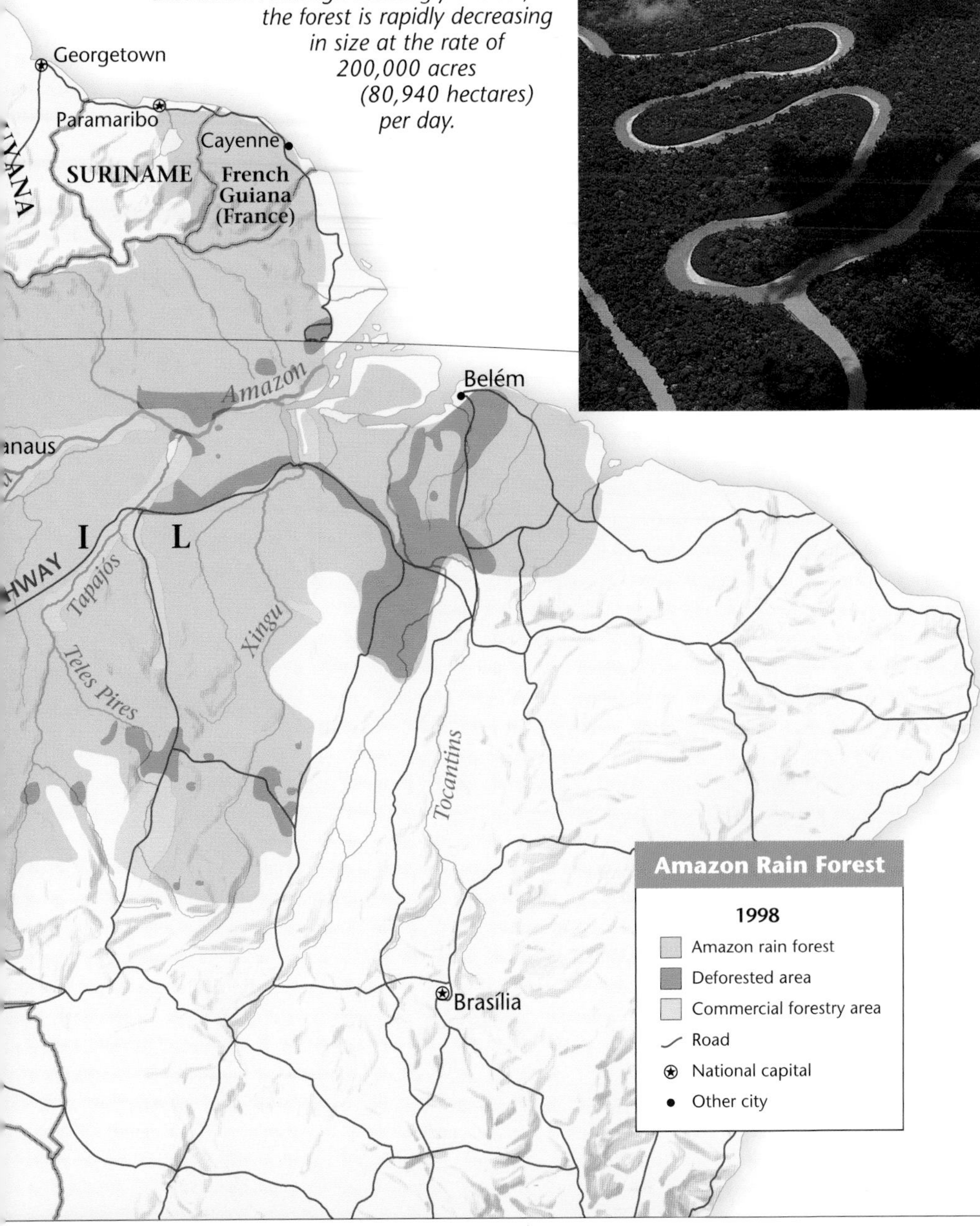

Georgetown

Paramaribo

Cayenne

SURINAME

French Guiana (France)

GUYANA

Amazon

Belém

anaus

HWAY

B R A Z I L

Tapajós

Teles Pires

Xingu

Tocantins

Brasília

Amazon Rain Forest

1998

- Amazon rain forest
- Deforested area
- Commercial forestry area
- / Road
- ⊛ National capital
- • Other city

▲ **Slow-moving,** this three-toed sloth spends most of its life in the treetops. It is one of the many unusual species of animals that make their homes in the forests of the Amazon Basin.

▲ **Slash-and-burn** is a method used in the tropics for clearing land for farms. But the soil is poor in nutrients, and good yields are short-lived.

▲ **Mining operations,** such as this tin mine, remove forests to gain access to mineral deposits.

Europe

Smaller than every other continent except Australia, Europe is a mosaic of islands and peninsulas. In fact, Europe itself is one big peninsula, jutting westward from the huge landmass of Asia and nearly touching Africa to the south. Europe's ragged coastline measures more than one and a half times the length of the Equator—37,877 miles (60,955 km) to be exact—giving 30 of its 43 countries direct access to the sea.

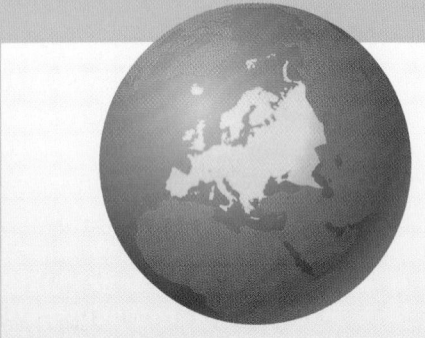

Facts & Figures

- **Land area:** 3,837,400 sq mi (9,938,000 sq km)

- **Population:** 727,758,000

- **Highest point:** Mount El'brus, Russia: 18,510 ft (5,642 m)

- **Lowest point:** Caspian Sea: 92 ft (28 m) below sea level

- **Longest river:** Volga, Russia: 2,290 mi (3,685 km)

- **Largest lake entirely in Europe:** Ladoga, Russia: 6,853 sq mi (17,703 sq km)

- **Number of independent countries:** 43 (including Russia)

- **Largest country entirely in Europe:** Ukraine 233,206 sq mi (604,001 sq km)

- **Smallest country:** Vatican City: 0.2 sq mi (0.4 sq km)

- **Most populous country entirely in Europe:** Germany: Pop. 82,141,000

- **Least populous country:** Vatican City: Pop. 1,000

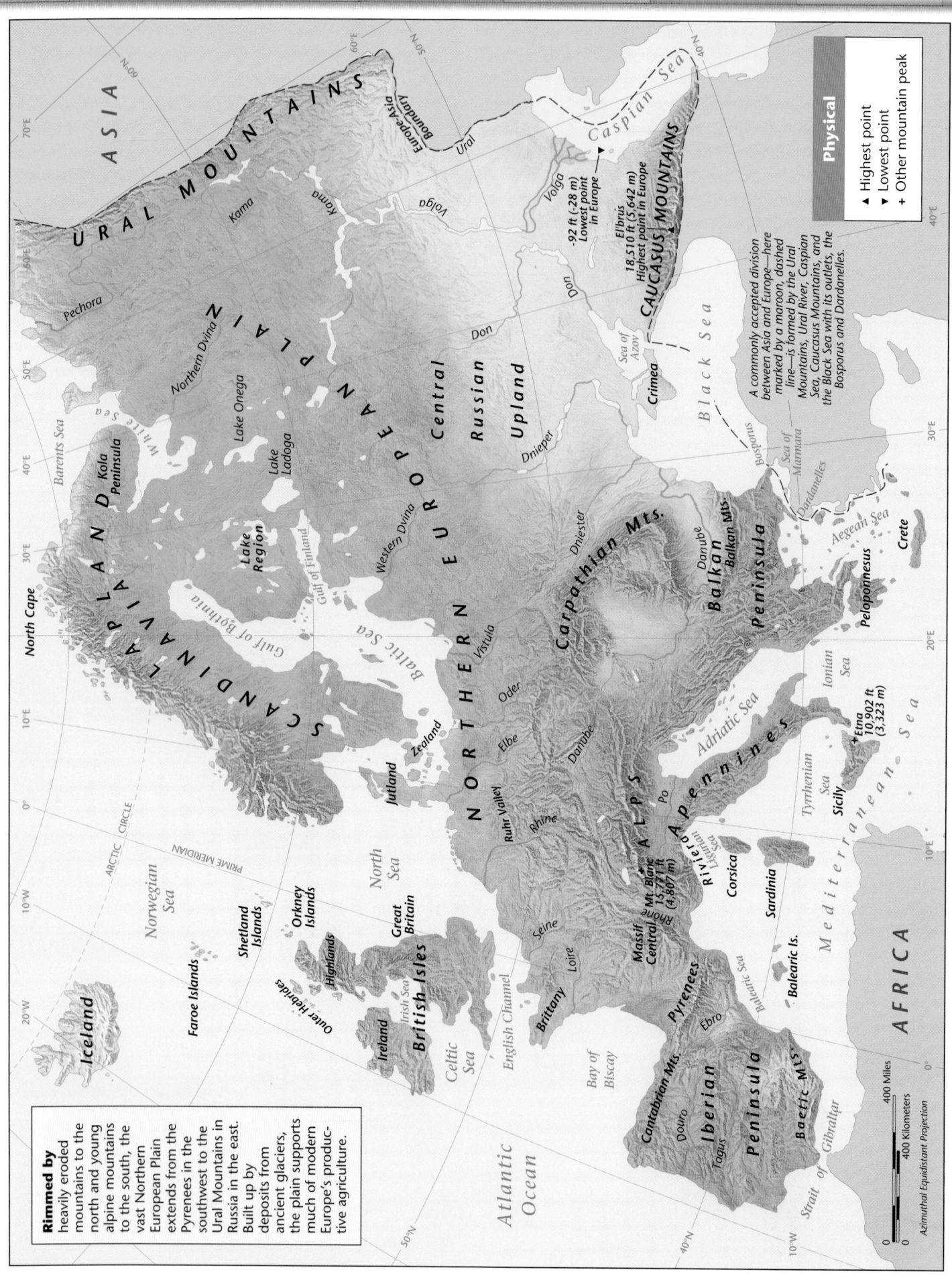

Physical

▲ Highest point
▼ Lowest point
+ Other mountain peak

A commonly accepted division between Asia and Europe—here marked by a maroon, dashed line—is formed by the Ural Mountains, Ural River, Caspian Sea, Caucasus Mountains, and the Black Sea with its outlets, the Bosporus and Dardanelles.

ASIA

URAL MOUNTAINS

Europe-Asia Boundary

Ural

Pechora

Kama

Kama

Volga

Volga

Northern Dvina

Lake Onega

Lake Ladoga

Don

Don

Dnieper

Central Russian Upland

NORTHERN EUROPEAN PLAIN

SCANDINAVIAN UPLAND

Barents Sea

White Sea

Kola Peninsula

North Cape

Lake Region

Gulf of Bothnia

Gulf of Finland

Western Dvina

Baltic Sea

Vistula

Oder

Elbe

Zealand

Jutland

Dniester

Carpathian Mts.

Danube

Danube

Balkan Mts.

Balkan Peninsula

Peloponnesus

Crete

Aegean Sea

Caspian Sea

-92 ft (-28 m) Lowest point in Europe

Elbrus 18,510 ft (5,642 m) Highest point in Europe

CAUCASUS MOUNTAINS

Crimea

Black Sea

Sea of Azov

Bosporus

Sea of Marmara

Dardanelles

Norwegian Sea

ARCTIC CIRCLE

PRIME MERIDIAN

Iceland

Faroe Islands

Shetland Islands

Orkney Islands

Highlands

Outer Hebrides

Great Britain

British Isles

Ireland

Irish Sea

North Sea

Celtic Sea

English Channel

Brittany

Seine

Loire

Bay of Biscay

Ruhr Valley

Rhine

Massif Central

Mt. Blanc 15,771 ft (4,807 m)

Rhône

ALPS

Riviera

Po

L. Geneva

Apennines

Corsica

Sardinia

Tyrrhenian Sea

Sicily

+Etna 10,902 ft (3,323 m)

Adriatic Sea

Ionian Sea

Mediterranean Sea

Balearic Sea

Balearic Is.

Pyrenees

Cantabrian Mts.

Douro

Ebro

Iberian Peninsula

Tagus

Baetic Mts.

Strait of Gibraltar

Atlantic Ocean

AFRICA

Rimmed by heavily eroded mountains to the north and young alpine mountains to the south, the vast Northern European Plain extends from the Pyrenees in the southwest to the Ural Mountains in Russia in the east. Built up by deposits from ancient glaciers, the plain supports much of modern Europe's productive agriculture.

400 Miles

400 Kilometers

Azimuthal Equidistant Projection

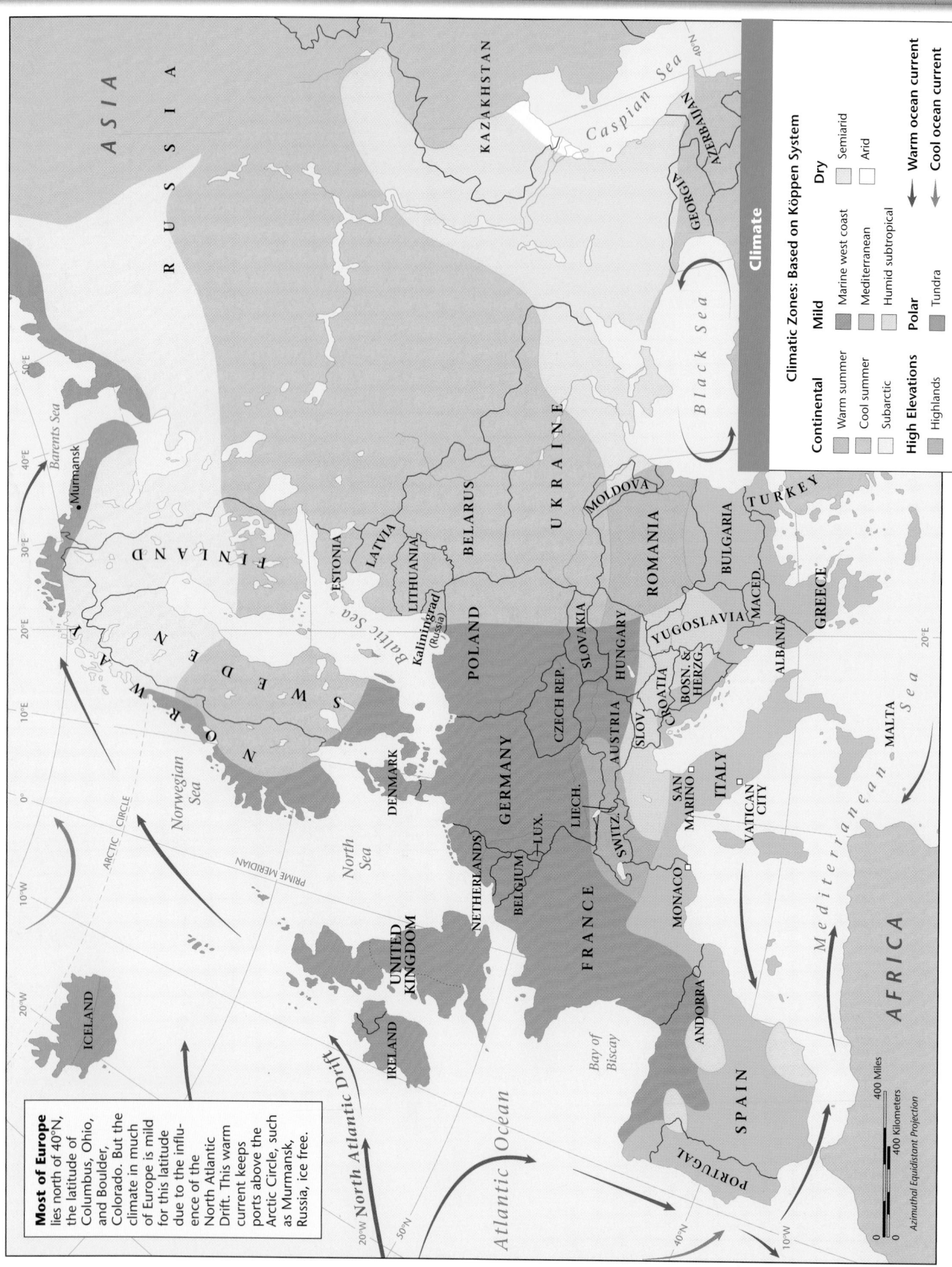

Most of Europe lies north of 40°N, the latitude of Columbus, Ohio, and Boulder, Colorado. But the climate in much of Europe is mild for this latitude due to the influence of the North Atlantic Drift. This warm current keeps ports above the Arctic Circle, such as Murmansk, Russia, ice free.

Climate

Climatic Zones: Based on Köppen System

Continental
- Warm summer
- Cool summer
- Subarctic

High Elevations
- Highlands

Mild
- Marine west coast
- Mediterranean
- Humid subtropical

Polar
- Tundra

Dry
- Semiarid
- Arid

→ Warm ocean current
→ Cool ocean current

Azimuthal Equidistant Projection

0   400 Miles
0   400 Kilometers

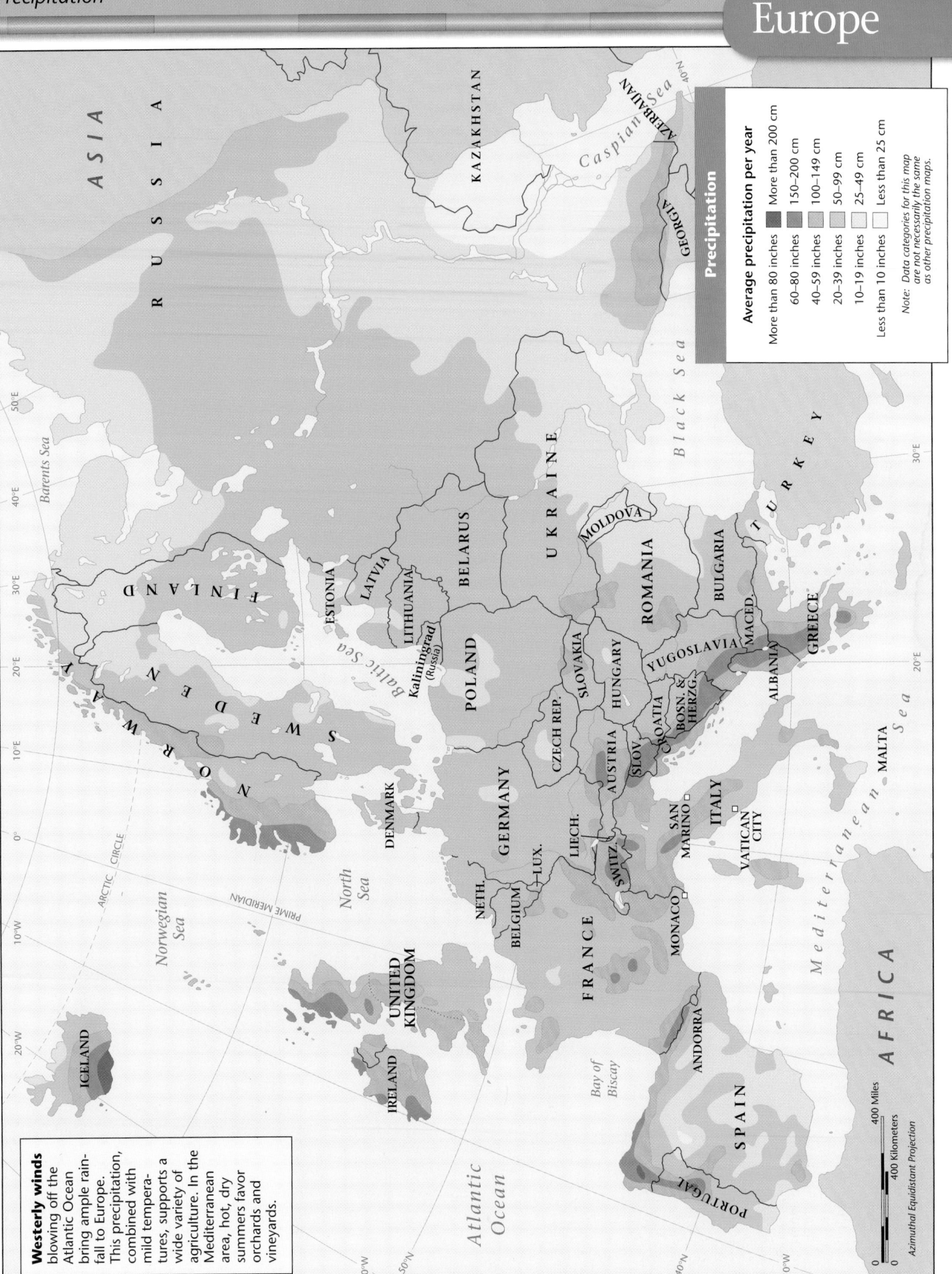

Precipitation

Average precipitation per year

More than 80 inches — More than 200 cm
60–80 inches — 150–200 cm
40–59 inches — 100–149 cm
20–39 inches — 50–99 cm
10–19 inches — 25–49 cm
Less than 10 inches — Less than 25 cm

Note: Data categories for this map are not necessarily the same as other precipitation maps.

Westerly winds blowing off the Atlantic Ocean bring ample rainfall to Europe. This precipitation, combined with mild temperatures, supports a wide variety of agriculture. In the Mediterranean area, hot, dry summers favor orchards and vineyards.

ASIA

RUSSIA

KAZAKHSTAN

Caspian Sea

AZERBAIJAN

GEORGIA

TURKEY

Black Sea

Barents Sea

FINLAND

ESTONIA
LATVIA
LITHUANIA
Kaliningrad (Russia)

BELARUS

UKRAINE

MOLDOVA

ROMANIA

BULGARIA

MACED.

GREECE

ALBANIA

YUGOSLAVIA

POLAND

CZECH REP.

SLOVAKIA

HUNGARY

CROATIA

BOSN. & HERZG.

SLOV.

AUSTRIA

Baltic Sea

SWEDEN

NORWAY

DENMARK

GERMANY

NETH.

BELGIUM

LUX.

LIECH.

SWITZ.

FRANCE

SAN MARINO

MONACO

ITALY

VATICAN CITY

MALTA

Mediterranean Sea

AFRICA

ANDORRA

SPAIN

PORTUGAL

Bay of Biscay

Atlantic Ocean

North Sea

Norwegian Sea

IRELAND

UNITED KINGDOM

ICELAND

ARCTIC CIRCLE

PRIME MERIDIAN

400 Miles
400 Kilometers
0
0
Azimuthal Equidistant Projection

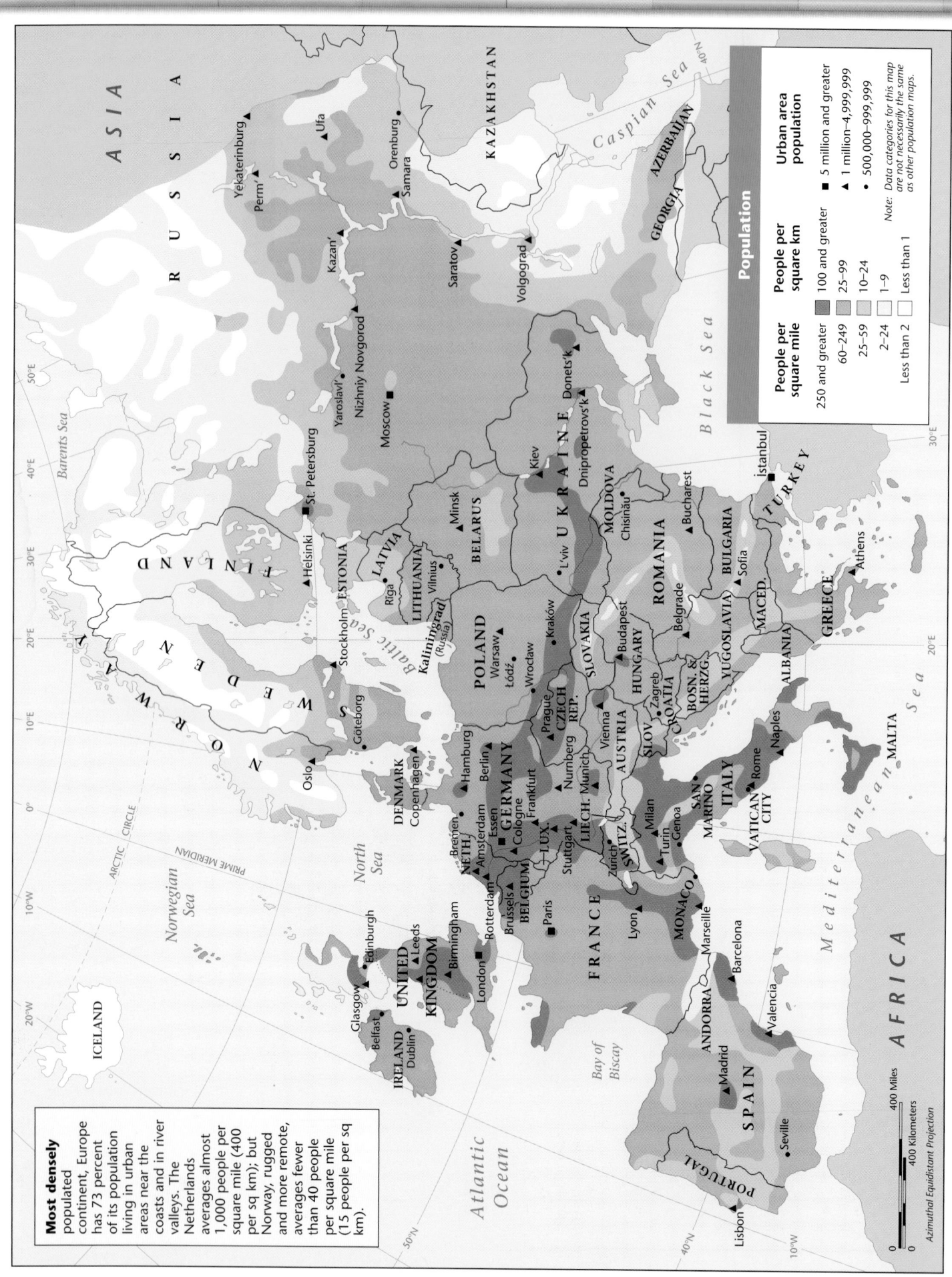

Population

People per square mile
- 250 and greater
- 60–249
- 25–59
- 2–24
- Less than 2

People per square km
- 100 and greater
- 25–99
- 10–24
- 1–9
- Less than 1

Urban area population
- ■ 5 million and greater
- ▲ 1 million–4,999,999
- ● 500,000–999,999

Note: Data categories for this map are not necessarily the same as other population maps.

Most densely populated continent, Europe has 73 percent of its population living in urban areas near the coasts and in river valleys. The Netherlands averages almost 1,000 people per square mile (400 per sq km); but Norway, rugged and more remote, averages fewer than 40 people per square mile (15 people per sq km).

Azimuthal Equidistant Projection

Europe

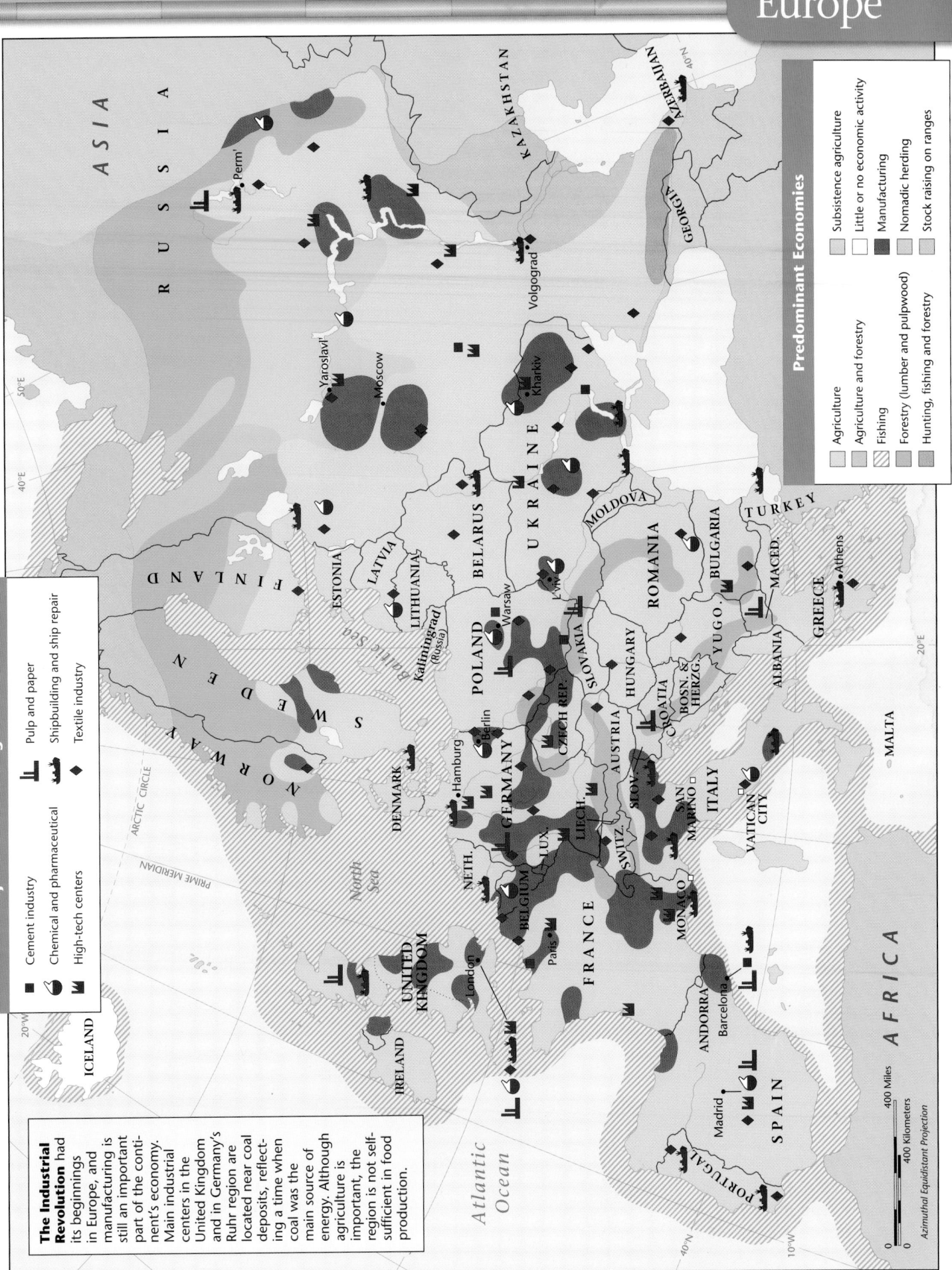

Major Manufacturing Centers

- ■ Cement industry
- ◖ Chemical and pharmaceutical
- ⚒ High-tech centers
- ⊥⊤ Pulp and paper
- ⚓ Shipbuilding and ship repair
- ◆ Textile industry

ICELAND

The Industrial Revolution had its beginnings in Europe, and manufacturing is still an important part of the continent's economy. Main industrial centers in the United Kingdom and in Germany's Ruhr region are located near coal deposits, reflecting a time when coal was the main source of energy. Although agriculture is important, the region is not self-sufficient in food production.

Predominant Economies

- Agriculture
- Agriculture and forestry
- ▨ Fishing
- Forestry (lumber and pulpwood)
- Hunting, fishing and forestry
- Subsistence agriculture
- Little or no economic activity
- Manufacturing
- Nomadic herding
- Stock raising on ranges

ASIA
RUSSIA
KAZAKHSTAN
AZERBAIJAN
GEORGIA
• Perm'
Volgograd •
Yaroslavl'
• Moscow
Kharkiv •
UKRAINE
MOLDOVA
BELARUS
ESTONIA
LATVIA
LITHUANIA
Kaliningrad (Russia)
POLAND
Warsaw •
ROMANIA
BULGARIA
TURKEY
MACED.
GREECE
Athens •
ALBANIA
YUGO.
BOSN. & HERZG.
CROATIA
HUNGARY
SLOVAKIA
CZECH REP.
AUSTRIA
SLOV.
ITALY
SAN MARINO
VATICAN CITY
SWITZ.
LIECH.
GERMANY
Berlin •
Hamburg •
DENMARK
LUX.
BELGIUM
MONACO
FRANCE
Paris •
ANDORRA
Barcelona •
SPAIN
Madrid •
PORTUGAL
NETH.
UNITED KINGDOM
London •
IRELAND
North Sea
Atlantic Ocean
NORWAY
SWEDEN
FINLAND
Baltic Sea
ARCTIC CIRCLE
PRIME MERIDIAN
AFRICA
MALTA

400 Miles
400 Kilometers
Azimuthal Equidistant Projection

50°E
40°E
20°E
20°W
10°W
40°N

FOCUS ON

European Union

In the years following World War II, the countries of Europe looked for ways to restore political stability to the continent while rebuilding their war-ravaged economies. The first step toward the European Union was taken in 1950 when France proposed creating common institutions to govern coal and steel production in Europe jointly. In 1951 France, West Germany, Italy, Belgium, Netherlands, and Luxembourg created the European Coal and Steel Community with the goal of bringing former adversaries together. In 1965 that organization became the European Community (EC).

The Maastricht Treaty took effect in 1993, establishing today's European Union (EU) and paving the way for a common foreign policy and a single European currency. The treaty also laid plans for the open flow of people, products, and services among the member countries. Since 1993, three more countries have joined the EU, bringing the total number of members to 15 (see map). As of the year 2000, 12 other countries were actively seeking admission: Bulgaria, Cypress, Czech Republic, Estonia, Hungary, Latvia, Lithuania, Poland, Romania, Slovakia, Slovenia, and Turkey.

▲ **Main trade outlet** for Germany's heavily industrialized Ruhr Valley, the port of Rotterdam in the Netherlands accommodates massive supertankers and container ships.

Web Link for information on the European Union: www.europa.eu.int

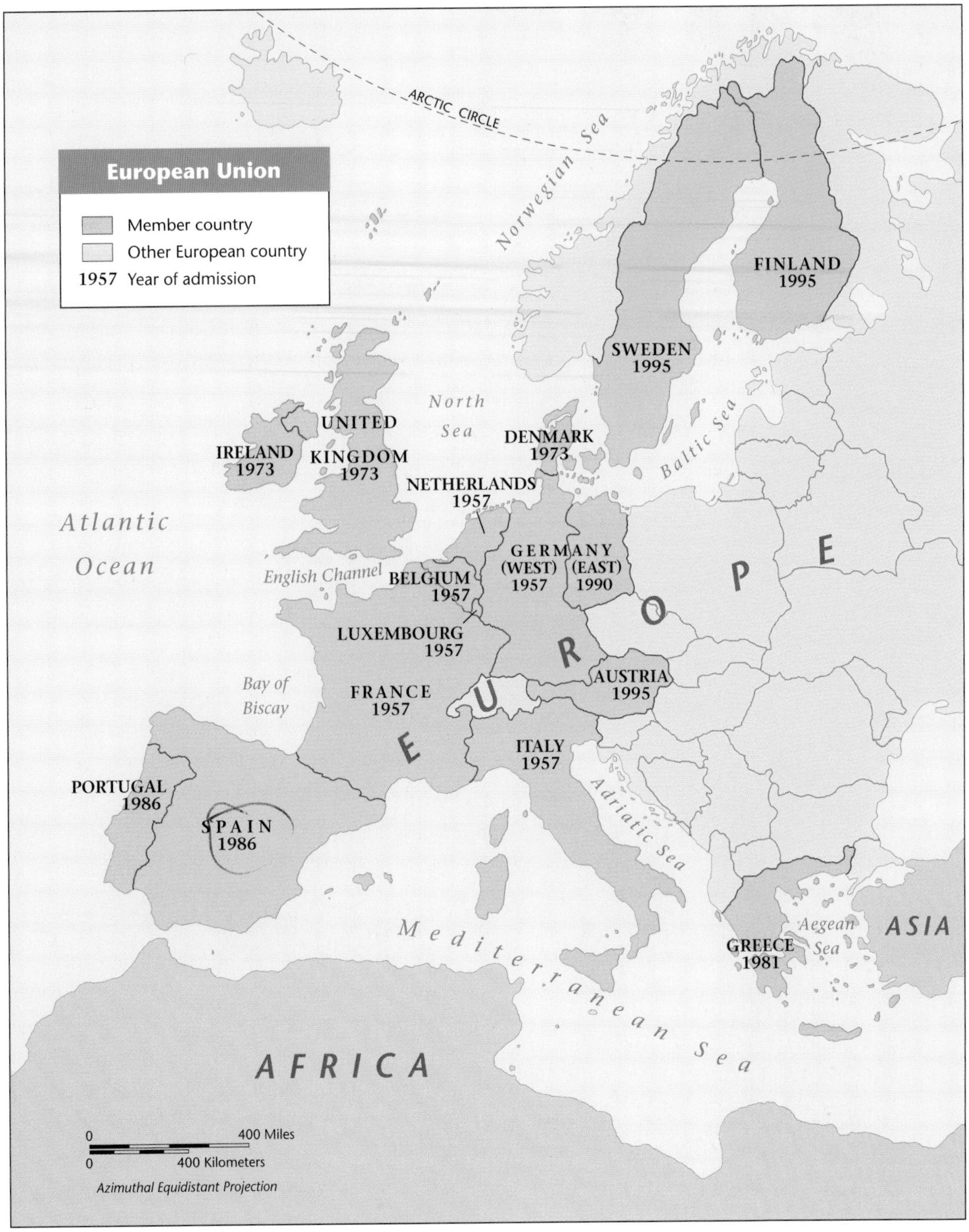

European Union

- Member country
- Other European country
- 1957 Year of admission

(Map of Europe showing EU member countries and years of admission)

FINLAND 1995
SWEDEN 1995
UNITED KINGDOM 1973
IRELAND 1973
DENMARK 1973
NETHERLANDS 1957
BELGIUM 1957
GERMANY (WEST) 1957
GERMANY (EAST) 1990
LUXEMBOURG 1957
FRANCE 1957
AUSTRIA 1995
ITALY 1957
PORTUGAL 1986
SPAIN 1986
GREECE 1981

North Sea
Norwegian Sea
Baltic Sea
Atlantic Ocean
English Channel
Bay of Biscay
Adriatic Sea
Aegean Sea
Mediterranean Sea
ARCTIC CIRCLE
EUROPE
ASIA
AFRICA

0 — 400 Miles
0 — 400 Kilometers
Azimuthal Equidistant Projection

Symbols of New Unity

THE FLAG of the Council of Europe, a circle of gold stars on a field of blue, was adopted as a symbol of unity first by the EC and then by the EU. Another important step toward European unity came in 1999 with the introduction of a common currency—the euro—which is scheduled to begin circulating in January 2002.

European Union's Share of World Trade

Acting as a trade bloc, the European Union is a major player in the global economy. With only a little more than six percent of the world's population, the EU accounts for about twice the trade of the U.S. and Canada combined or of Asia. The three regions together account for more than 80 percent of world trade in both products and services.

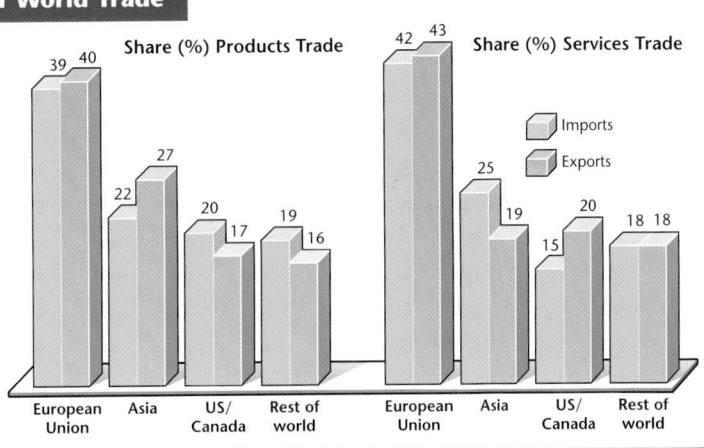

Share (%) Products Trade

	European Union	Asia	US/Canada	Rest of world
Imports	39	22	20	19
Exports	40	27	17	16

Share (%) Services Trade

	European Union	Asia	US/Canada	Rest of world
Imports	42	25	15	18
Exports	43	19	20	18

Africa

From space, Africa appears divided into three regions: the northern third, dominated by the vast Sahara, largest hot desert in the world; a central green band of rain forests and tropical grasslands; and more dry lands to the south. Africa itself may be dividing literally: The Great Rift Valley, which runs from the Red Sea through the volcanic Afar Triangle to the lake district in the south (see map page 85), eventually may split apart the continent.

Facts & Figures

▶ **Land area:** 11,609,000 sq mi (30,065,000 sq km)

▶ **Population:** 800,245,000

▶ **Highest point:** Mount Kilimanjaro, Tanzania: 19,340 ft (5,895 m)

▶ **Lowest point:** Lake Assal, Djibouti: 512 ft (156 m) below sea level

▶ **Longest river:** Nile: 4,241 mi (6,825 km)

▶ **Largest Lake:** Victoria: 26,836 sq mi (69,500 sq km)

▶ **Number of independent countries:** 53

▶ **Largest country:** Sudan: 963,600 sq mi (2,495,712 sq km)

▶ **Smallest country:** Seychelles: 175 sq mi (453 sq km)

▶ **Most populous country:** Nigeria: Pop. 123,338,000

▶ **Least populous country:** Seychelles: Pop. 82,000

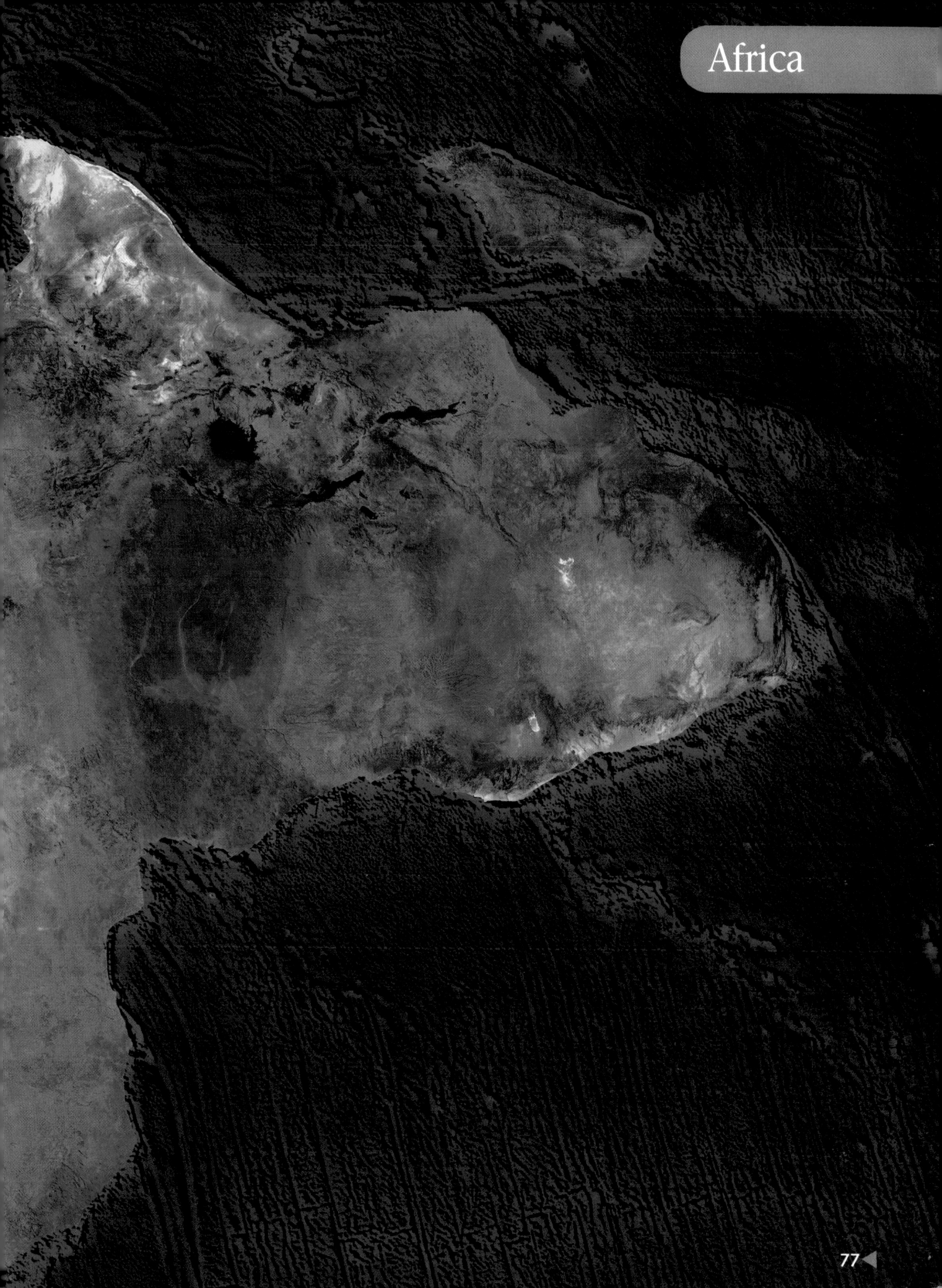

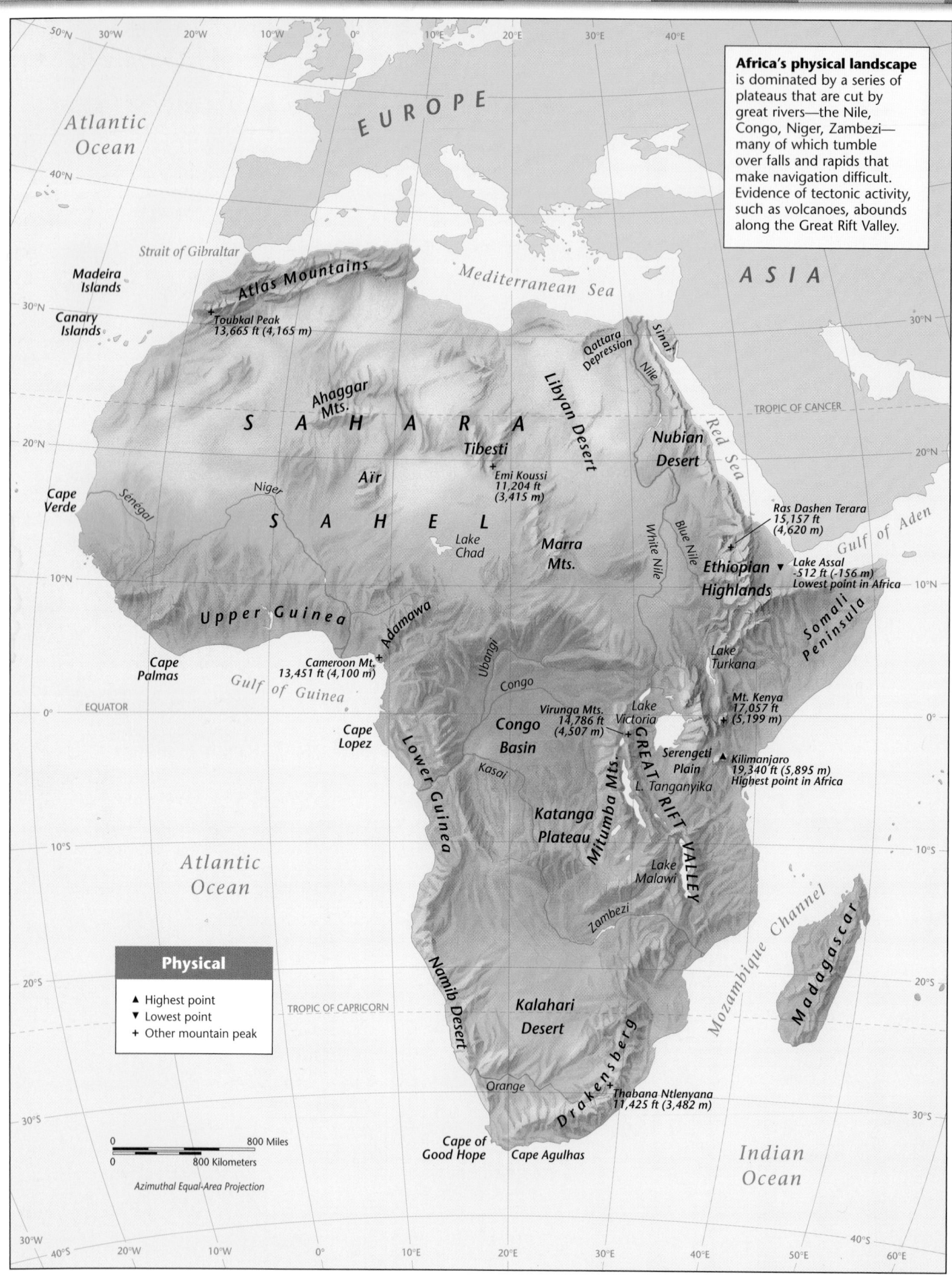

Africa's physical landscape is dominated by a series of plateaus that are cut by great rivers—the Nile, Congo, Niger, Zambezi—many of which tumble over falls and rapids that make navigation difficult. Evidence of tectonic activity, such as volcanoes, abounds along the Great Rift Valley.

EUROPE

ASIA

Atlantic Ocean

Mediterranean Sea

Strait of Gibraltar

Madeira Islands

Canary Islands

Atlas Mountains
+ Toubkal Peak
13,665 ft (4,165 m)

Qattara Depression

Sinai

Nile

TROPIC OF CANCER

Ahaggar Mts.

S A H A R A

Libyan Desert

Nubian Desert

Red Sea

Tibesti

Aïr

+ Emi Koussi
11,204 ft
(3,415 m)

Niger

Cape Verde

Sénégal

S A H E L

Lake Chad

Marra Mts.

White Nile

Blue Nile

Ras Dashen Terara
15,157 ft
(4,620 m)

Gulf of Aden

Lake Assal
-512 ft (-156 m)
Lowest point in Africa

Ethiopian Highlands

Somali Peninsula

Upper Guinea

Adamawa

Ubangi

Cape Palmas

Cameroon Mt.
13,451 ft (4,100 m)

Gulf of Guinea

Congo

Lake Turkana

Mt. Kenya
17,057 ft
(5,199 m)

EQUATOR

Cape Lopez

Congo Basin

Virunga Mts.
14,786 ft
(4,507 m)

Lake Victoria

GREAT RIFT VALLEY

Kasai

Lower Guinea

Serengeti Plain

Kilimanjaro
19,340 ft (5,895 m)
Highest point in Africa

L. Tanganyika

Mitumba Mts.

Katanga Plateau

Atlantic Ocean

Lake Malawi

Zambezi

Mozambique Channel

Madagascar

Namib Desert

Physical

▲ Highest point
▼ Lowest point
+ Other mountain peak

TROPIC OF CAPRICORN

Kalahari Desert

Drakensberg

Orange

+ Thabana Ntlenyana
11,425 ft (3,482 m)

0   800 Miles
0   800 Kilometers

Azimuthal Equal-Area Projection

Cape of Good Hope

Cape Agulhas

Indian Ocean

Africa

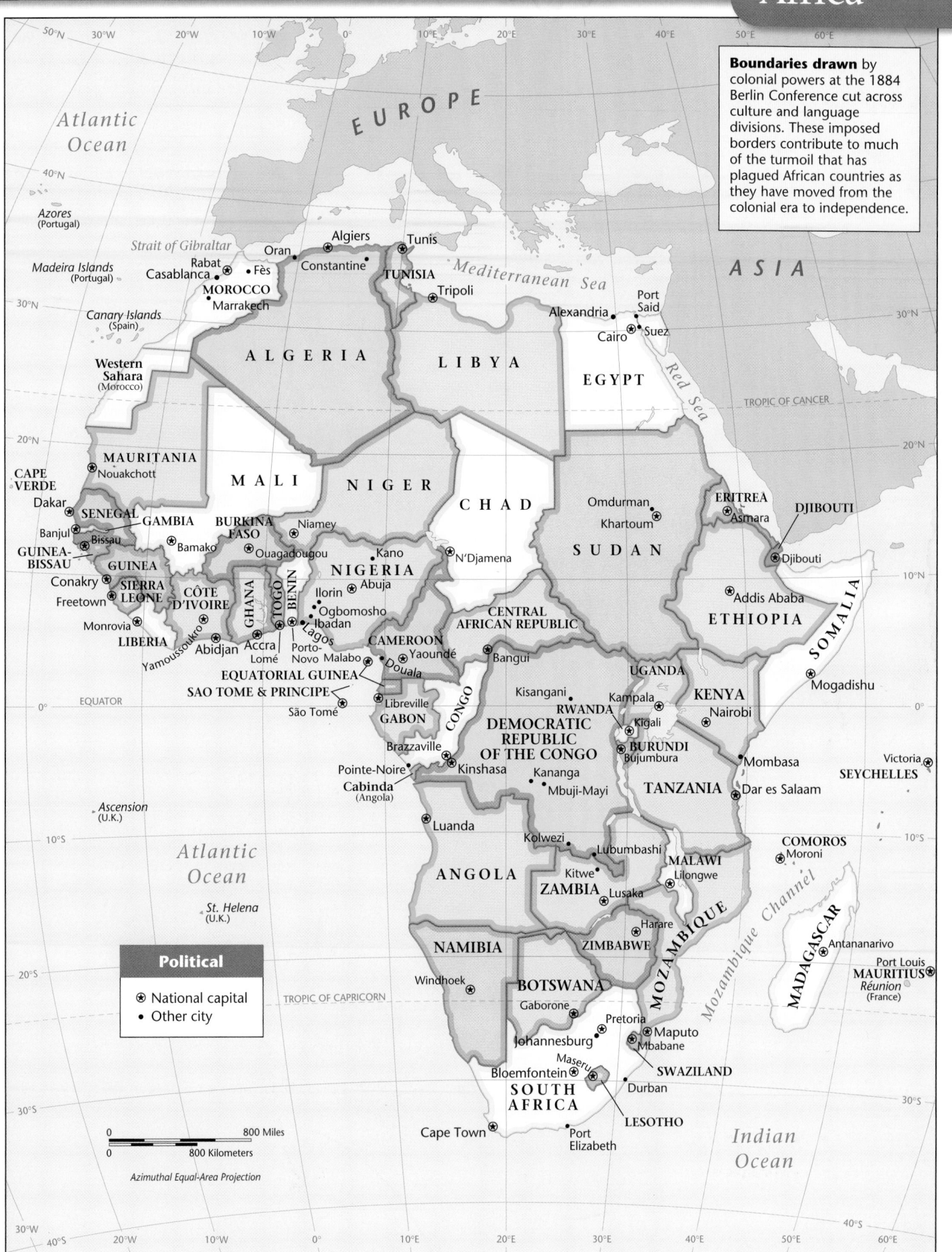

Boundaries drawn by colonial powers at the 1884 Berlin Conference cut across culture and language divisions. These imposed borders contribute to much of the turmoil that has plagued African countries as they have moved from the colonial era to independence.

EUROPE

ASIA

Atlantic Ocean

Azores (Portugal)

Madeira Islands (Portugal)

Canary Islands (Spain)

Western Sahara (Morocco)

Strait of Gibraltar

Mediterranean Sea

Algiers
Tunis
Oran
Constantine
TUNISIA
Tripoli
Rabat
Casablanca Fès
MOROCCO
Marrakech

ALGERIA

LIBYA

EGYPT

Alexandria
Port Said
Cairo Suez

Red Sea

TROPIC OF CANCER

MAURITANIA
Nouakchott

CAPE VERDE

Dakar
SENEGAL GAMBIA
Banjul
Bissau
GUINEA-BISSAU
GUINEA
Conakry
SIERRA LEONE
Freetown
Monrovia
LIBERIA
Yamoussoukro
Abidjan
CÔTE D'IVOIRE
GHANA
TOGO
BENIN
Accra
Lomé
Porto-Novo

MALI

Bamako
BURKINA FASO
Ouagadougou
Niamey

NIGER

Kano
NIGERIA
Ilorin
Abuja
Ogbomosho
Ibadan
Lagos
Malabo

CHAD

N'Djamena

SUDAN

Omdurman
Khartoum

ERITREA
Asmara

DJIBOUTI
Djibouti

Addis Ababa

ETHIOPIA

SOMALIA

CENTRAL AFRICAN REPUBLIC

CAMEROON
Yaoundé
Douala
EQUATORIAL GUINEA
SAO TOME & PRINCIPE
São Tomé
Libreville
GABON
CONGO
Brazzaville
Pointe-Noire
Cabinda (Angola)

Bangui

Kisangani

UGANDA
Kampala

RWANDA
Kigali
BURUNDI
Bujumbura

KENYA
Nairobi

Mogadishu

SEYCHELLES
Victoria

DEMOCRATIC REPUBLIC OF THE CONGO

Kinshasa
Kananga
Mbuji-Mayi

Kolwezi
Lubumbashi
Kitwe
ZAMBIA
Lusaka

TANZANIA
Dar es Salaam
Mombasa

COMOROS
Moroni

Luanda

ANGOLA

MALAWI
Lilongwe

Harare
ZIMBABWE

MOZAMBIQUE

Mozambique Channel

MADAGASCAR
Antananarivo

MAURITIUS
Port Louis
Réunion (France)

NAMIBIA
Windhoek

BOTSWANA
Gaborone
Pretoria
Johannesburg
Maseru
Bloemfontein
SOUTH AFRICA
Cape Town
Port Elizabeth
Durban
Maputo
Mbabane
SWAZILAND
LESOTHO

Atlantic Ocean

Ascension (U.K.)

St. Helena (U.K.)

EQUATOR

TROPIC OF CAPRICORN

Indian Ocean

Political

⊛ National capital
• Other city

0   800 Miles
0   800 Kilometers

Azimuthal Equal-Area Projection

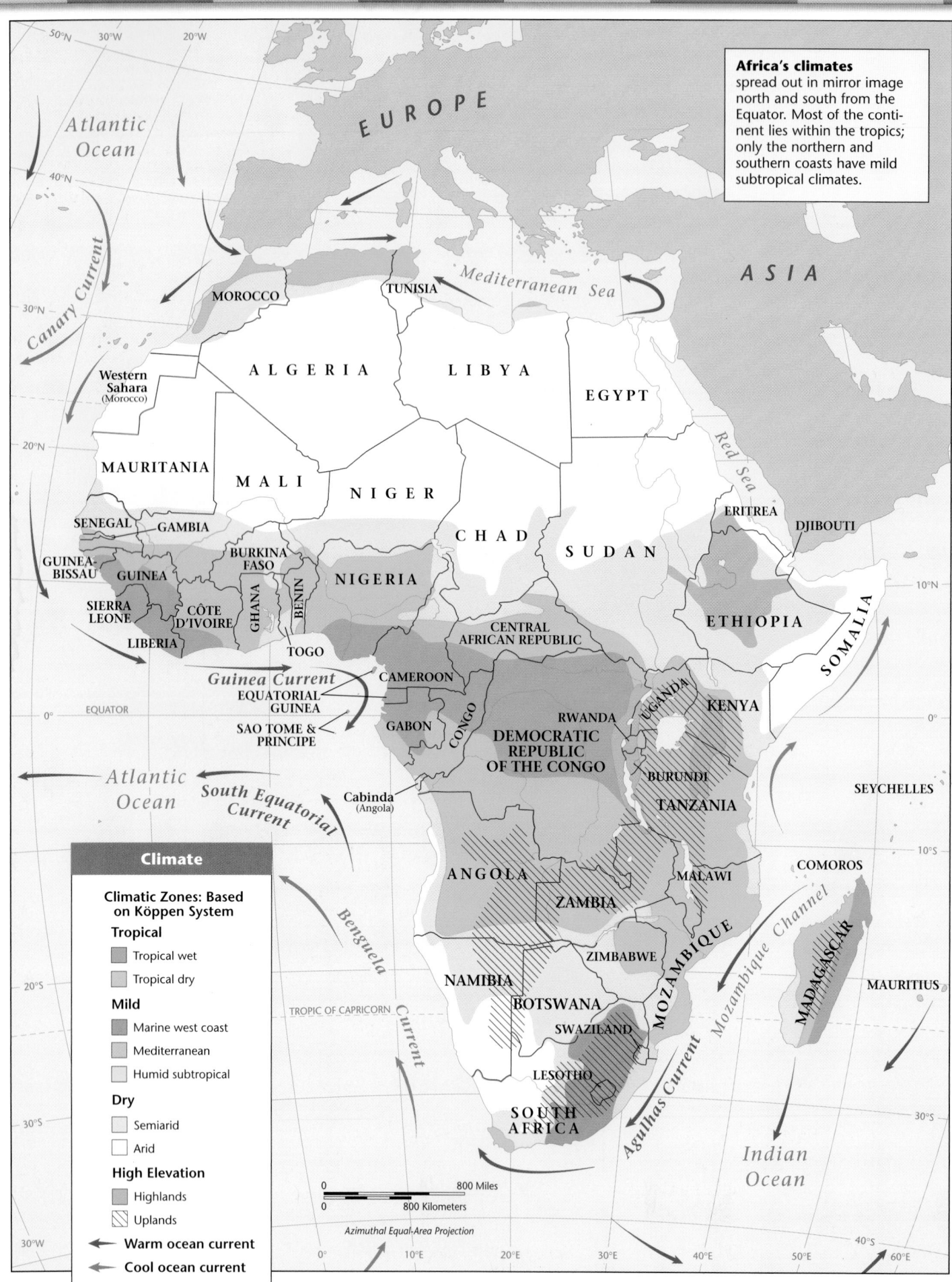

Climate

Africa's climates spread out in mirror image north and south from the Equator. Most of the continent lies within the tropics; only the northern and southern coasts have mild subtropical climates.

EUROPE

ASIA

Atlantic Ocean

Canary Current

Mediterranean Sea

MOROCCO

TUNISIA

ALGERIA

LIBYA

EGYPT

Western Sahara (Morocco)

MAURITANIA

MALI

NIGER

CHAD

SUDAN

Red Sea

ERITREA

DJIBOUTI

SENEGAL

GAMBIA

BURKINA FASO

NIGERIA

ETHIOPIA

GUINEA-BISSAU

GUINEA

GHANA

BENIN

CENTRAL AFRICAN REPUBLIC

SOMALIA

SIERRA LEONE

CÔTE D'IVOIRE

LIBERIA

TOGO

Guinea Current

CAMEROON

EQUATORIAL GUINEA

SAO TOME & PRINCIPE

GABON

CONGO

DEMOCRATIC REPUBLIC OF THE CONGO

RWANDA

UGANDA

KENYA

BURUNDI

TANZANIA

SEYCHELLES

EQUATOR

Atlantic Ocean

South Equatorial Current

Cabinda (Angola)

ANGOLA

ZAMBIA

MALAWI

COMOROS

Benguela Current

NAMIBIA

BOTSWANA

ZIMBABWE

MOZAMBIQUE

Mozambique Channel

MADAGASCAR

MAURITIUS

TROPIC OF CAPRICORN

SWAZILAND

Agulhas Current

LESOTHO

SOUTH AFRICA

Indian Ocean

Climate

Climatic Zones: Based on Köppen System

Tropical
- Tropical wet
- Tropical dry

Mild
- Marine west coast
- Mediterranean
- Humid subtropical

Dry
- Semiarid
- Arid

High Elevation
- Highlands
- Uplands

← Warm ocean current
← Cool ocean current

0   800 Miles
0   800 Kilometers

Azimuthal Equal-Area Projection

Africa

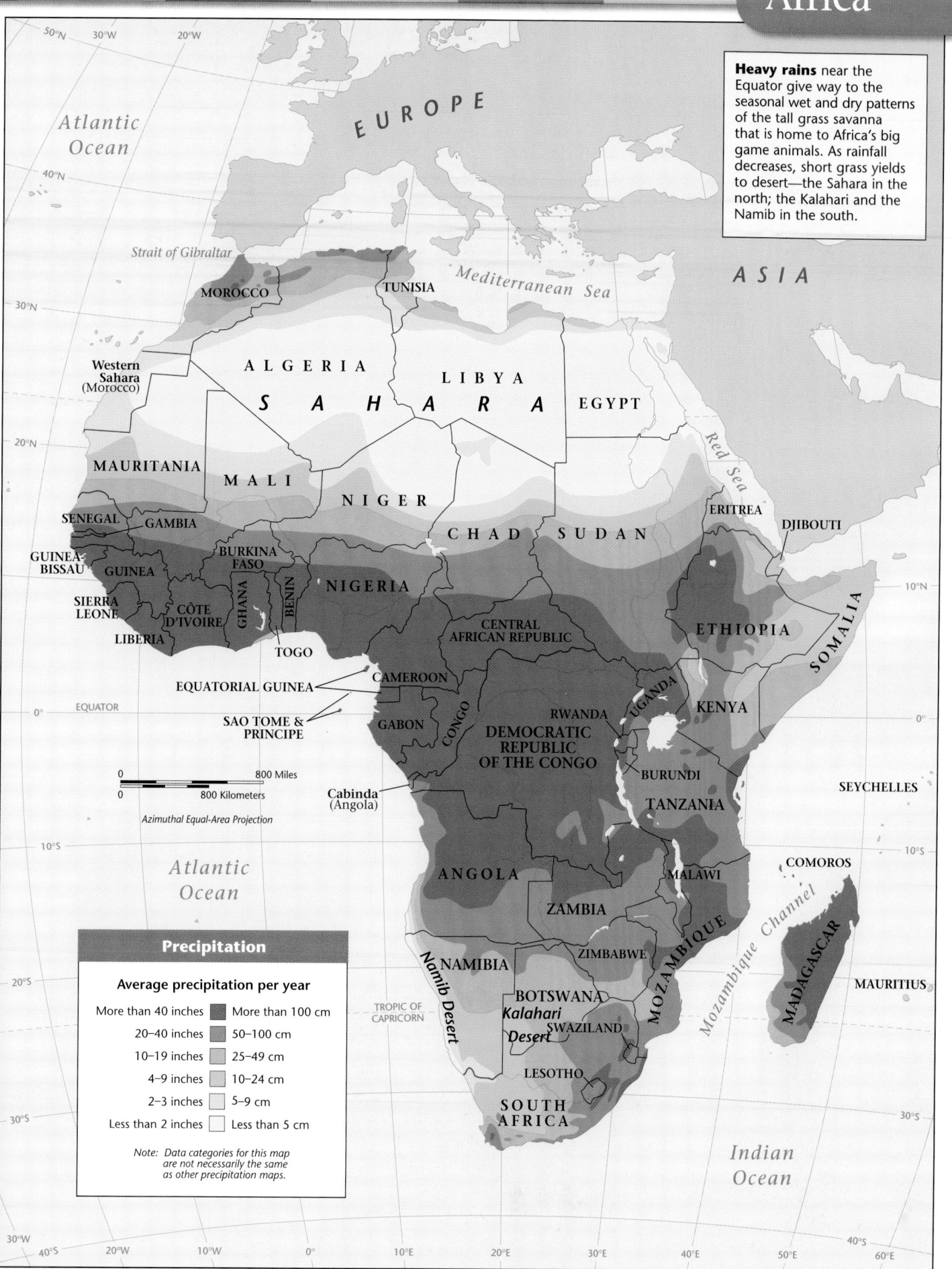

Heavy rains near the Equator give way to the seasonal wet and dry patterns of the tall grass savanna that is home to Africa's big game animals. As rainfall decreases, short grass yields to desert—the Sahara in the north; the Kalahari and the Namib in the south.

Atlantic Ocean

EUROPE

Strait of Gibraltar

Mediterranean Sea

ASIA

MOROCCO
TUNISIA
Western Sahara (Morocco)
ALGERIA
LIBYA
EGYPT
SAHARA
Red Sea
MAURITANIA
MALI
NIGER
CHAD
SUDAN
ERITREA
DJIBOUTI
SENEGAL
GAMBIA
GUINEA-BISSAU
GUINEA
BURKINA FASO
GHANA
BENIN
NIGERIA
SIERRA LEONE
CÔTE D'IVOIRE
LIBERIA
TOGO
CENTRAL AFRICAN REPUBLIC
ETHIOPIA
SOMALIA
EQUATORIAL GUINEA
CAMEROON
SAO TOME & PRINCIPE
GABON
CONGO
DEMOCRATIC REPUBLIC OF THE CONGO
RWANDA
UGANDA
KENYA
EQUATOR
BURUNDI
TANZANIA
SEYCHELLES
Cabinda (Angola)

0   800 Miles
0   800 Kilometers
Azimuthal Equal-Area Projection

ANGOLA
ZAMBIA
MALAWI
COMOROS
NAMIBIA
ZIMBABWE
MOZAMBIQUE
Mozambique Channel
MADAGASCAR
MAURITIUS
Namib Desert
BOTSWANA
Kalahari Desert
SWAZILAND
TROPIC OF CAPRICORN
LESOTHO
SOUTH AFRICA
Atlantic Ocean
Indian Ocean

Precipitation

Average precipitation per year

More than 40 inches	More than 100 cm
20–40 inches	50–100 cm
10–19 inches	25–49 cm
4–9 inches	10–24 cm
2–3 inches	5–9 cm
Less than 2 inches	Less than 5 cm

Note: Data categories for this map are not necessarily the same as other precipitation maps.

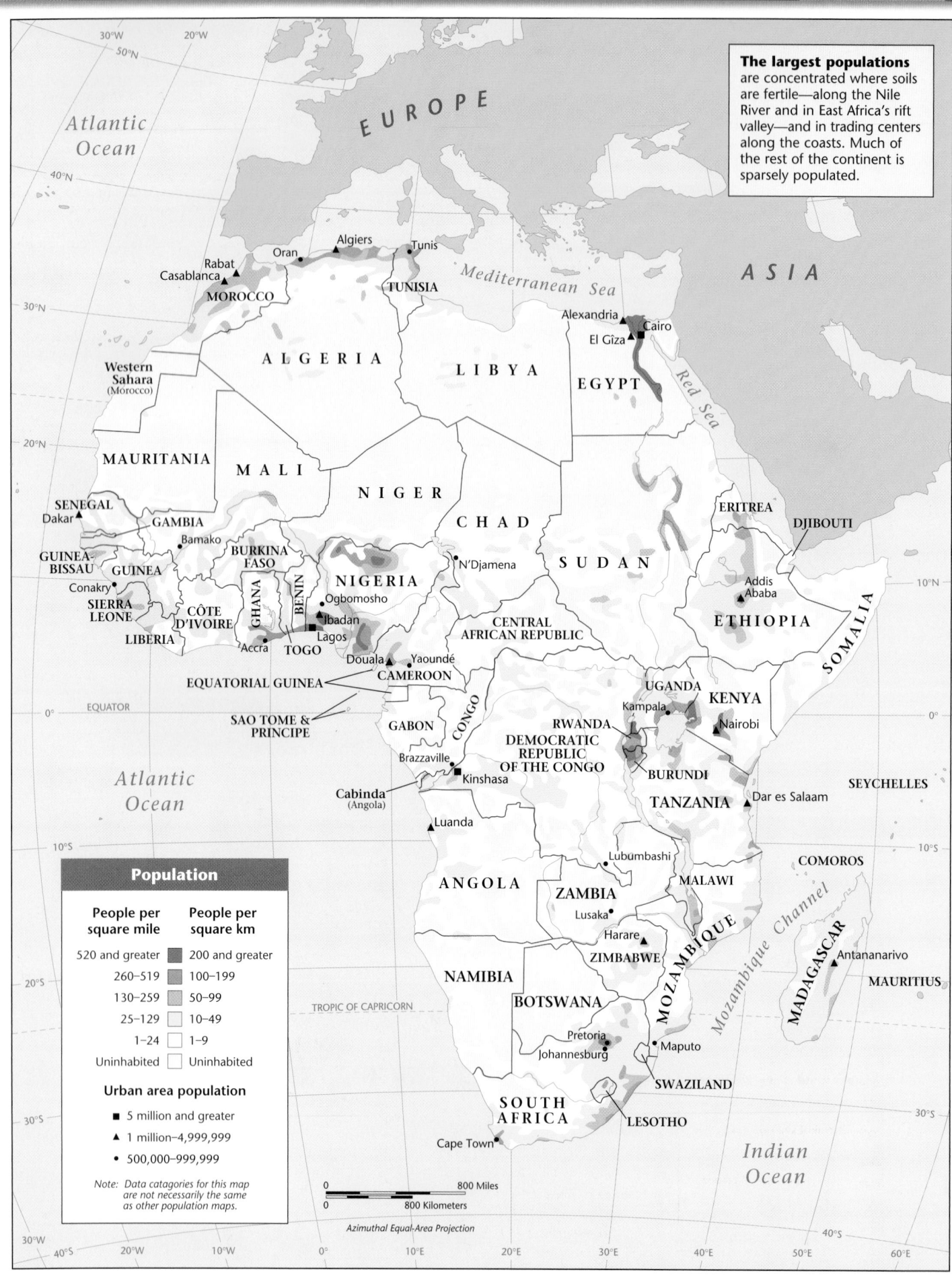

The largest populations are concentrated where soils are fertile—along the Nile River and in East Africa's rift valley—and in trading centers along the coasts. Much of the rest of the continent is sparsely populated.

EUROPE

ASIA

Atlantic Ocean

Mediterranean Sea

Red Sea

Atlantic Ocean

Indian Ocean

Mozambique Channel

Population

People per square mile	**People per square km**
520 and greater	200 and greater
260–519	100–199
130–259	50–99
25–129	10–49
1–24	1–9
Uninhabited	Uninhabited

Urban area population

■ 5 million and greater
▲ 1 million–4,999,999
• 500,000–999,999

Note: Data catagories for this map are not necessarily the same as other population maps.

0   800 Miles
0   800 Kilometers

Azimuthal Equal-Area Projection

MOROCCO
Rabat
Casablanca
Oran
Algiers
Tunis
TUNISIA
Western Sahara (Morocco)
ALGERIA
LIBYA
EGYPT
Alexandria
El Gîza
Cairo
MAURITANIA
MALI
NIGER
CHAD
SUDAN
ERITREA
DJIBOUTI
SENEGAL
Dakar
GAMBIA
Bamako
BURKINA FASO
GUINEA-BISSAU
GUINEA
Conakry
SIERRA LEONE
LIBERIA
CÔTE D'IVOIRE
GHANA
BENIN
TOGO
Accra
NIGERIA
Ogbomosho
Ibadan
Lagos
N'Djamena
CENTRAL AFRICAN REPUBLIC
Addis Ababa
ETHIOPIA
SOMALIA
Douala
Yaoundé
CAMEROON
EQUATORIAL GUINEA
SAO TOME & PRINCIPE
GABON
CONGO
Brazzaville
Kinshasa
Cabinda (Angola)
Luanda
DEMOCRATIC REPUBLIC OF THE CONGO
UGANDA
Kampala
RWANDA
BURUNDI
KENYA
Nairobi
TANZANIA
Dar es Salaam
SEYCHELLES
Lubumbashi
ANGOLA
ZAMBIA
Lusaka
MALAWI
COMOROS
MOZAMBIQUE
Harare
ZIMBABWE
NAMIBIA
BOTSWANA
Pretoria
Johannesburg
Maputo
SWAZILAND
LESOTHO
SOUTH AFRICA
Cape Town
MADAGASCAR
Antananarivo
MAURITIUS
EQUATOR
TROPIC OF CAPRICORN

Africa

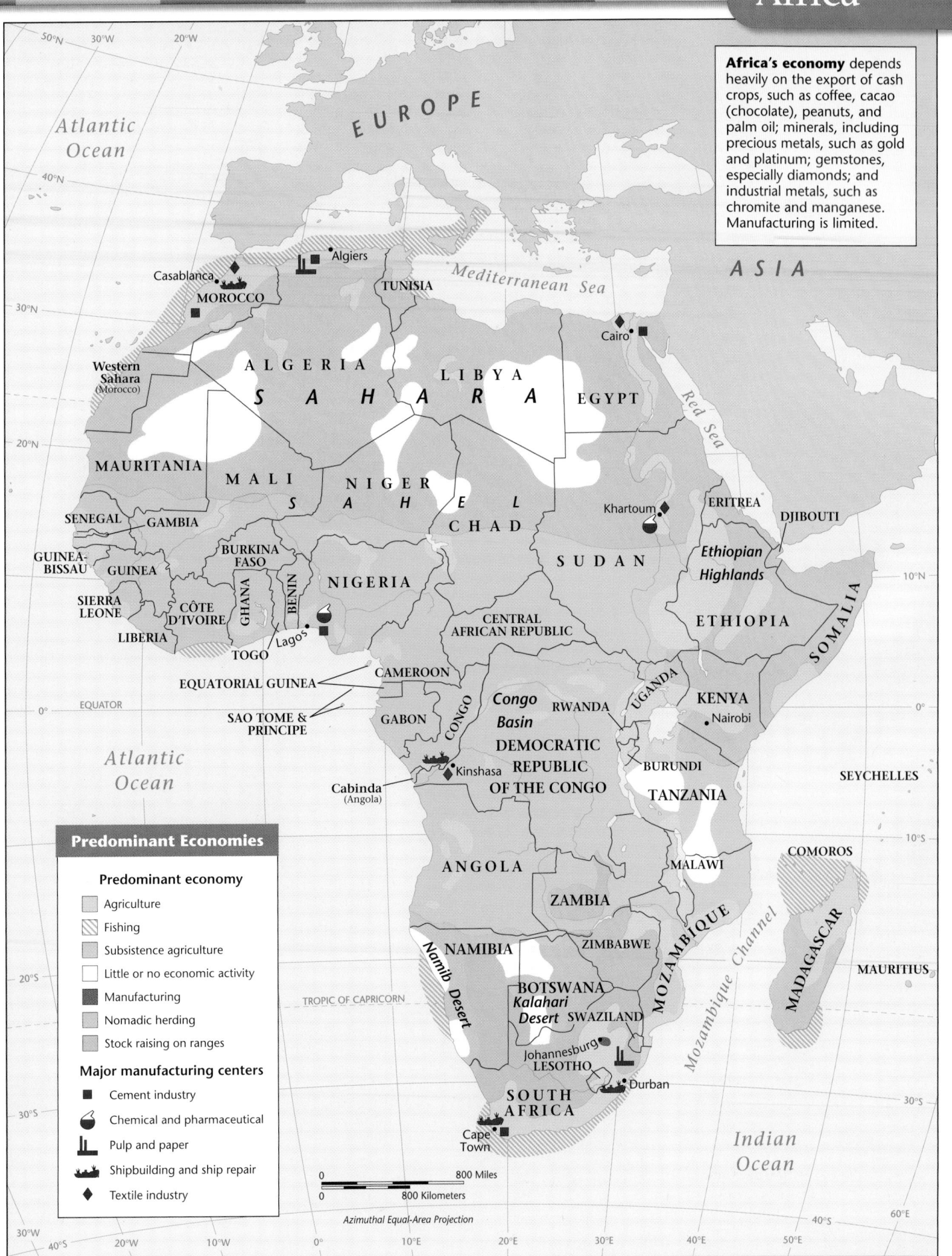

Africa's economy depends heavily on the export of cash crops, such as coffee, cacao (chocolate), peanuts, and palm oil; minerals, including precious metals, such as gold and platinum; gemstones, especially diamonds; and industrial metals, such as chromite and manganese. Manufacturing is limited.

Predominant Economies

Predominant economy

- Agriculture
- Fishing
- Subsistence agriculture
- Little or no economic activity
- Manufacturing
- Nomadic herding
- Stock raising on ranges

Major manufacturing centers

- Cement industry
- Chemical and pharmaceutical
- Pulp and paper
- Shipbuilding and ship repair
- Textile industry

800 Miles
800 Kilometers

Azimuthal Equal-Area Projection

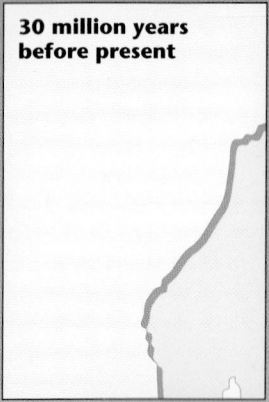

30 million years before present

The Arabian Peninsula and Africa were joined as one landmass 30 million years ago.

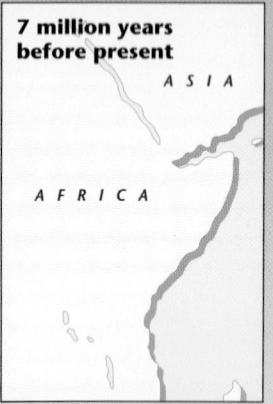

7 million years before present

ASIA

AFRICA

Fiery-hot magma rising from within Earth caused rifting that began to push apart the land along what is now the Red Sea.

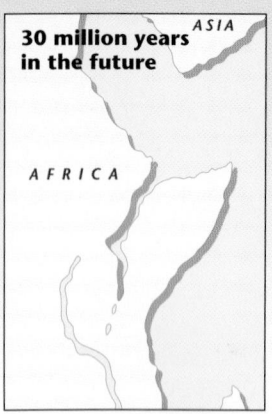

30 million years in the future

ASIA

AFRICA

Long, narrow lakes could become a single channel if rifting continues and causes the Somali Plate to break away.

FOCUS ON

The Great Rift Valley

More than a hundred million years ago, Gondwana, the southern part of the supercontinent Pangaea, began to break apart. Landmasses that we know today as South America, Antarctica, Australia, and the Indian subcontinent slowly moved away, propelled by tectonic forces originating deep within Earth (see map page 14). The part of Gondwana that was left behind is what we know as Africa.

The forces that tore apart Gondwana continue today, especially in East Africa where the Great Rift Valley marks the boundary of what many earth scientists believe eventually will be a new sea that will separate part of eastern and southern Africa from the rest of the continent.

▶ **Volcanic cones,** in the tiny country of Djibouti, mark the area where active tectonic rifting may someday result in the formation of a new ocean.

▼ **Colorful flamingos** are attracted to rift valley lakes, where high evaporation rates help create alkaline waters. The birds feed on brine shrimp and various kinds of algae.

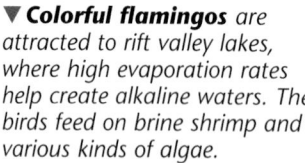

▶ **Subsistence farmers,** many of them women, grow staple crops of maize (corn) and beans in the fertile volcanic soils. Large commercial farms produce cash crops, such as coffee and sisal.

Web Link for information on the Great Rift: www.robinsonresearch.com/AFRICA/THE_LAND/Rift_Val.htm

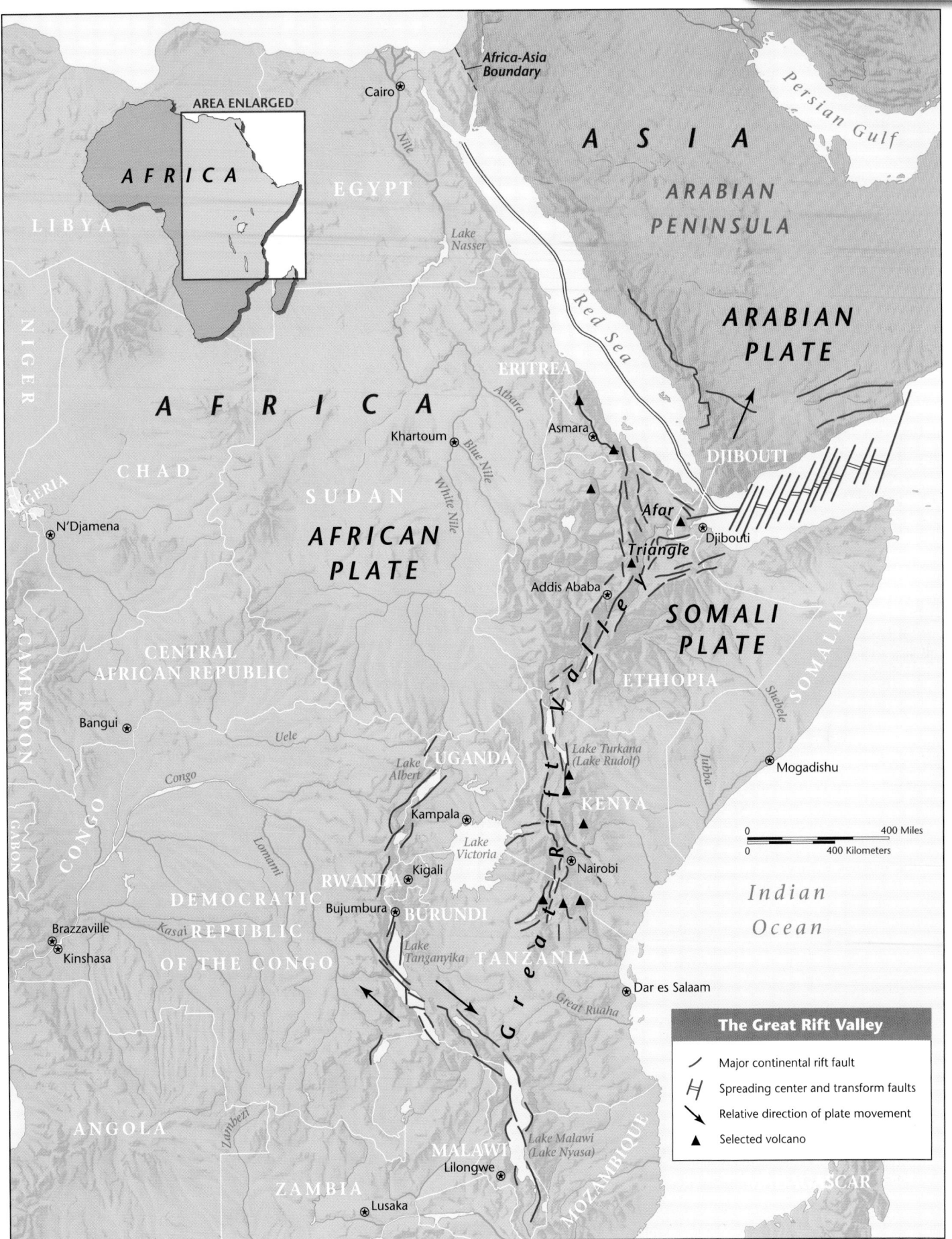

AREA ENLARGED

AFRICA

LIBYA

NIGER

CHAD

CAMEROON

CENTRAL
AFRICAN REPUBLIC

Bangui

GABON

CONGO

Brazzaville
Kinshasa

DEMOCRATIC
REPUBLIC
OF THE CONGO

ANGOLA

ZAMBIA

Lusaka

N'Djamena

EGYPT

Cairo

Lake
Nasser

Nile

Khartoum

SUDAN

AFRICAN
PLATE

White Nile

Blue Nile

Athara

Uele

Congo

Lomami

Kasai

Zambezi

Lake
Albert

UGANDA

Kampala

Lake
Victoria

RWANDA

Kigali

Bujumbura

BURUNDI

Lake
Tanganyika

TANZANIA

MALAWI

Lilongwe

Lake Malawi
(Lake Nyasa)

Africa-Asia
Boundary

Red Sea

ERITREA

Asmara

Afar

Triangle

Addis Ababa

Djibouti

DJIBOUTI

ETHIOPIA

Shebele

Juba

SOMALIA

SOMALI
PLATE

Mogadishu

Lake Turkana
(Lake Rudolf)

KENYA

Nairobi

Great Ruaha

Dar es Salaam

ASIA

ARABIAN
PENINSULA

Persian
Gulf

ARABIAN
PLATE

Indian
Ocean

MOZAMBIQUE

SCAR

Great Rift Valley

| 0 | | 400 Miles |
| 0 | | 400 Kilometers |

The Great Rift Valley

/   Major continental rift fault

H   Spreading center and transform faults

→   Relative direction of plate movement

▲   Selected volcano

Asia

From the frozen shores of the Arctic Ocean to the equatorial islands of Indonesia, Asia stretches across 90 degrees of latitude. From the Ural Mountains to the Pacific Ocean it covers more than 150 degrees of longitude. Here, three of history's great culture hearths emerged in the valleys of the Tigris-Euphrates, the Indus, and the Yellow (Huang) Rivers. Today, Asia is home to more than 60 percent of Earth's people and some of the world's fastest growing economies.

Facts & Figures

▶ **Land area:** 17,213,300 sq mi (44,579,000 sq km)

▶ **Population:** 3,684,490,000

▶ **Highest point:** Mount Everest, China-Nepal: 29,035 ft (8,850 m)

▶ **Lowest point:** Dead Sea, Israel-Jordan: 1,349 ft (411 m) below sea level

▶ **Longest river:** Yangtze (Chang), China: 3,964 mi (6,380 km)

▶ **Largest lake entirely in Asia:** Baikal, Russia: 12,163 sq mi (31,500 sq km)

▶ **Number of independent countries:** 46 (excluding Russia)

▶ **Largest country entirely in Asia:** China: 3,705,820 sq mi (9,598,032 sq km)

▶ **Smallest country:** Maldives: 115 sq mi (298 sq km)

▶ **Most populous country:** China: Pop. 1,264,536,000

▶ **Least populous country:** Maldives: Pop. 286,000

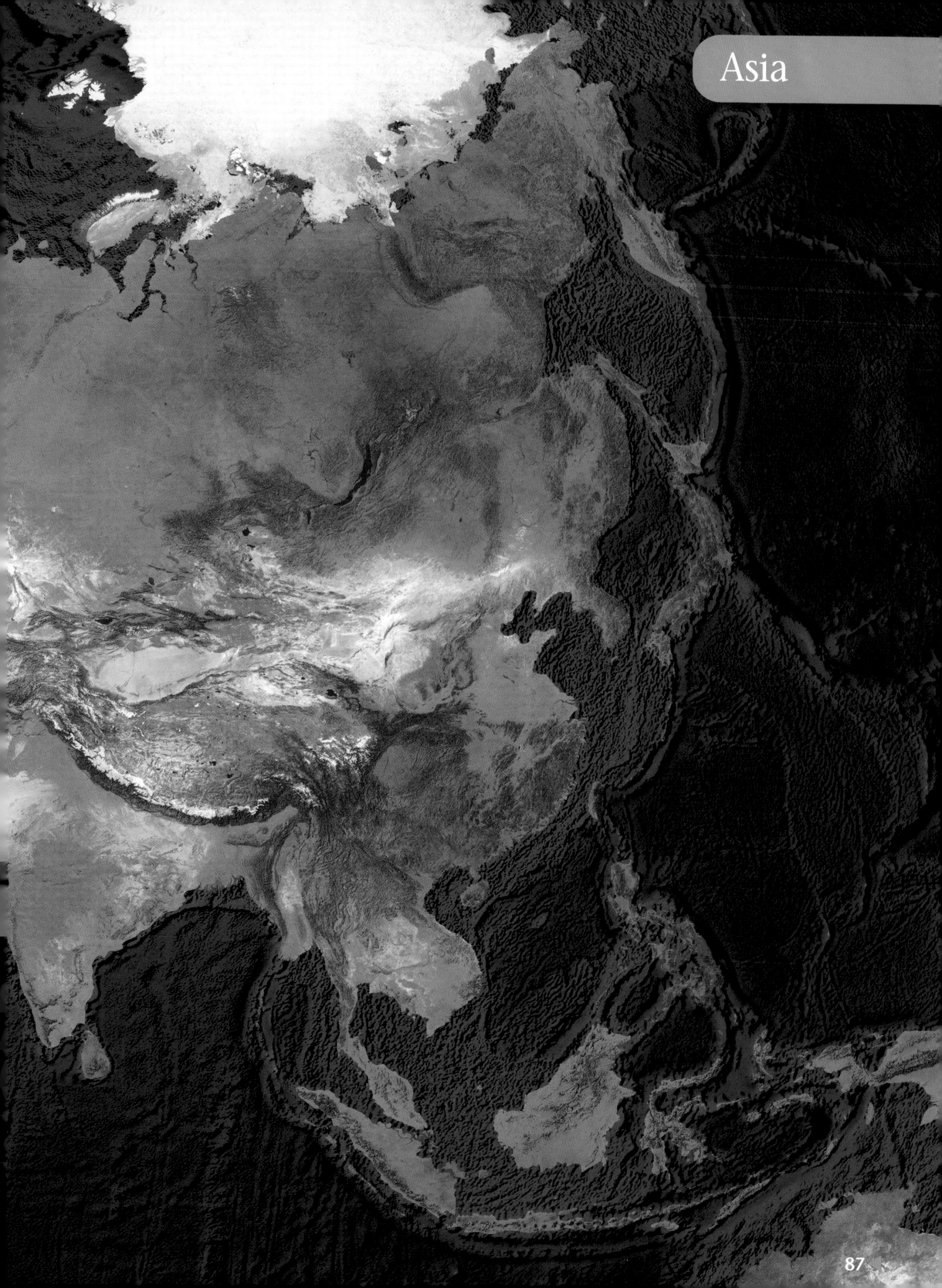

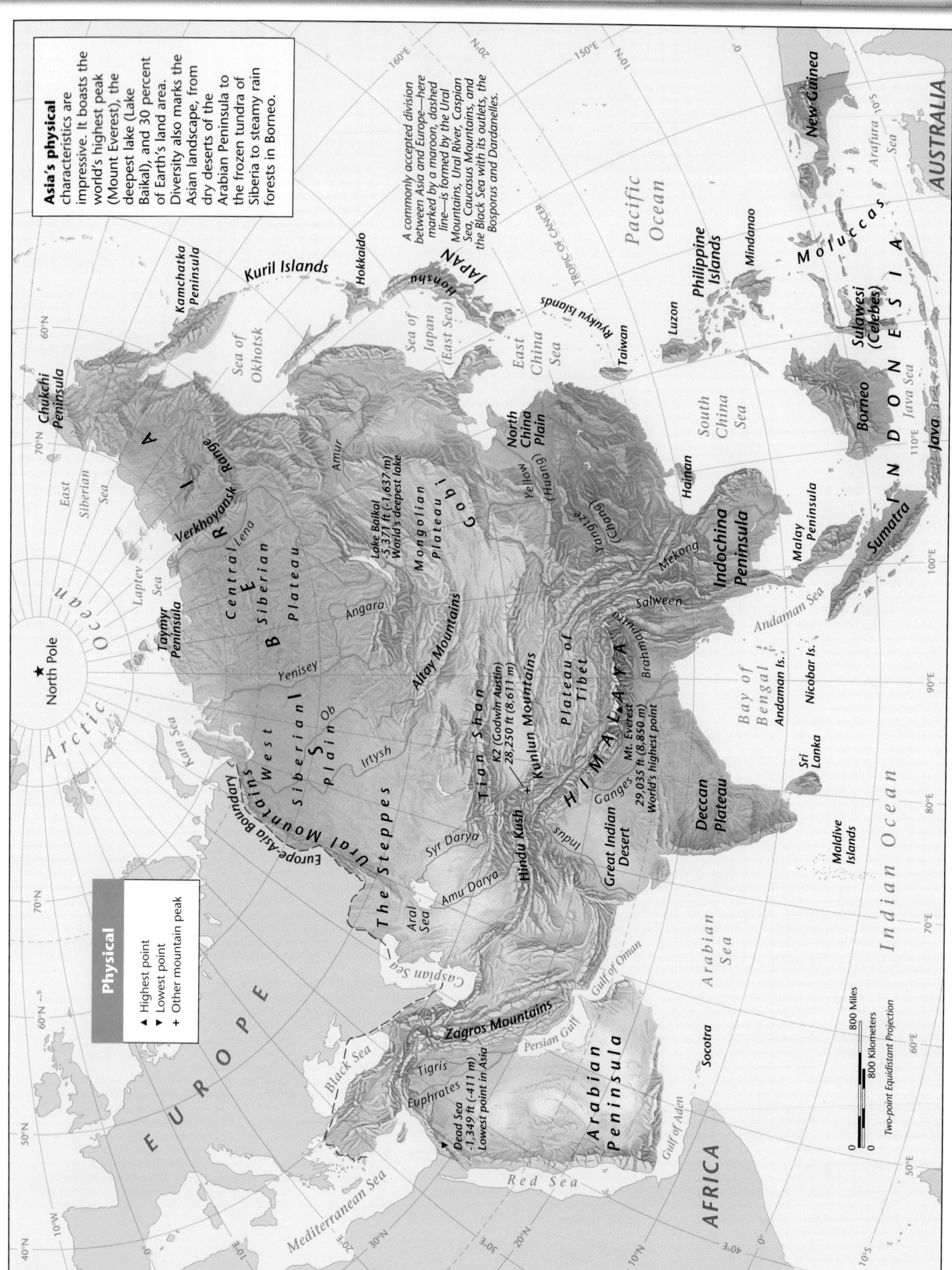

Asia's physical characteristics are impressive. It boasts the world's highest peak (Mount Everest), the deepest lake (Lake Baikal), and 30 percent of Earth's land area. Diversity also marks the Asian landscape, from the frozen tundra of Siberia to steamy rain forests in Borneo.

A commonly accepted division between Asia and Europe—here marked by a maroon, dashed line—is formed by the Ural Mountains, Ural River, Caspian Sea, Caucasus Mountains, and the Black Sea with its outlets, the Bosporus and Dardanelles.

Physical

- ▲ Highest point
- ▼ Lowest point
- + Other mountain peak

Two-point Equidistant Projection

800 Miles

800 Kilometers

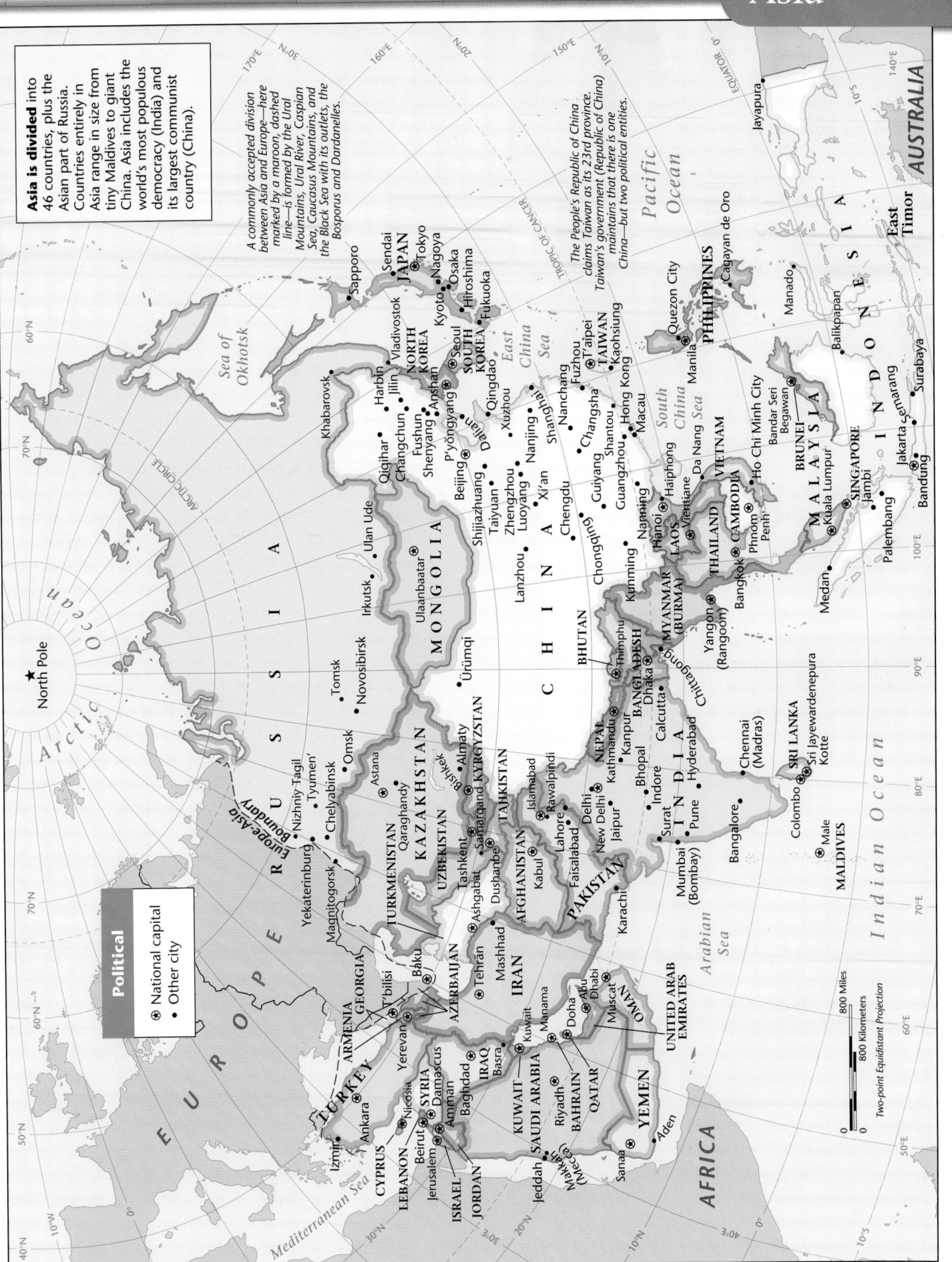

Asia is divided into 46 countries, plus the Asian part of Russia. Countries entirely in Asia range in size from tiny Maldives to giant China. Asia includes the world's most populous democracy (India) and its largest communist country (China).

A commonly accepted division between Asia and Europe—here marked by a maroon, dashed line—is formed by the Ural Mountains, Ural River, Caspian Sea, Caucasus Mountains, and the Black Sea with its outlets, the Bosporus and Dardanelles.

The People's Republic of China claims Taiwan as its 23rd province. Taiwan's government (Republic of China) maintains that there is one China—but two political entities.

Political

⊛ National capital
• Other city

Two-point Equidistant Projection

800 Miles
800 Kilometers

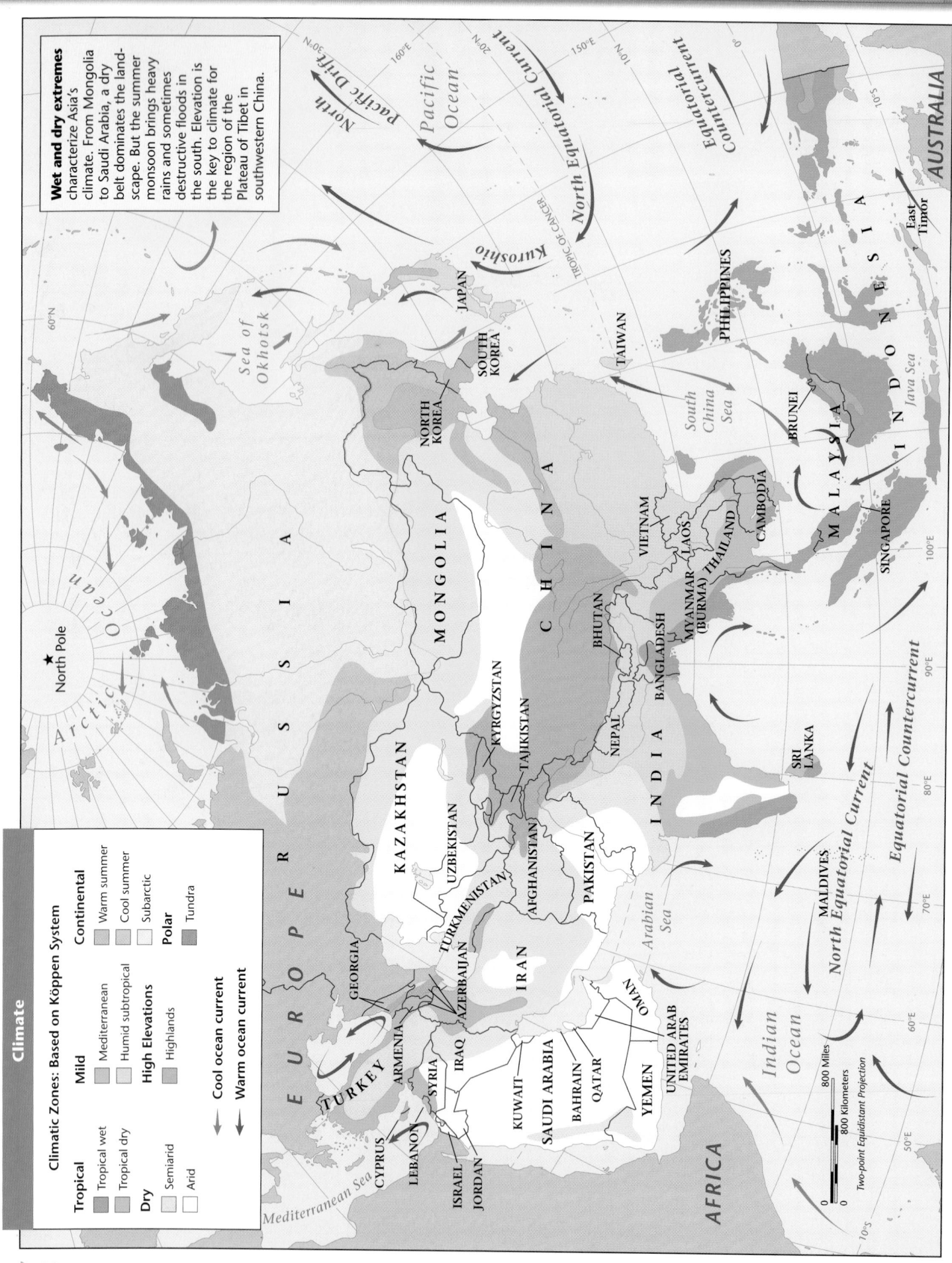

Asia

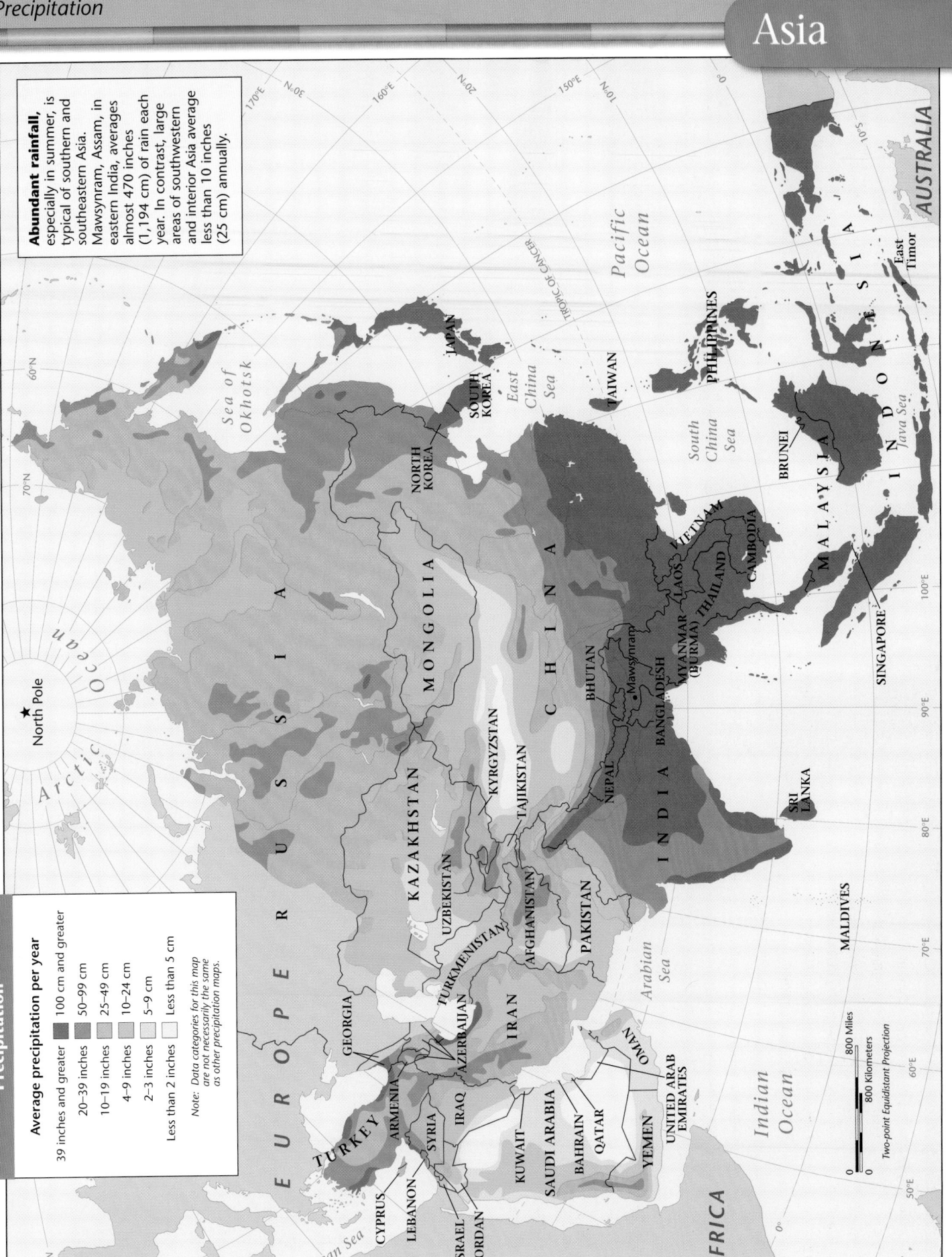

Abundant rainfall, especially in summer, is typical of southern and southeastern Asia. Mawsynram, Assam, in eastern India, averages almost 470 inches (1,194 cm) of rain each year. In contrast, large areas of southwestern and interior Asia average less than 10 inches (25 cm) annually.

Average precipitation per year

- 39 inches and greater — 100 cm and greater
- 20–39 inches — 50–99 cm
- 10–19 inches — 25–49 cm
- 4–9 inches — 10–24 cm
- 2–3 inches — 5–9 cm
- Less than 2 inches — Less than 5 cm

Note: Data categories for this map are not necessarily the same as other precipitation maps.

800 Miles

800 Kilometers

Two-point Equidistant Projection

EUROPE

RUSSIA

KAZAKHSTAN

MONGOLIA

CHINA

North Pole

Arctic Ocean

Sea of Okhotsk

JAPAN

SOUTH KOREA

NORTH KOREA

East China Sea

TAIWAN

Pacific Ocean

TROPIC OF CANCER

PHILIPPINES

South China Sea

BRUNEI

MALAYSIA

INDONESIA

East Timor

Java Sea

AUSTRALIA

VIETNAM

LAOS

CAMBODIA

THAILAND

MYANMAR (BURMA)

Mawsynram

BANGLADESH

BHUTAN

NEPAL

INDIA

SRI LANKA

SINGAPORE

MALDIVES

UZBEKISTAN

KYRGYZSTAN

TAJIKISTAN

TURKMENISTAN

AFGHANISTAN

PAKISTAN

Arabian Sea

GEORGIA

AZERBAIJAN

ARMENIA

IRAN

OMAN

UNITED ARAB EMIRATES

TURKEY

IRAQ

SYRIA

KUWAIT

SAUDI ARABIA

BAHRAIN

QATAR

YEMEN

Indian Ocean

CYPRUS

LEBANON

ISRAEL

JORDAN

Mediterranean Sea

AFRICA

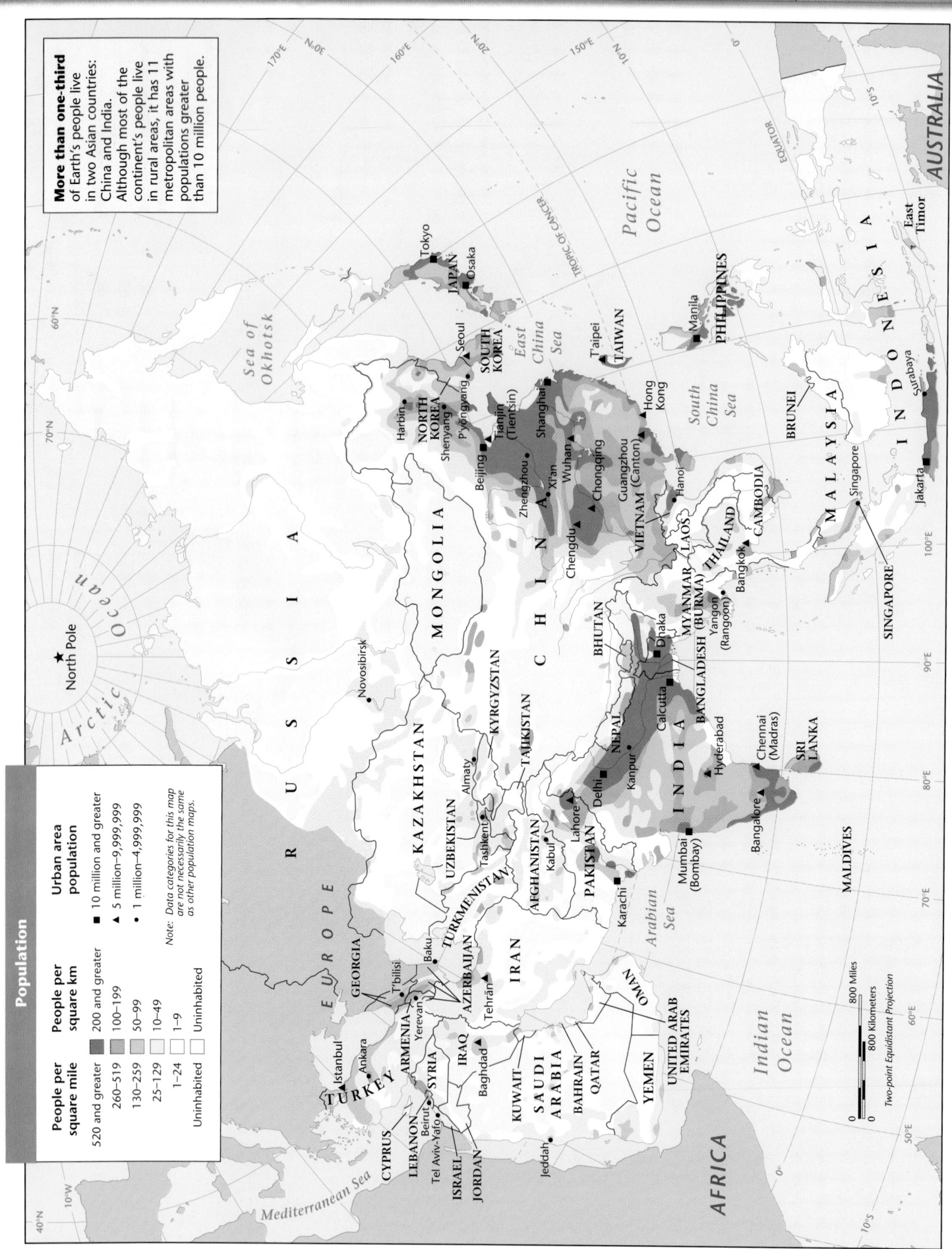

Asia

Nomadic herding, farming, and other subsistence activities define the economic lifestyle of the majority of Asia's people. But Asia also includes some of the world's industrial giants, such as Japan and South Korea.

Predominant Economies

- Agriculture
- Agriculture and forestry
- Fishing
- Forestry (lumber and pulpwood)
- Hunting, fishing and forestry
- Subsistence agriculture
- Little or no economic activity
- Manufacturing
- Nomadic herding
- Stock raising on ranges

Major Manufacturing Centers

- Cement industry
- Chemical and pharmaceutical
- High-tech centers
- Pulp and paper
- Shipbuilding and ship repair
- Textile industry

800 Miles
800 Kilometers
Two-point Equidistant Projection

North Pole

Arctic Ocean

Sea of Okhotsk

Pacific Ocean

East China Sea

South China Sea

Indian Ocean

Arabian Sea

Mediterranean Sea

Labels: SIBERIA, RUSSIA, EUROPE, TURKEY, GEORGIA, ARMENIA, AZERBAIJAN, SYRIA, CYPRUS, LEBANON, ISRAEL, JORDAN, IRAQ, Baghdad, KUWAIT, SAUDI ARABIA, BAHRAIN, QATAR, YEMEN, UNITED ARAB EMIRATES, OMAN, IRAN, Tehrān, TURKMENISTAN, AFGHANISTAN, PAKISTAN, Karachi, UZBEKISTAN, Tashkent, KAZAKHSTAN, Chelyabinsk, Novosibirsk, Krasnoyarsk, KYRGYZSTAN, TAJIKISTAN, Plateau of Tibet, CHINA, MONGOLIA, Gobi, HIMALAYA, NEPAL, BHUTAN, INDIA, Bhopal, Mumbai (Bombay), Chennai (Madras), Calcutta, BANGLADESH, SRI LANKA, MALDIVES, MYANMAR (BURMA), Yangon (Rangoon), LAOS, THAILAND, Bangkok, CAMBODIA, VIETNAM, MALAYSIA, SINGAPORE, BRUNEI, INDONESIA, Jakarta, PHILIPPINES, Manila, East Timor, AUSTRALIA, NORTH KOREA, SOUTH KOREA, Seoul, JAPAN, Tokyo, Beijing, Shanghai, Hong Kong, TAIWAN, AFRICA

TROPIC OF CANCER

World Heritage Sites

I n 1972, the United Nations Educational, Scientific and Cultural Organization (UNESCO) adopted a treaty, signed by more than 150 countries, dedicated to the preservation of cultural and natural sites of "outstanding universal value" that are "testimonies to an enduring past." These sites are designated as World Heritage Sites because they are part of the universal heritage of people everywhere.

Since much of human history is rooted in Asia, the continent is home to many of the best known World Heritage Sites, including the Taj Mahal, in India, and the temple complex at Angkor in Cambodia. Some of the world's endangered and vulnerable animals, such as the tiger and the komodo dragon, are native to Asia, and their habitats also are preserved as World Heritage Sites.

In December 1999, the World Heritage List included 630 sites in 118 countries. Among these, 148 sites are in Asian countries, including four in the part of Russia that lies east of the Ural Mountains.

▲ **Cappadocia,** *a centuries-old complex of caves, dwellings, and Christian churches carved into ancient volcanic rock in central Turkey, is an example of a mixed World Heritage Site.*

World Heritage Sites

These sites are chosen for their universal value. Cultural sites reflect unusual human ingenuity or represent the traditions or values of an established culture or civilization. Natural sites are often examples of important geological processes or the habitats of endangered species. A few sites are selected because they combine cultural and natural characteristics.

Natural
Cultural
Mixed

	Australia/ Oceania	U.S./ Canada	Africa	Latin America	Asia	Europe
Natural	12	18	32	22	25	19
Cultural	5	13	49	61	117	240
Mixed	0	0	2	3	6	6

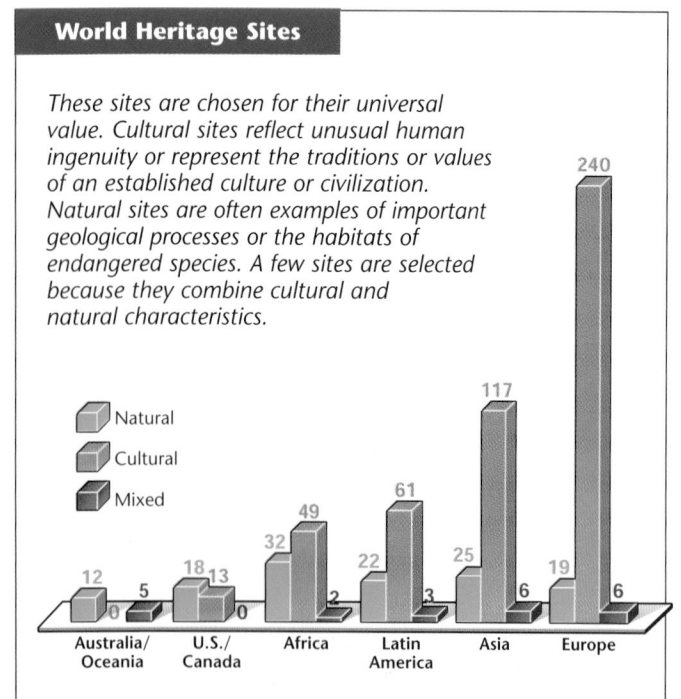

▲ **Angkor Wat,** *which is part of a cultural site in Cambodia, honors the Hindu god Vishnu. Nearby temples at Angkor Thom are Buddhist.*

Web Link for information on World Heritage Sites: www.unesco.org/whc/

Asia's World Heritage Sites

- ● Cultural site
- ▲ Natural site
- ■ Mixed site

LEBANON
1 Byblos
2 Baalbek
3 Anjar
4 Tyre
5 Ouadi Qadisha (the Holy Valley) and The Forest of the Cedars of God (Horsh Arz el-Rab)

TURKEY
1 Göreme National Park and Cappadocia
2 Great Mosque and Hospital of Divriği
3 Nemrud Dagh

CYPRUS
1 Paphos
2 Painted Churches in the Troodos Region

INDIA
1 Taj Mahal
2 Agra Fort
3 Fatehpur Sikri
4 Nanda Devi N.P.
5 Darjeeling Himalayan Railway
6 Manas Wildlife Sanctuary
7 Monuments at Khajuraho

SOUTH KOREA
1 Hwasong Fortress
2 Haiensa Temple
3 Sokkuram Grotto and Pulguksa Temple

CHINA
1 Temple of Confucius, Cemetery of Confucius, and Kong Family Mansion in Qufu
2 Ancient Building Complex in the Wudang Mts.

Arctic Ocean

EUROPE

RUSSIA

ASIA

KAZAKHSTAN

MONGOLIA

CHINA

Sea of Okhotsk

Pacific Ocean

Sea of Japan

JAPAN

Volcanoes of Kamchatka

Virgin Komi Forests

Historic Areas of Istanbul

Troy
Safranbolu
Western Caucasus
Bagrati Cathedral and Gelati Monastery
Upper Svaneti
Hattusha
GEORGIA
Georgia City-Museum Reserve of Mts'khet'a
Monastery of Haghpat
ARMENIA
AZERBAIJAN
CYPRUS
Aleppo
Site of Palmyra
SYRIA
Ancient city of Bosra
Ancient city of Damascus
JORDAN
Petra
Qusein Amra
IRAQ
Hatra
Tchoga Zanbil
KUWAIT
SAUDI ARABIA
BAHRAIN
QATAR
UNITED ARAB EMIRATES
Bahla Fort
YEMEN
OMAN
Old Walled City of Shibam
Old Walled City of Zabid

TURKMENISTAN
UZBEK.
Itchan Kala
Historic Centre of Bukhoro
Meidan Emam, Isfahan
"Ancient Merv"
Persepolis
IRAN
Takht-i-Bahi/Sahr-i-Bahol
Fort and Shalamar Gardens
Monuments of Thatta
AFGHANISTAN
Rohtas Fort
Taxila
Bat, Al-Khutm and Al-Ayn
Arabian Oryx Sanctuary
Ruins at Mohenjo Daro
PAKISTAN
KYRGYZSTAN
TAJIKISTAN

Golden Mountains of Altay
Lake Baikal

Lumbini, Birthplace of Buddha
Keoladeo N.P.
NEPAL
Royal Chitwan N.P.
Kathmandu Valley
Buddhist Monastery at Sanchih
BHUTAN
Sagarmatha N.P., Mt. Everest
Potala Palace, Lhasa
Kaziranga N.P.
BANGLADESH
Sundarbans N.P.
Ruins of the Buddhist Vihara
Bagherhat
INDIA
Ellora Caves
Elephanta Caves
Ajanta Caves
Sun Temple, Konarak
Monuments at Pattadakal
Churches & Convents of Goa
Monuments at Hampi
Brihadisvara Temple, Tanjore
Monuments at Mahabalipuram
Ancient City of Sigiriya
Golden Temple of Dambulla
Sinharaja Forest Reserve
SRI LANKA
Sacred City of Anuradhap
Ancient City of Polonnaruwa
Sacred City of Kandy
Old Town of Galle
MALDIVES

Mogao Caves
The Great Wall
Peking Man Site
Chongmyo Shrine
Ch'angdokkung Palace
Seoul
Summer Palace
Temple of Heaven
Imperial Palace
Beijing
NORTH KOREA
Mountain Resort
SOUTH KOREA
Mt. Taishan
Ancient City of Pingya
Mausoleum of the First Qin Emperor
Jiuzhaigou Valley
Huanglong
Dazu Rock Carvings
Lushan N.P.
Mt. Huangshan
Mt. Wuyi
Mt. Emei and Leshan Giant Buddha
Wulingyuan
Old Town of Lijiang
Classical Gardens of Suzhou
TAIWAN

Shirakami-Sanchi
Shrines and Temples of Nikko
Historic Villages of Shirakawa-go and Gokayama
Historic Monuments of Ancient Kyoto (Kyoto, Uji and Otsu Cities)
Himeji-jo
Buddhist Monuments in the Horyuji Area
Historic Monuments of Ancient Nara
Hiroshima Peace Memorial (Genbaku Dome)
Itsukushima Shinto Shrine
Yakushima

East China Sea

Historic Town of Vigan
Rice Terraces of the Philippine Cordilleras
Baroque Churches of the Philippines
PHILIPPINES
South China Sea
Ha Long Bay
Louangphabang
Hue
Hoi An, Ancient Town
My Son Sanctuary
Puerto-Princesa Subterranean River N.P.
Tubbataha Reef Marine Park
MYANMAR (BURMA)
Ban Chiang
Historic Town of Sukhothai
Thungyai-Huai Kha Khaeng Wildlife Sanctuaries
LAOS
Angkor
CAMBODIA
VIETNAM
Historic City of Ayutthaya
THAILAND
BRUNEI
MALAYSIA
SINGAPORE
INDONESIA
Lorentz N.P.
Borobudur Temple Compounds
Ujung Kulon N.P.
Sangiran Early Man Site
Prambanan Temple Compounds
Komodo N.P.
Java Sea

Indian Ocean
Arabian Sea
Bay of Bengal

0   1000 Miles
0   1000 Kilometers
Two-point Equidistant Projection

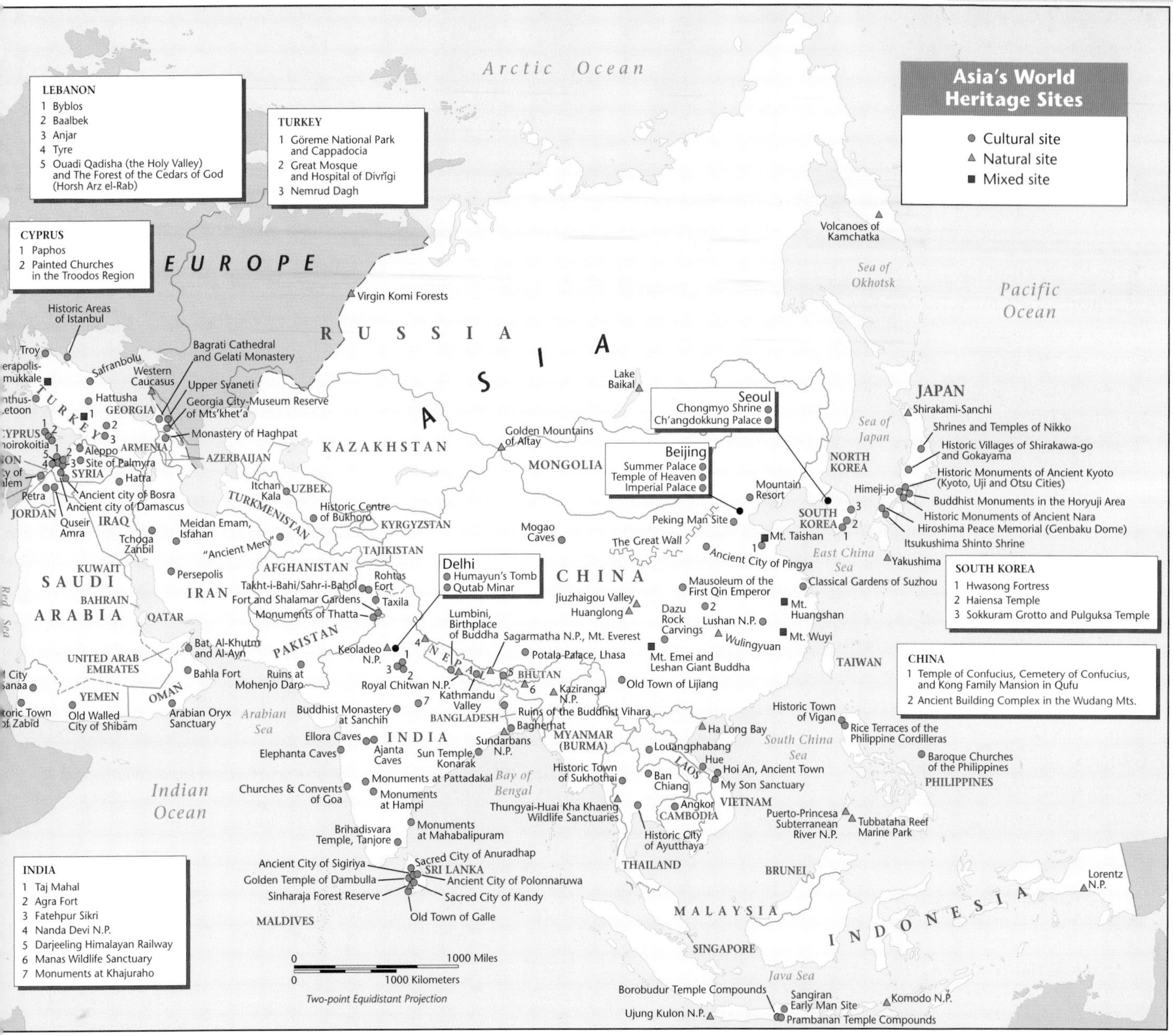

▲ **The Taj Mahal,** a cultural site in India, is an outstanding example of Muslim architecture in a country most often associated with Hinduism.

▲ **Tubbataha Reef Marine Park,** a natural site in the Philippines, is habitat for birds, sea turtles, and fish.

Australia & Oceania

Smallest of Earth's great landmasses, Australia is the only continent that is both a continent and a country. It is part of the greater region of Oceania, which includes New Zealand, the eastern part of New Guinea, and hundreds of smaller islands scattered across the Pacific Ocean. Although Hawaii is politically part of the United States, geographically and culturally it is part of Oceania.

Facts & Figures

- ▶ **Land area:** 3,284,000 sq mi (8,505,000 sq km)

- ▶ **Population:** 30,663,000

- ▶ **Highest point:** Mount Wilhelm, Papua New Guinea: 14,793 ft (4,509 m)

- ▶ **Lowest point:** Lake Eyre, Australia: 52 ft (16 m) below sea level

- ▶ **Longest river:** Murray-Darling, Australia: 2,911 mi (4,685 km)

- ▶ **Largest lake:** Lake Eyre, Australia: 3,430 sq mi (8,884 sq km)

- ▶ **Number of independent countries:** 14

- ▶ **Largest country:** Australia: 2,968,000 sq mi (7,687,000 sq km)

- ▶ **Smallest country:** Nauru: 8 sq mi (21 sq km)

- ▶ **Most populous country:** Australia: Pop. 19,195,000

- ▶ **Least populous country:** Nauru: Pop. 12,000

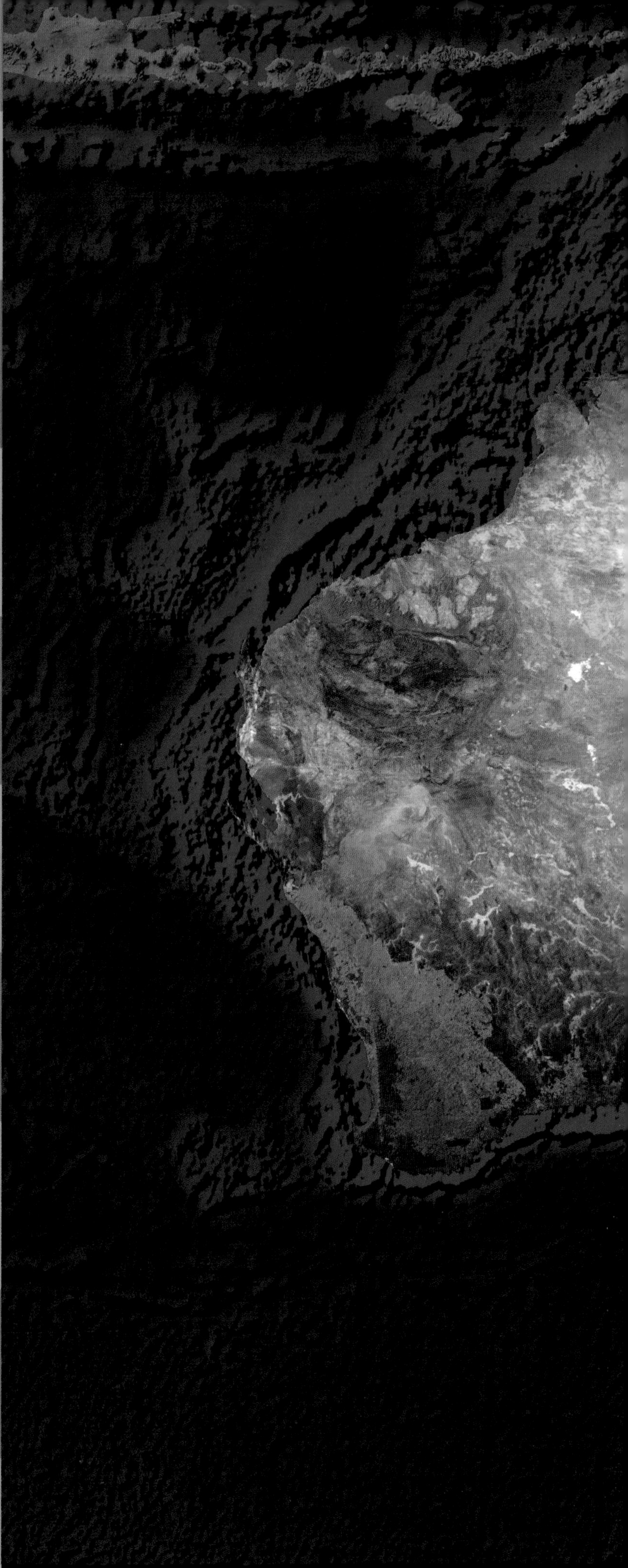

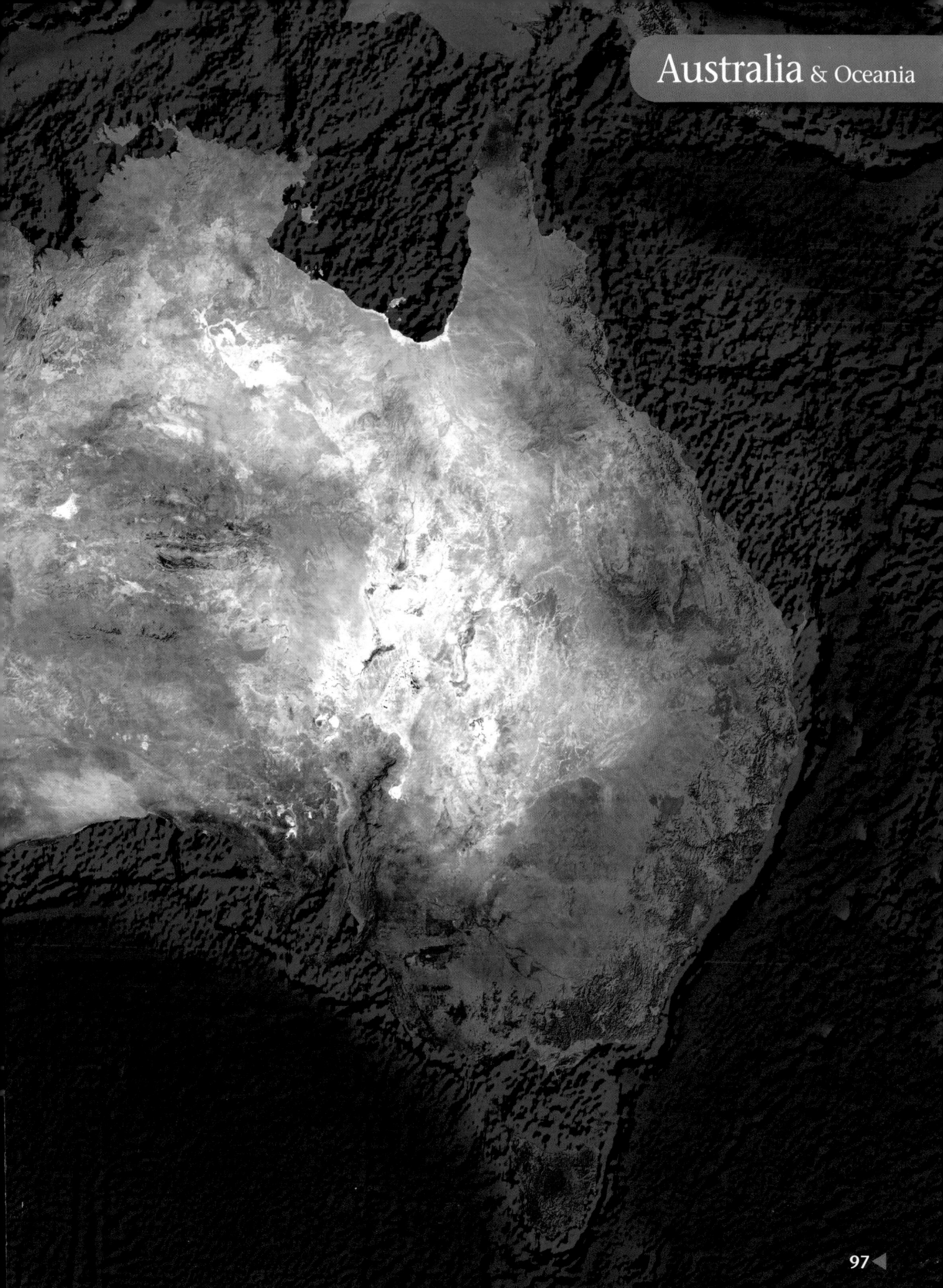

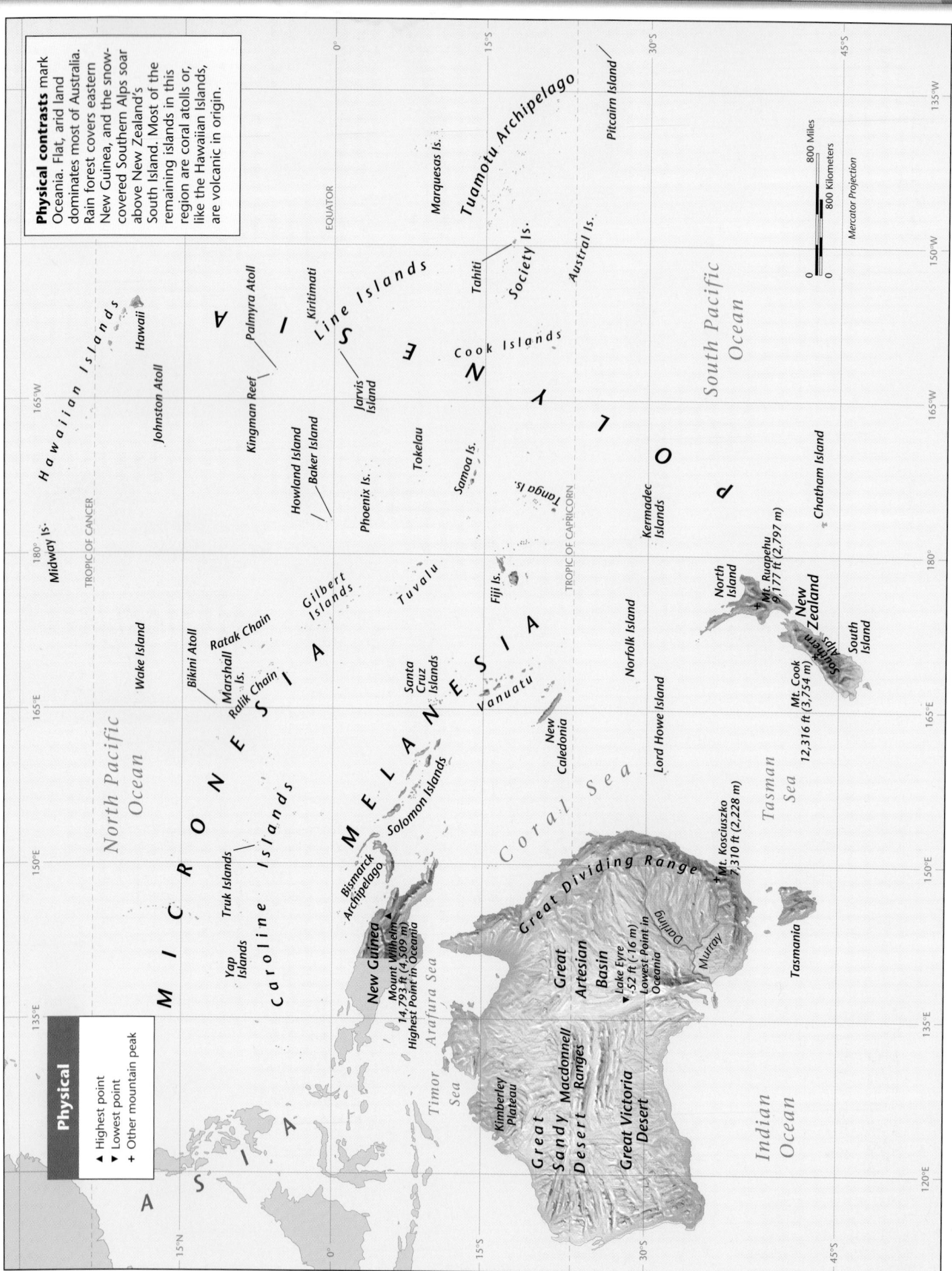

Physical contrasts mark Oceania. Flat, arid land dominates most of Australia. Rain forest covers eastern New Guinea, and the snow-covered Southern Alps soar above New Zealand's South Island. Most of the remaining islands in this region are coral atolls or, like the Hawaiian Islands, are volcanic in origin.

Physical

▲ Highest point
▼ Lowest point
+ Other mountain peak

800 Miles
800 Kilometers
Mercator Projection

EQUATOR

TROPIC OF CANCER

TROPIC OF CAPRICORN

North Pacific Ocean

South Pacific Ocean

Indian Ocean

Coral Sea

Tasman Sea

Arafura Sea

Timor Sea

ASIA

MICRONESIA

MELANESIA

POLYNESIA

Hawaiian Islands
Hawaii

Midway Is.

Johnston Atoll

Palmyra Atoll
Kingman Reef

Kiritimati

Line Islands

Marquesas Is.

Tuamotu Archipelago

Pitcairn Island

Tahiti
Society Is.
Austral Is.

Cook Islands

Jarvis Island

Howland Island
Baker Island

Phoenix Is.

Tokelau

Samoa Is.

Tonga Is.

Wake Island

Bikini Atoll
Ratak Chain
Marshall Is.
Ralik Chain

Gilbert Islands

Tuvalu

Fiji Is.

Yap Islands
Truk Islands

Caroline Islands

Santa Cruz Islands

Vanuatu

New Caledonia

Norfolk Island

Lord Howe Island

Kermadec Islands

Chatham Island

North Island
Mt. Ruapehu
9,177 ft (2,797 m)
New Zealand
Southern Alps
South Island

Mt. Cook
12,316 ft (3,754 m)

Bismarck Archipelago

Solomon Islands

New Guinea
▲ Mount Wilhelm
14,793 ft (4,509 m)
Highest Point in Oceania

Great Dividing Range

+ Mt. Kosciuszko
7,310 ft (2,228 m)

Great Artesian Basin

Lake Eyre
▼ 52 ft (-16 m)
Lowest Point in Oceania

Darling

Murray

Kimberley Plateau

Great Sandy Desert

Macdonnell Ranges

Great Victoria Desert

Tasmania

Australia & Oceania

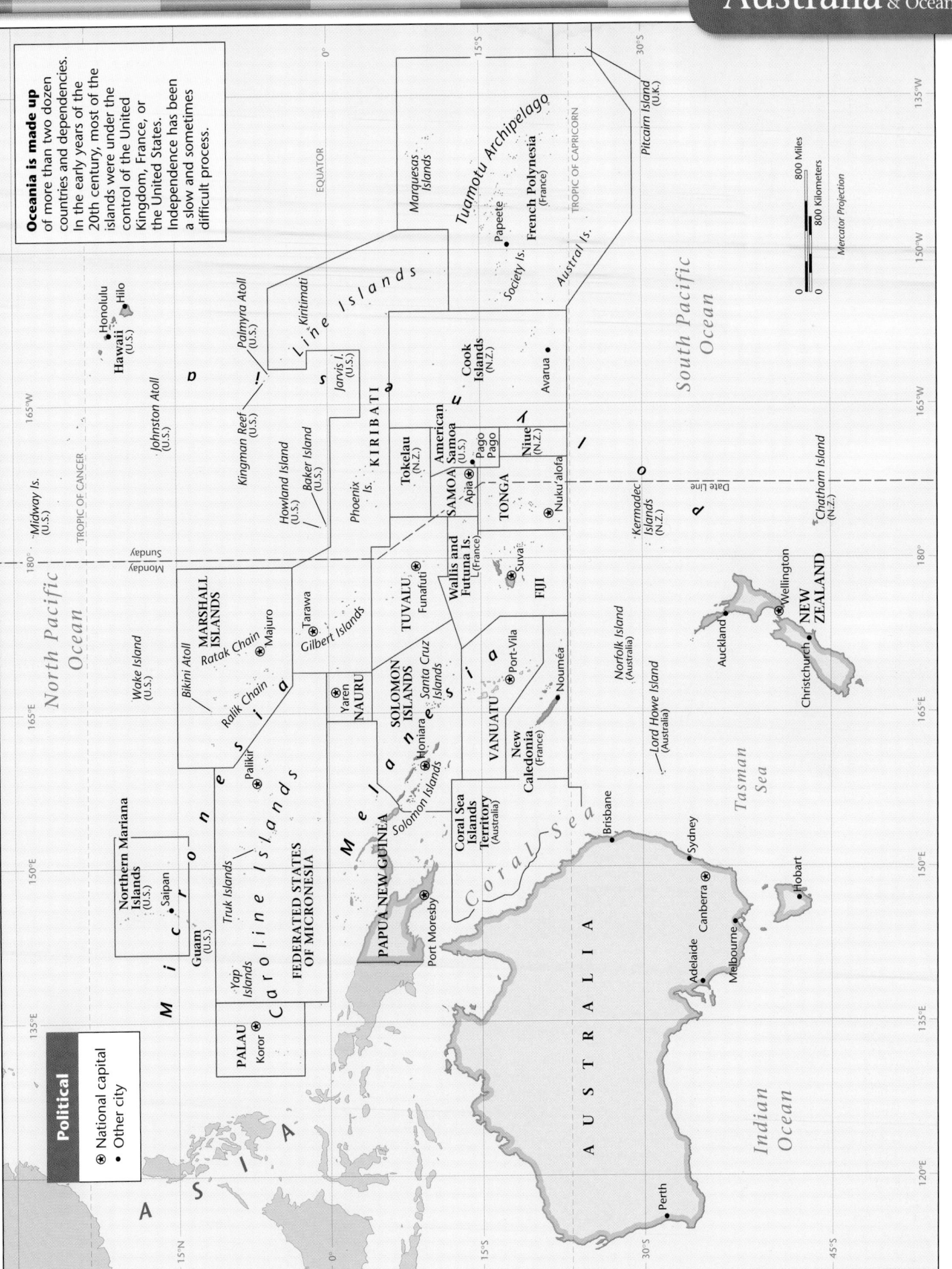

Oceania is made up of more than two dozen countries and dependencies. In the early years of the 20th century, most of the islands were under the control of the United Kingdom, France, or the United States. Independence has been a slow and sometimes difficult process.

Political

⊛ National capital

• Other city

Marquesas Islands

Tuamotu Archipelago

Papeete ● **French Polynesia** (France)

Society Is.

Austral Is.

TROPIC OF CAPRICORN

Pitcairn Island (U.K.)

South Pacific Ocean

Honolulu ● Hilo ●
Hawaii (U.S.)

Johnston Atoll (U.S.)

Palmyra Atoll (U.S.)

Kiritimati

Line Islands

Jarvis I. (U.S.)

Kingman Reef (U.S.)

Baker Island (U.S.)

Howland Island (U.S.)

Phoenix Is.

KIRIBATI

Tokelau (N.Z.)

American Samoa (U.S.)

Pago Pago

SAMOA ⊛ Apia

TONGA ⊛ Nuku'alofa

Niue (N.Z.)

Nuku'alofa

Cook Islands (N.Z.)

● Avarua

Date Line

Kermadec Islands (N.Z.)

Chatham Island (N.Z.)

North Pacific Ocean

Midway Is. (U.S.)

TROPIC OF CANCER

Sunday
Monday

Wake Island (U.S.)

Bikini Atoll

MARSHALL ISLANDS

Ratak Chain

Majuro ⊛

Ralik Chain

Tarawa ●

Gilbert Islands

TUVALU ● Funafuti

Wallis and Futuna Is. (France)

Suva ● **FIJI**

NAURU ⊛ Yaren

SOLOMON ISLANDS
Honiara ⊛

Santa Cruz Islands

VANUATU
Port-Vila ⊛

New Caledonia (France)

Nouméa ●

Norfolk Island (Australia)

Lord Howe Island (Australia)

Tasman Sea

Auckland ●

NEW ZEALAND

Wellington ⊛

Christchurch ●

Northern Mariana Islands (U.S.)

Saipan ●

Truk Islands

FEDERATED STATES OF MICRONESIA

Palikir ⊛

Yap Islands

Guam (U.S.)

Caroline Islands

PALAU ⊛ Koror

PAPUA NEW GUINEA

Port Moresby ●

Solomon Islands

Coral Sea Islands Territory (Australia)

Coral Sea

Brisbane ●

Sydney ●

AUSTRALIA

Adelaide ● Canberra ⊛

Melbourne ●

Hobart ●

Indian Ocean

Perth ●

A S I A

Micronesia

Melanesia

Polynesia

EQUATOR

800 Miles
800 Kilometers
Mercator Projection

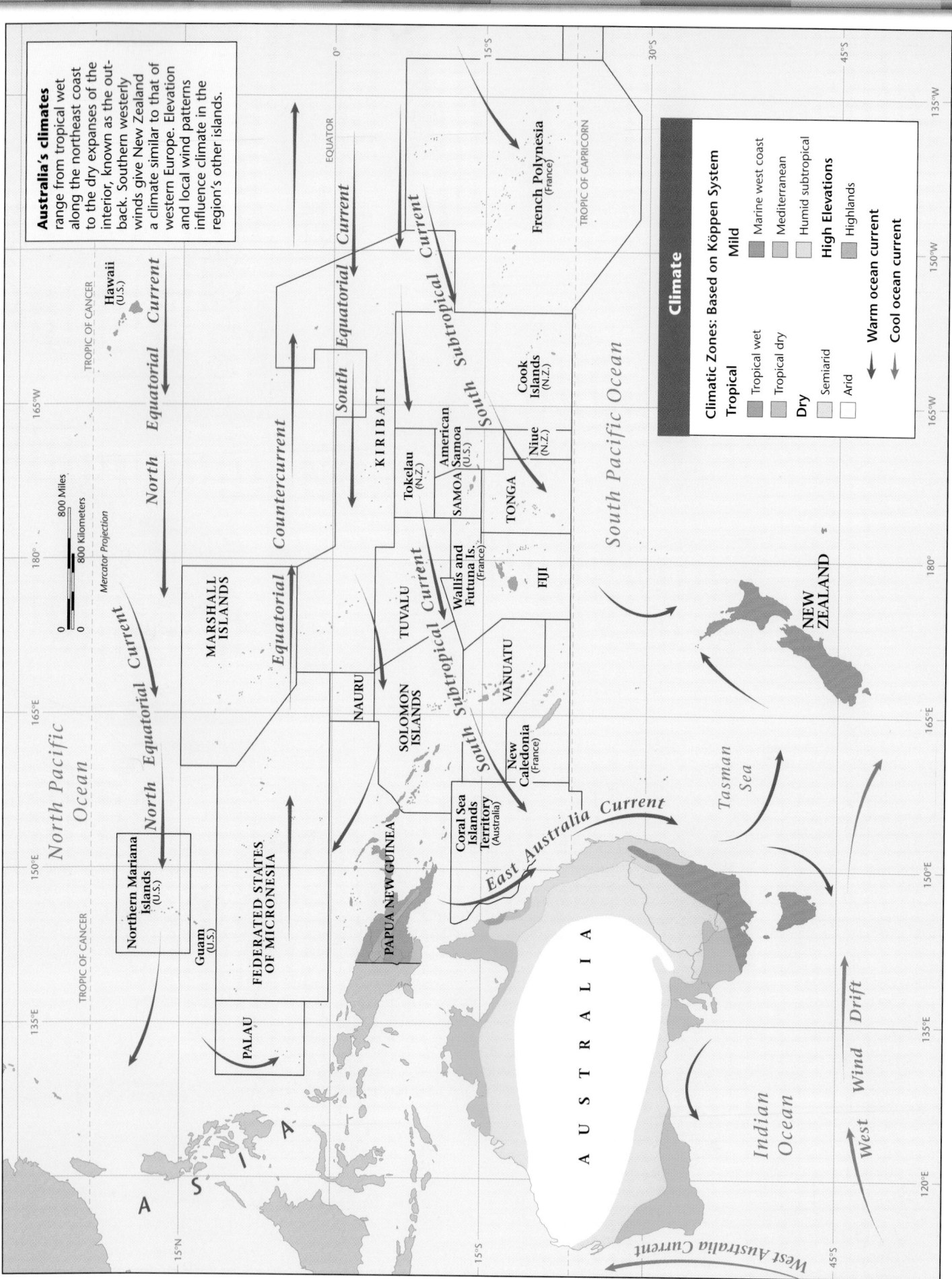

Australia's climates range from tropical wet along the northeast coast to the dry expanses of the interior, known as the outback. Southern westerly winds give New Zealand a climate similar to that of western Europe. Elevation and local wind patterns influence climate in the region's other islands.

Climate

Climatic Zones: Based on Köppen System

Tropical
- Tropical wet
- Tropical dry

Dry
- Semiarid
- Arid

Mild
- Marine west coast
- Mediterranean
- Humid subtropical

High Elevations
- Highlands

→ Warm ocean current
→ Cool ocean current

800 Miles
800 Kilometers
Mercator Projection

North Pacific Ocean
South Pacific Ocean
Indian Ocean
Tasman Sea

EQUATOR
TROPIC OF CANCER
TROPIC OF CAPRICORN

North Equatorial Current
North Equatorial Current
Equatorial Countercurrent
Equatorial Current
South Equatorial Current
South Subtropical Current
South Subtropical Current
East Australia Current
West Australia Current
West Wind Drift

Hawaii (U.S.)
French Polynesia (France)
Cook Islands (N.Z.)
Niue (N.Z.)
American Samoa (U.S.)
SAMOA
Tokelau (N.Z.)
KIRIBATI
TONGA
FIJI
Wallis and Futuna Is. (France)
TUVALU
NAURU
MARSHALL ISLANDS
SOLOMON ISLANDS
VANUATU
New Caledonia (France)
Coral Sea Islands Territory (Australia)
PAPUA NEW GUINEA
FEDERATED STATES OF MICRONESIA
Guam (U.S.)
Northern Mariana Islands (U.S.)
PALAU
NEW ZEALAND
AUSTRALIA
ASIA

15°N
0°
15°S
30°S
45°S

135°E
150°E
165°E
180°
165°W
150°W
135°W
120°E

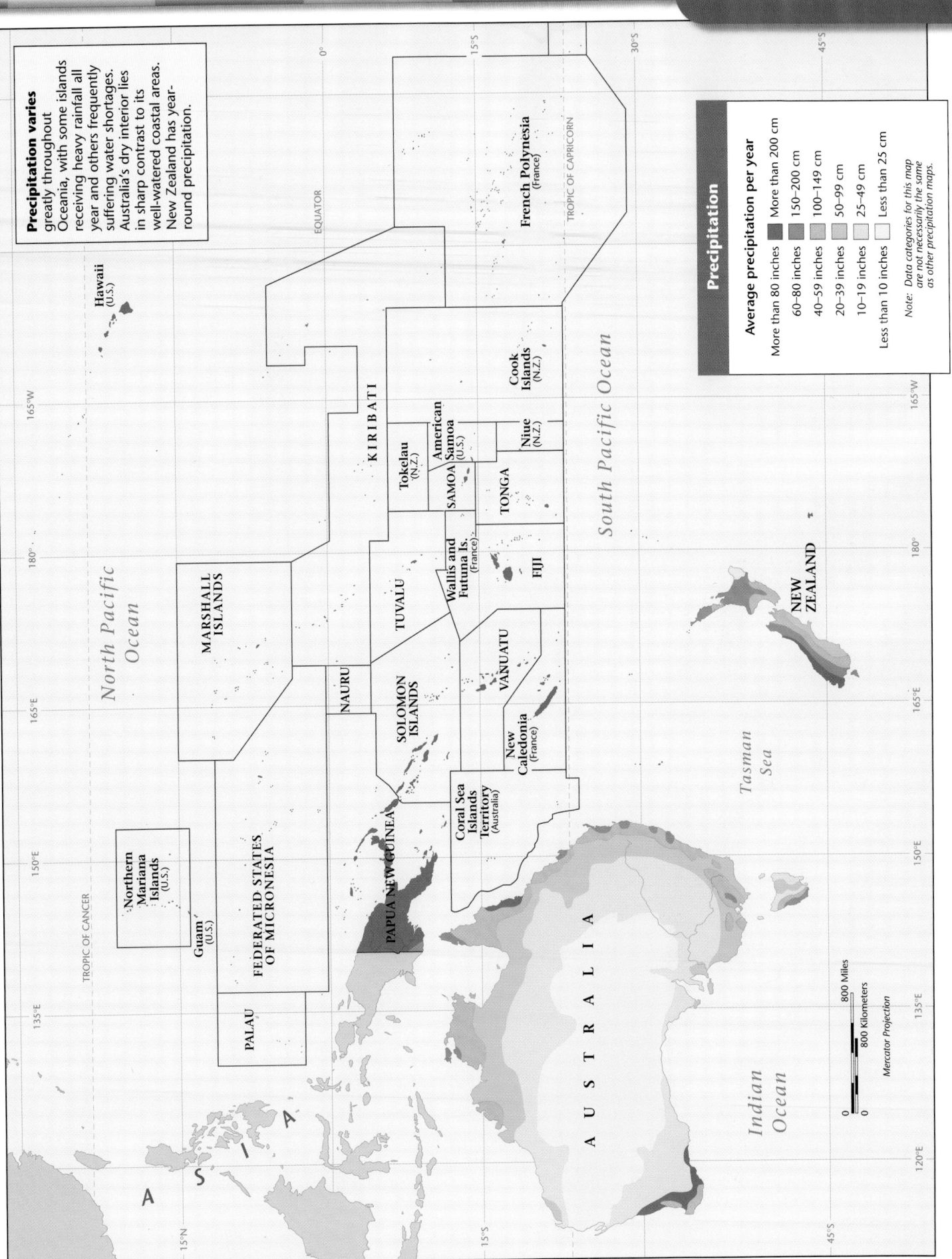

Precipitation varies greatly throughout Oceania, with some islands receiving heavy rainfall all year and others frequently suffering water shortages. Australia's dry interior lies in sharp contrast to its well-watered coastal areas. New Zealand has year-round precipitation.

Hawaii (U.S.)

North Pacific Ocean

TROPIC OF CANCER

Northern Mariana Islands (U.S.)

Guam (U.S.)

PALAU

FEDERATED STATES OF MICRONESIA

MARSHALL ISLANDS

KIRIBATI

NAURU

TUVALU

SOLOMON ISLANDS

PAPUA NEW GUINEA

Coral Sea Islands Territory (Australia)

Tokelau (N.Z.)

American Samoa (U.S.)

SAMOA

Wallis and Futuna Is. (France)

FIJI

VANUATU

New Caledonia (France)

TONGA

Niue (N.Z.)

Cook Islands (N.Z.)

French Polynesia (France)

TROPIC OF CAPRICORN

South Pacific Ocean

EQUATOR

A S I A

A U S T R A L I A

Indian Ocean

Tasman Sea

NEW ZEALAND

Precipitation

Average precipitation per year

More than 80 inches — More than 200 cm
60–80 inches — 150–200 cm
40–59 inches — 100–149 cm
20–39 inches — 50–99 cm
10–19 inches — 25–49 cm
Less than 10 inches — Less than 25 cm

Note: Data categories for this map are not necessarily the same as other precipitation maps.

800 Miles

800 Kilometers

Mercator Projection

120°E 135°E 150°E 165°E 180° 165°W

15°N 0° 15°S 30°S 45°S

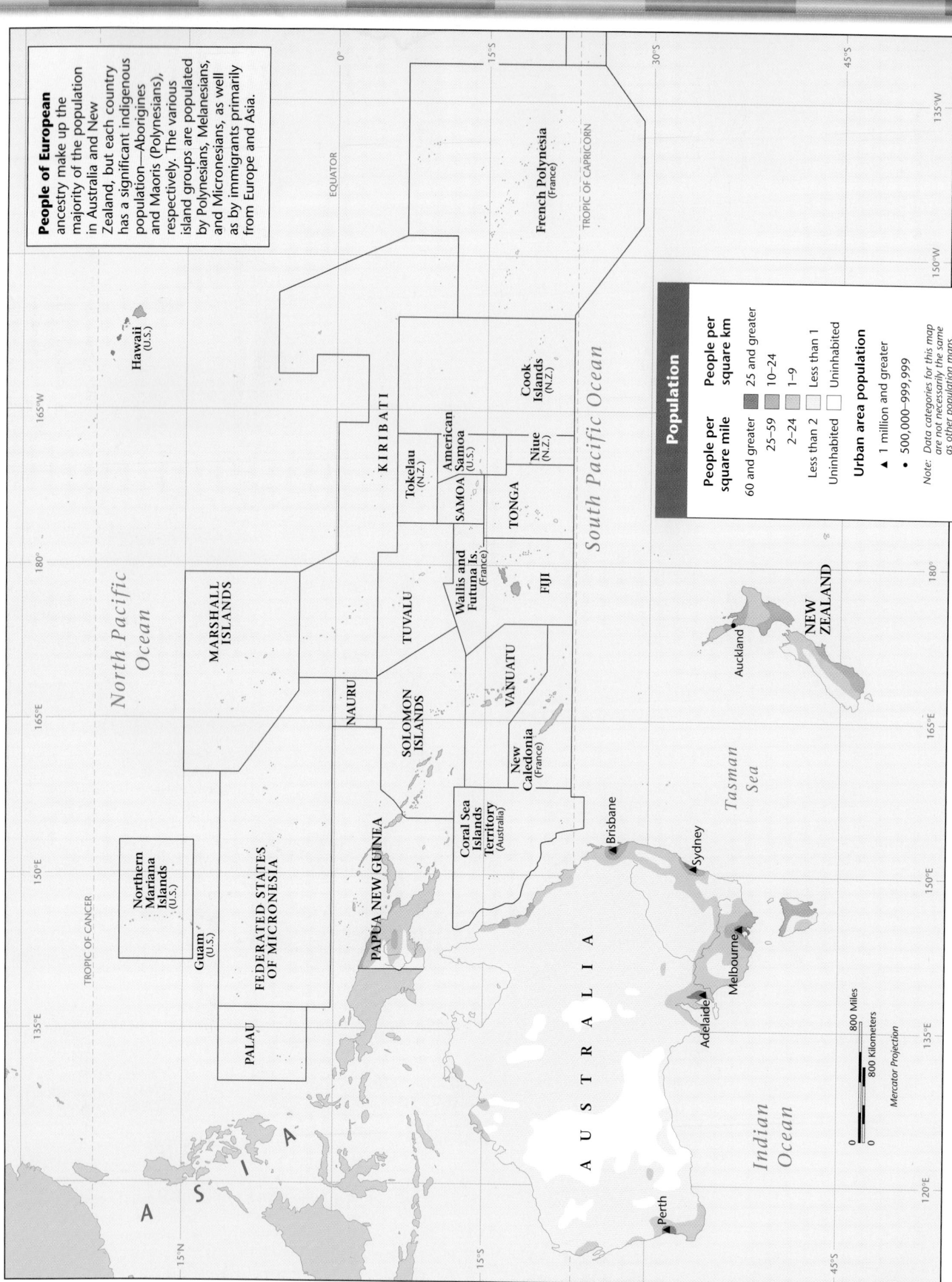

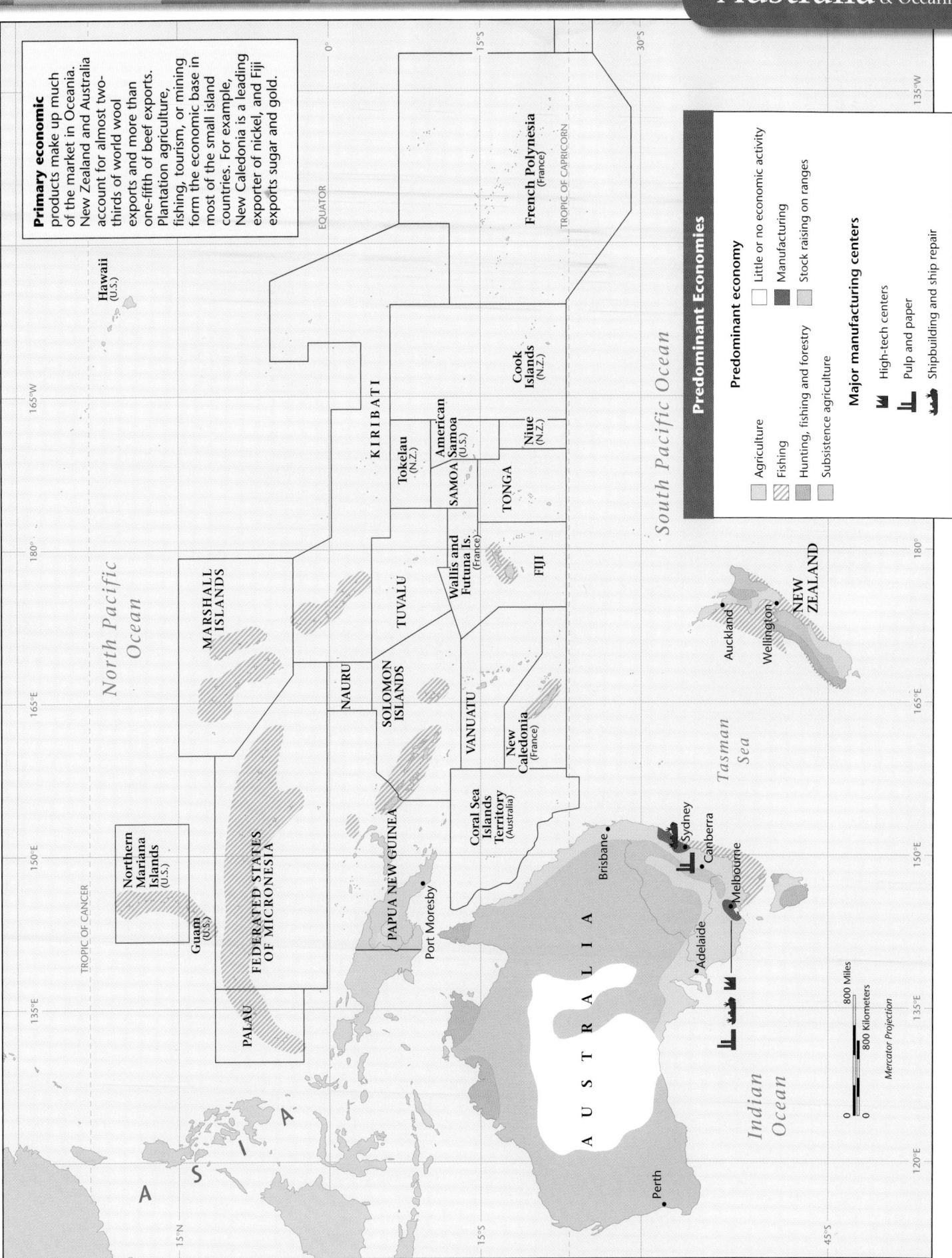

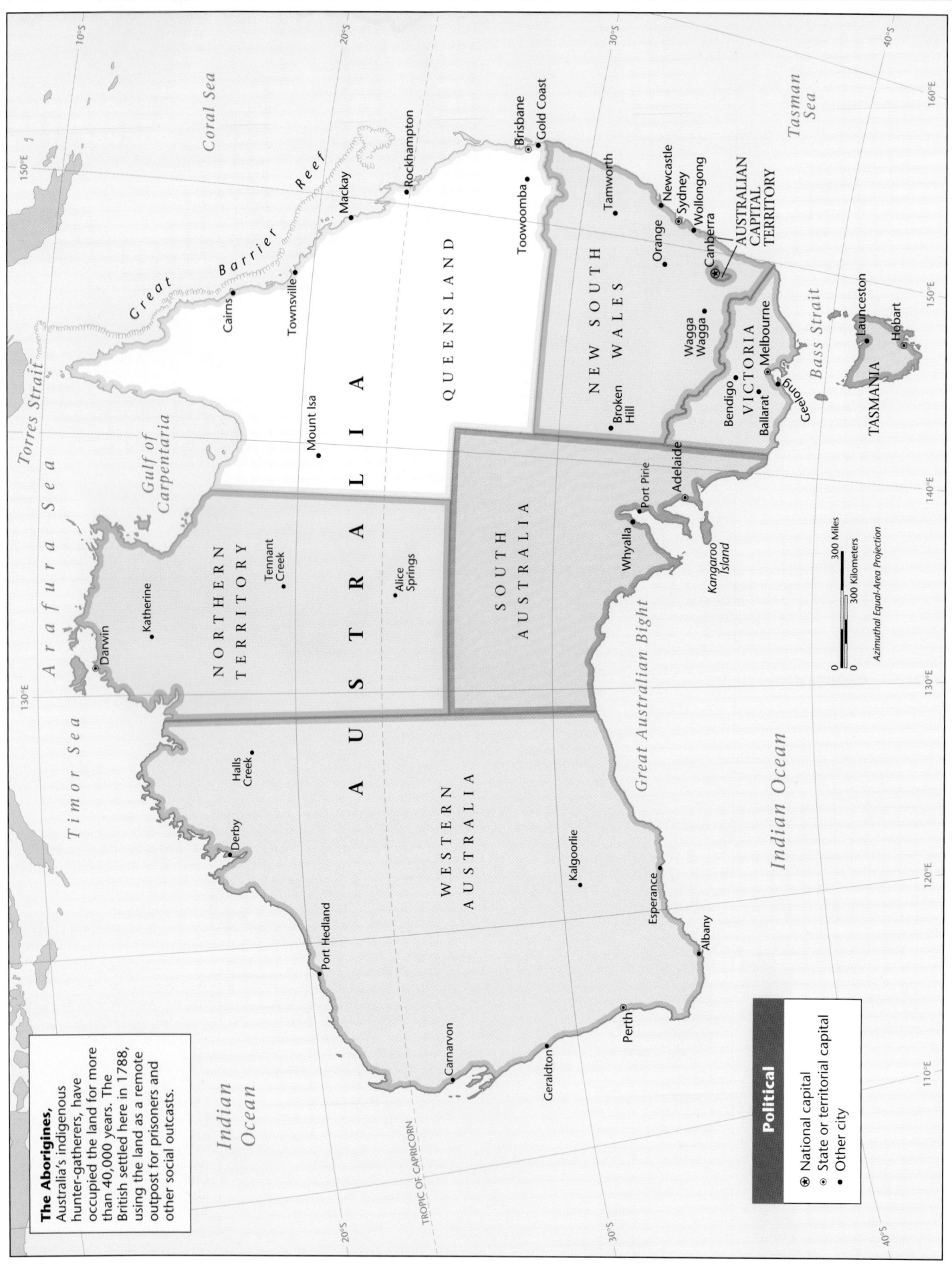

The Aborigines, Australia's indigenous hunter-gatherers, have occupied the land for more than 40,000 years. The British settled here in 1788, using the land as a remote outpost for prisoners and other social outcasts.

Political

⊛ National capital
◉ State or territorial capital
• Other city

Coral Sea

Great Barrier Reef

Torres Strait

Gulf of Carpentaria

Arafura Sea

Timor Sea

Indian Ocean

Tasman Sea

Bass Strait

Indian Ocean

Great Australian Bight

Brisbane
Gold Coast
Rockhampton
Mackay
Toowoomba
Tamworth
Newcastle
Sydney
Wollongong
Orange
Canberra
AUSTRALIAN CAPITAL TERRITORY
Cairns
Townsville

QUEENSLAND

NEW SOUTH WALES

Wagga Wagga
Broken Hill
Bendigo
VICTORIA
Ballarat
Melbourne
Geelong

Launceston
Hobart
TASMANIA

Mount Isa

A U S T R A L I A

NORTHERN TERRITORY
Tennant Creek
Alice Springs
Katherine
Darwin

SOUTH AUSTRALIA
Adelaide
Port Pirie
Whyalla
Kangaroo Island

WESTERN AUSTRALIA
Halls Creek
Derby
Port Hedland
Carnarvon
Geraldton
Perth
Albany
Esperance
Kalgoorlie

300 Miles
300 Kilometers
Azimuthal Equal-Area Projection

TROPIC OF CAPRICORN

150°E
140°E
130°E
120°E
110°E
160°E
10°S
20°S
30°S
40°S

Political

⊛ National capital
• Other city

Kaitaia
Kerikeri
Whangarei

Great Barrier Island

Tasman Sea

Takapuna
Waitemata
Auckland
Manukau

North Island

Hamilton
Mount Maunganui
Tauranga
Whakatane
Rotorua

Taupo
Gisborne

New Plymouth
Raetihi
Napier
Hastings
Wanganui
Feilding
Palmerston North
Porirua
Levin
Masterton
Nelson
Upper Hutt
Lower Hutt
Picton
Wellington
Blenheim
Cook Strait
Westport

150 Miles
150 Kilometers

Azimuthal Equal-Area Projection

Molesworth

Greymouth
Parnassus
Kaikoura
Hokitika
Arthur's Pass

Pacific Ocean

Fox Glacier
Franz Josef Glacier
Christchurch
Lyttelton
Haast
Ashburton

Timaru

Canterbury Bight

Milford Sound
Wanaka

Oamaru

South Island

Dunedin
Gore
Balclutha
Invercargill

Foveaux Strait

Stewart Island

35°S
35°S
170°E
175°E
40°S
40°S
45°S
165°E
170°E
175°E

Two large islands
and several smaller ones
make up New Zealand.
The country averages 37
people per square mile
(14 people per sq km), but
most of the population
lives in urban areas. The
economy relies on primary
activities, such as raising
sheep, dairying, and
forestry. Wellington,
Christchurch, and other
place-names reflect a
strong British influence.

Time Zones & the Date Line

The *Fiji Times*, a newspaper published in Suva, capital of the Fiji Islands, carries the message "The First Newspaper Published in the World Today" on the front page of each edition. How can this newspaper from a small island country make such a claim? Fiji and most of the other islands that make up Oceania, including Australia and New Zealand, lie west of the date line, an invisible boundary designated to mark the beginning of each new day. The date line is just part of the system we have adopted to keep track of the passage of days.

For most of human history, people determined time by observing the position of the sun in the sky. Slight differences in time did not matter until, in the mid-19th century, the spread of railroads and telegraph lines changed forever the importance of time. High-speed transportation and communications required schedules, and schedules required that everyone agree on the time.

In 1884, an international conference, convened in Washington, D.C., established an international system of 24 time zones based on the fact that Earth turns from west to east 15 degrees of longitude every hour. Each time zone has a central meridian and is 15 degrees wide, $7\frac{1}{2}$ degrees to either side of the named central meridian.

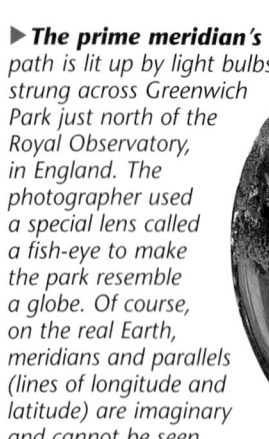

▶ **The prime meridian's** path is lit up by light bulbs strung across Greenwich Park just north of the Royal Observatory, in England. The photographer used a special lens called a fish-eye to make the park resemble a globe. Of course, on the real Earth, meridians and parallels (lines of longitude and latitude) are imaginary and cannot be seen.

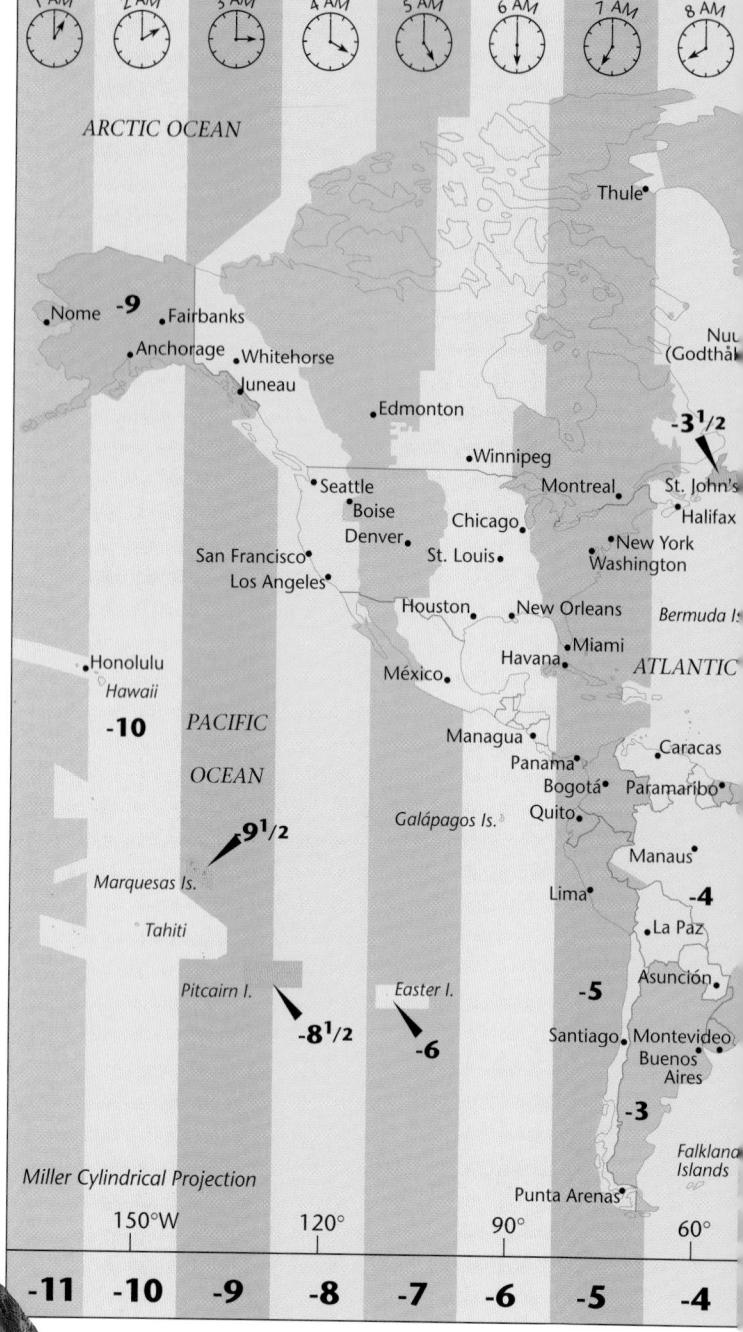

▲ **A system of standard time** put trains on schedules, which helped reduce the chance of collisions and the loss of lives and property caused by them.

Web Link for information on time zones: http://tycho.usno.navy.mil/tzones.html

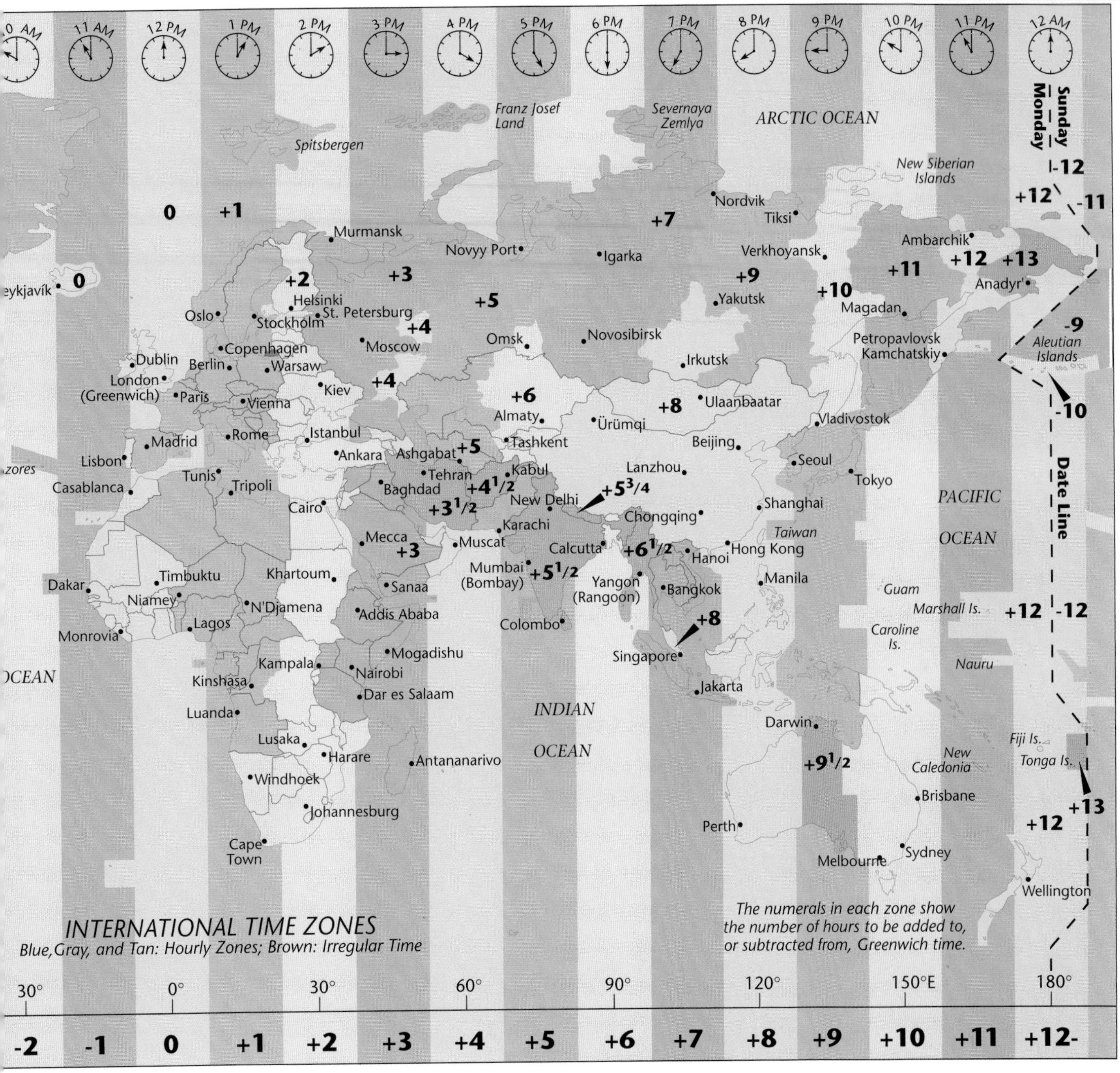

INTERNATIONAL TIME ZONES

Blue, Gray, and Tan: Hourly Zones; Brown: Irregular Time

The numerals in each zone show the number of hours to be added to, or subtracted from, Greenwich time.

30°	0°	30°	60°	90°	120°	150°E	180°
-2	-1	0	+1	+2	+3	+4	+5	+6	+7	+8	+9	+10	+11	+12-

Date Line

The date line (180°) is directly opposite the prime meridian (0°). As Earth rotates, each new day officially begins as the 180° line passes 12 midnight. If you travel *west* across the date line, you advance one day; if you travel *east* across the date line, you fall back one day.

Notice on the map how the line zigs to the east as it passes through the South Pacific so that the islands of Fiji will not be split between two different days. Also notice that India is 5½ hours ahead of Greenwich time, and China has only one time zone, even though the country spans more than 60 degrees of longitude. These differences are the result of decisions made at the country level.

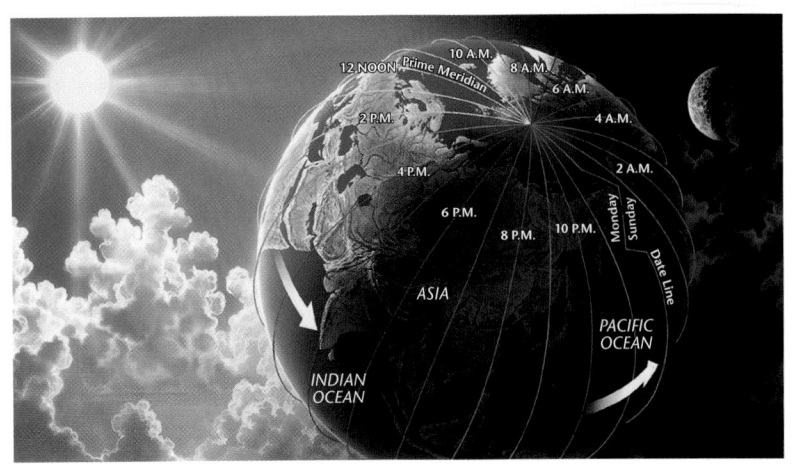

Antarctica

About 180 million years ago Antarctica broke away from the ancient supercontinent Gondwana. Slowly the continent drifted to its present location at the southernmost point on Earth. Approximately 98 percent of the continent lies under permanent ice sheets that are nearly 3 miles (5 km) thick in places. It is estimated that if all of Antarctica's ice were to melt, the global ocean level would rise more than 200 feet (60 m).

Facts & Figures

- ▶ **Land area:** 5,100,400 sq mi (13,209,000 sq km)

- ▶ **Population:** no permanent residents

- ▶ **Highest point:** Vinson Massif: 16,067 ft (4,897 m)

- ▶ **Lowest point:** Bentley Subglacial Trench: 8,366 ft (2,550 m) below sea level

- ▶ **Number of independent countries:** 0

- ▶ **Number of countries claiming land:** 7

- ▶ **Number of countries operating research stations:** 23

- ▶ **Number of research stations:** 44

- ▶ **Coldest temperature recorded:** minus 128.6°F (minus 89°C), July 21, 1983

- ▶ **Average precipitation on the polar plateau:** less than 2 in (5 cm) per year

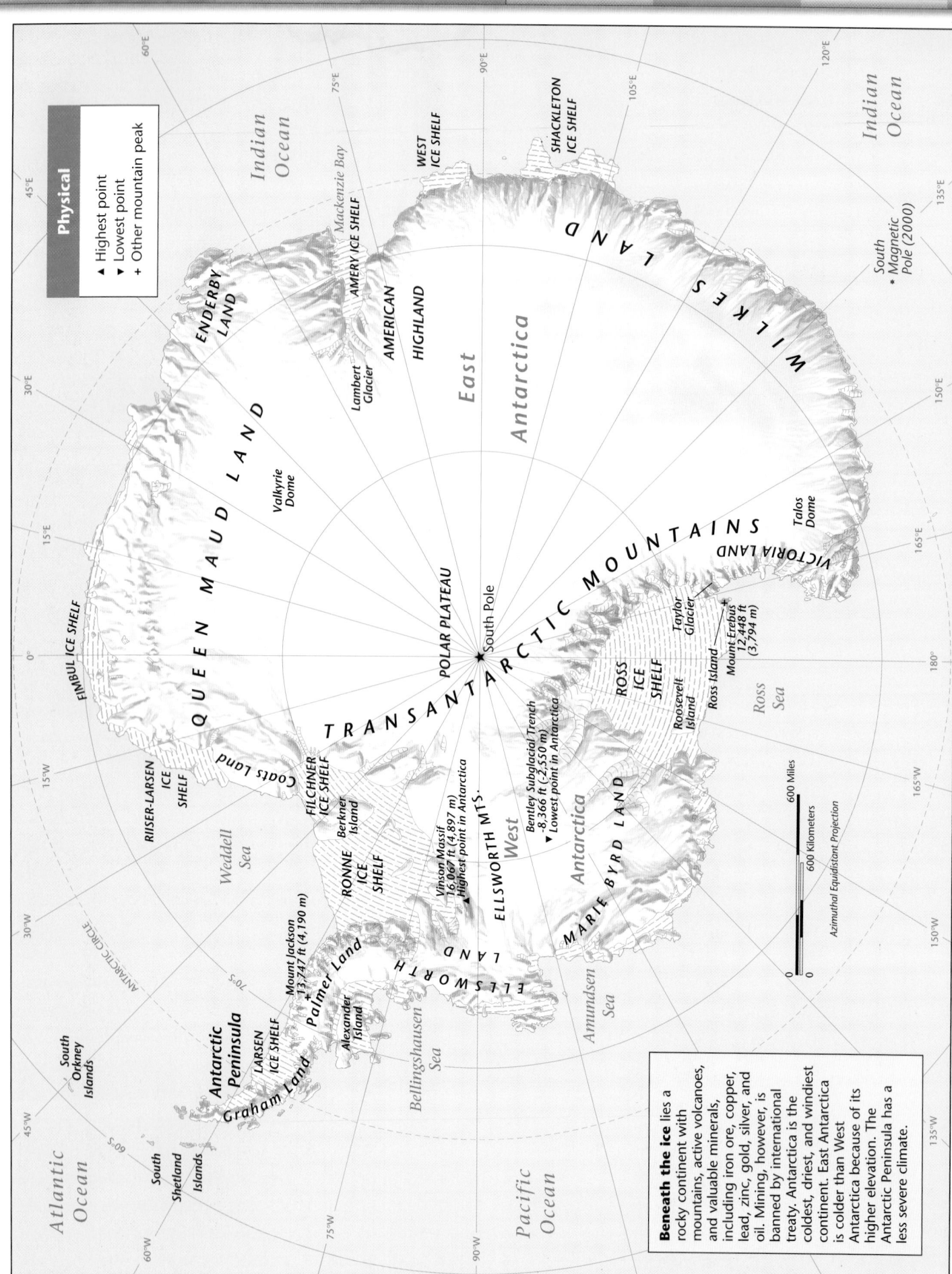

Physical

- ▲ Highest point
- ▼ Lowest point
- + Other mountain peak

Atlantic Ocean

Indian Ocean

Indian Ocean

Pacific Ocean

ENDERBY LAND

QUEEN MAUD LAND

Mackenzie Bay

Lambert Glacier

AMERY ICE SHELF

WEST ICE SHELF

SHACKLETON ICE SHELF

AMERICAN HIGHLAND

WILKES LAND

East Antarctica

Valkyrie Dome

Talos Dome

POLAR PLATEAU

South Pole

South Magnetic Pole (2000)

VICTORIA LAND

FIMBUL ICE SHELF

TRANSANTARCTIC MOUNTAINS

Taylor Glacier

+ Mount Erebus 12,448 ft (3,794 m)

ROSS ICE SHELF

Roosevelt Island

Ross Island

Ross Sea

RIISER-LARSEN ICE SHELF

Coats Land

FILCHNER ICE SHELF

Berkner Island

Weddell Sea

RONNE ICE SHELF

Vinson Massif 16,067 ft (4,897 m) ▲ Highest point in Antarctica

ELLSWORTH MTS.

West Antarctica

Bentley Subglacial Trench -8,366 ft (-2,550 m) ▼ Lowest point in Antarctica

MARIE BYRD LAND

ELLSWORTH LAND

South Orkney Islands

Mount Jackson + 13,747 ft (4,190 m)

Antarctic Peninsula

Palmer Land

Alexander Island

LARSEN ICE SHELF

Graham Land

Bellingshausen Sea

Amundsen Sea

South Shetland Islands

ANTARCTIC CIRCLE

600 Miles

600 Kilometers

Azimuthal Equidistant Projection

Beneath the ice lies a rocky continent with mountains, active volcanoes, and valuable minerals, including iron ore, copper, lead, zinc, gold, silver, and oil. Mining, however, is banned by international treaty. Antarctica is the coldest, driest, and windiest continent. East Antarctica is colder than West Antarctica because of its higher elevation. The Antarctic Peninsula has a less severe climate.

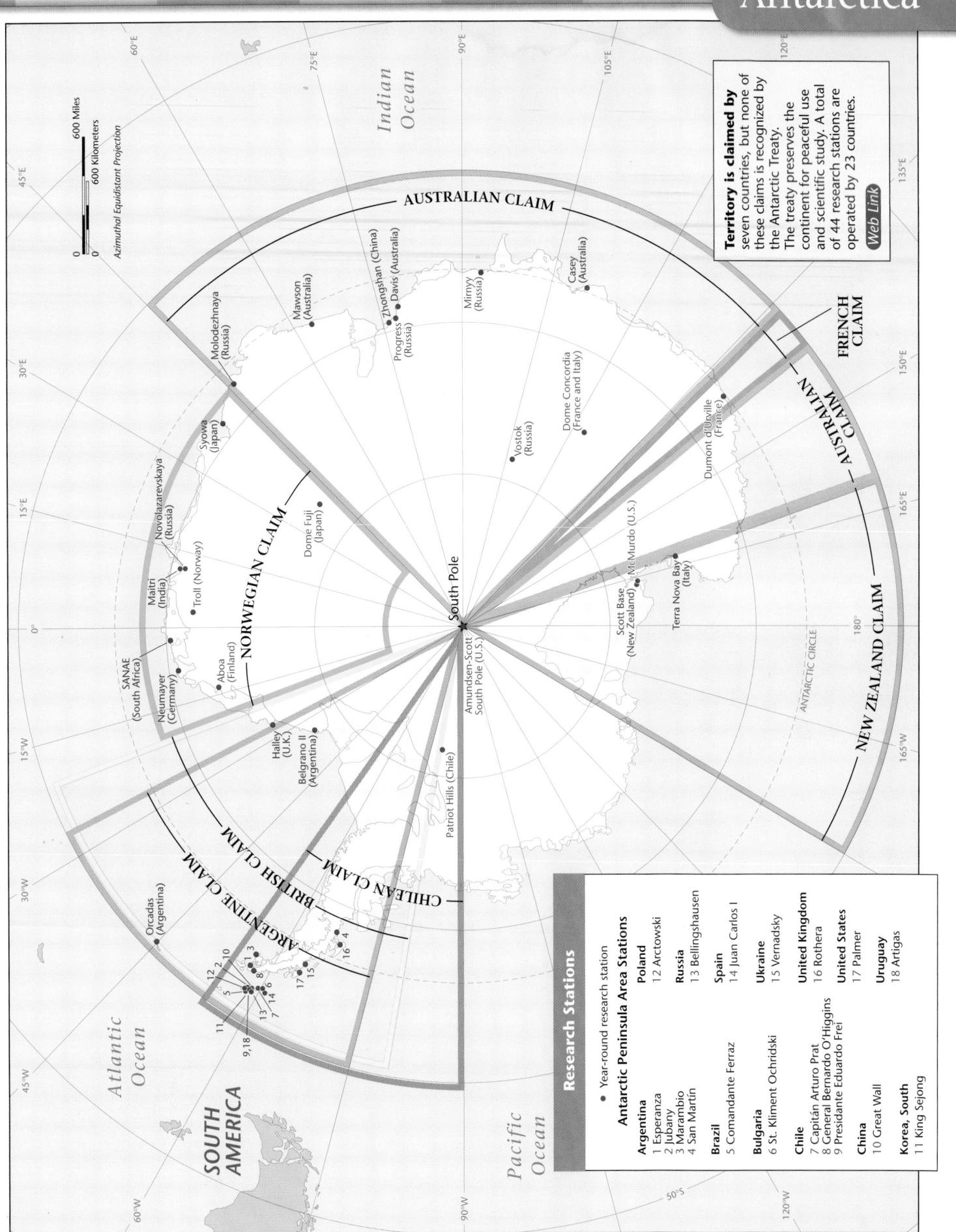

AUSTRALIAN CLAIM

FRENCH CLAIM

AUSTRALIAN CLAIM

NEW ZEALAND CLAIM

NORWEGIAN CLAIM

BRITISH CLAIM

ARGENTINE CLAIM

CHILEAN CLAIM

Territory is claimed by seven countries, but none of these claims is recognized by the Antarctic Treaty. The treaty preserves the continent for peaceful use and scientific study. A total of 44 research stations are operated by 23 countries.

Web Link

Indian Ocean

Atlantic Ocean

Pacific Ocean

SOUTH AMERICA

ANTARCTIC CIRCLE

South Pole

600 Miles
600 Kilometers
Azimuthal Equidistant Projection

Mawson (Australia)
Zhongshan (China)
Davis (Australia)
Progress (Russia)
Mirnyy (Russia)
Casey (Australia)
Molodezhnaya (Russia)
Dome Concordia (France and Italy)
Vostok (Russia)
Dumont d'Urville (France)
Syowa (Japan)
Novolazarevskaya (Russia)
Dome Fuji (Japan)
Maitri (India)
Troll (Norway)
McMurdo (U.S.)
Terra Nova Bay (Italy)
SANAE (South Africa)
Aboa (Finland)
Scott Base (New Zealand)
Neumayer (Germany)
Amundsen-Scott South Pole (U.S.)
Orcadas (Argentina)
Halley (U.K.)
Belgrano II (Argentina)
Patriot Hills (Chile)

Research Stations

• Year-round research station

Antarctic Peninsula Area Stations

Argentina
1 Esperanza
2 Jubany
3 Marambio
4 San Martín

Brazil
5 Comandante Ferraz

Bulgaria
6 St. Kliment Ochridski

Chile
7 Capitán Arturo Prat
8 General Bernardo O'Higgins
9 Presidente Eduardo Frei

China
10 Great Wall

Korea, South
11 King Sejong

Poland
12 Arctowski

Russia
13 Bellingshausen

Spain
14 Juan Carlos I

Ukraine
15 Vernadsky

United Kingdom
16 Rothera

United States
17 Palmer

Uruguay
18 Artigas

The flags and fact boxes below represent the world's 191 independent countries—those with national governments that are the highest legal authority over the land and people within their boundaries. The flags shown are national flags recognized by the United Nations. Area figures are for land only. They do not include surface areas for inland bodies of water. Population figures are for the year 2000 as provided by the Population Reference Bureau of the United States. The languages listed are either the ones most commonly spoken within a country or official languages of a country.

NORTH AMERICA

Antigua and Barbuda
Area: 170 sq mi
(440 sq km)
Population: 68,000
Capital: St. John's
Languages: English, local dialects

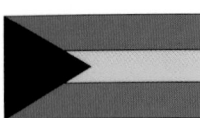

Bahamas
Area: 5,382 sq mi
(13,939 sq km)
Population: 310,000
Capital: Nassau
Languages: English, Creole

Barbados
Area: 166 sq mi
(430 sq km)
Population: 259,000
Capital: Bridgetown
Language: English

Belize
Area: 8,867 sq mi
(22,965 sq km)
Population: 254,000
Capital: Belmopan
Languages: English, Spanish, Mayan, Carib

Canada
Area: 3,849,670 sq mi
(9,970,610 sq km)
Population: 30,764,000
Capital: Ottawa
Languages: English, French (both official)

Costa Rica
Area: 19,730 sq mi
(51,100 sq km)
Population: 3,589,000
Capital: San José
Languages: Spanish, English

Cuba
Area: 42,804 sq mi
(110,861 sq km)
Population: 11,139,000
Capital: Havana
Language: Spanish

Dominica
Area: 290 sq mi
(751 sq km)
Population: 76,000
Capital: Roseau
Languages: English, French patois

Dominican Republic
Area: 18,816 sq mi
(48,734 sq km)
Population: 8,443,000
Capital: Santo Domingo
Language: Spanish

El Salvador
Area: 8,124 sq mi
(21,041 sq km)
Population: 6,280,000
Capital: San Salvador
Languages: Spanish, Nahuatl

Grenada
Area: 133 sq mi
(344 sq km)
Population: 98,000
Capital: St. George's
Languages: English, French patois

Guatemala
Area: 42,042 sq mi
(108,889 sq km)
Population: 12,670,000
Capital: Guatemala City
Languages: Spanish, Amerindian dialects

Haiti
Area: 10,714 sq mi
(27,750 sq km)
Population: 6,423,000
Capital: Port-au-Prince
Languages: French, Creole

Honduras
Area: 43,277 sq mi
(112,088 sq km)
Population: 6,130,000
Capital: Tegucigalpa
Languages: Spanish, Amerindian dialects

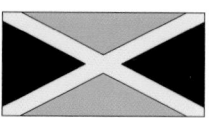

Jamaica
Area: 4,244 sq mi
(10,991 sq km)
Population: 2,609,000
Capital: Kingston
Languages: English, Creole

Mexico
Area: 756,066 sq mi
(1,958,201 sq km)
Population: 99,639,000
Capital: Mexico City
Languages: Spanish, regional indigenous languages

Nicaragua
Area: 50,193 sq mi
(129,999 sq km)
Population: 5,074,000
Capital: Managua
Languages: Spanish, English, Amerindian dialects

Panama
Area: 29,762 sq mi
(77,082 sq km)
Population: 2,857,000
Capital: Panama City
Languages: Spanish, English

St. Kitts and Nevis
Area: 101 sq mi
(261 sq km)
Population: 43,000
Capital: Basseterre
Language: English

St. Lucia
Area: 238 sq mi
(617 sq km)
Population: 157,000
Capital: Castries
Languages: English, French patois

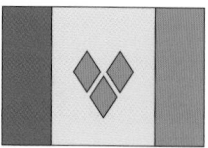

St. Vincent and the Grenadines
Area: 150 sq mi
(388 sq km)
Population: 112,000
Capital: Kingstown
Languages: English, French patois

Trinidad and Tobago
Area: 1,981 sq mi
(5,131 sq km)
Population: 1,295,000
Capital: Port of Spain
Languages: English, Hindi, French, Spanish

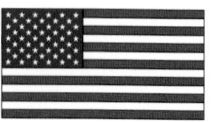

United States
Area: 3,717,796 sq mi
(9,629,091 sq km)
Population: 275,600,000
Capital: Washington, D.C.
Languages: English, Spanish

SOUTH AMERICA

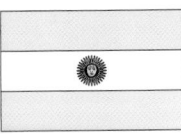

Argentina
Area: 1,068,302 sq mi (2,766,889 sq km)
Population: 37,048,000
Capital: Buenos Aires
Languages: Spanish, English, Italian, German

Bolivia
Area: 424,164 sq mi (1,098,581 sq km)
Population: 8,281,000
Capitals: La Paz, Sucre
Languages: Spanish, Quechua, Aymara (all official)

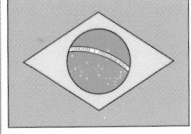

Brazil
Area: 3,286,488 sq mi (8,511,965 sq km)
Population: 170,115,000
Capital: Brasília
Languages: Portuguese, Spanish, English

Chile
Area: 292,135 sq mi (756,626 sq km)
Population: 15,211,000
Capital: Santiago
Language: Spanish

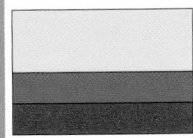

Colombia
Area: 439,737 sq mi (1,138,914 sq km)
Population: 40,037,000
Capital: Bogotá
Language: Spanish

Ecuador
Area: 109,484 sq mi (283,561 sq km)
Population: 12,646,000
Capital: Quito
Languages: Spanish, Quechua

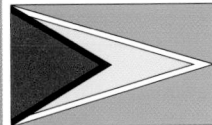

Guyana
Area: 83,000 sq mi (214,969 sq km)
Population: 698,000
Capital: Georgetown
Languages: English, Amerindian dialects

Paraguay
Area: 157,048 sq mi (406,752 sq km)
Population: 5,505,000
Capital: Asunción
Languages: Spanish, Guaraní

Peru
Area: 496,225 sq mi (1,285,217 sq km)
Population: 27,136,000
Capital: Lima
Languages: Spanish, Quechua (both official), Aymara

Suriname
Area: 63,037 sq mi (163,265 sq km)
Population: 434,000
Capital: Paramaribo
Languages: Dutch, English, Sranang Tongo (Taki-Taki), Hindustani, Javanese

Uruguay
Area: 68,037 sq mi (176,215 sq km)
Population: 3,313,000
Capital: Montevideo
Languages: Spanish, Portunol, Brazilero

Venezuela
Area: 352,144 sq mi (912,050 sq km)
Population: 24,170,000
Capital: Caracas
Language: Spanish

EUROPE

Albania
Area: 11,100 sq mi (28,748 sq km)
Population: 3,431,000
Capital: Tirana
Languages: Albanian, Greek

Andorra
Area: 175 sq mi (453 sq km)
Population: 67,000
Capital: Andorra la Vella
Languages: Catalan, French, Spanish

Austria
Area: 32,377 sq mi (83,856 sq km)
Population: 8,094,000
Capital: Vienna
Language: German

Belarus
Area: 80,154 sq mi (207,598 sq km)
Population: 10,004,000
Capital: Minsk
Languages: Belorussian, Russian

Belgium
Area: 11,783 sq mi (30,518 sq km)
Population: 10,246,000
Capital: Brussels
Languages: Flemish, French, German

Bosnia and Herzegovina
Area: 19,741 sq mi (51,129 sq km)
Population: 3,809,000
Capital: Sarajevo
Language: Serbo-Croat (Bosnian)

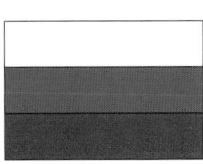

Bulgaria
Area: 42,823 sq mi (110,912 sq km)
Population: 8,152,000
Capital: Sofia
Language: Bulgarian

Croatia
Area: 21,829 sq mi (56,538 sq km)
Population: 4,600,000
Capital: Zagreb
Language: Serbo-Croat

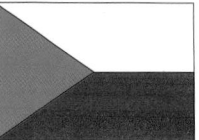

Czech Republic
Area: 30,450 sq mi (78,864 sq km)
Population: 10,275,000
Capital: Prague
Languages: Czech, Slovak

Denmark
Area: 16,638 sq mi (43,092 sq km)
Population: 5,330,000
Capital: Copenhagen
Languages: Danish, Faeroese, Greenlandic

Estonia
Area: 17,413 sq mi (45,099 sq km)
Population: 1,433,000
Capital: Tallinn
Languages: Estonian, Russian, Ukrainian

Finland
Area: 130,558 sq mi (338,145 sq km)
Population: 5,177,000
Capital: Helisinki
Languages: Finnish, Swedish (both official)

France
Area: 210,026 sq mi (543,965 sq km)
Population: 59,353,000
Capital: Paris
Language: French

Germany
Area: 137,857 sq mi
(357,046 sq km)
Population: 82,141,000
Capital: Berlin
Language: German

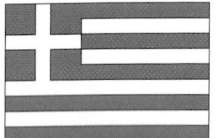

Greece
Area: 50,962 sq mi
(131,990 sq km)
Population: 10,596,000
Capital: Athens
Languages: Greek, English,
French

Hungary
Area: 35,919 sq mi
(93,030 sq km)
Population: 10,020,000
Capital: Budapest
Language: Hungarian

Iceland
Area: 39,769 sq mi
(103,001 sq km)
Population: 281,000
Capital: Reykjavík
Language: Icelandic

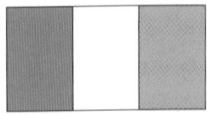

Ireland
Area: 27,137 sq mi
(70,284 sq km)
Population: 3,795,000
Capital: Dublin
Languages: English, Irish
(Gaelic)

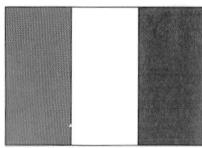

Italy
Area: 116,324 sq mi
(301,277 sq km)
Population: 57,820,000
Capital: Rome
Languages: Italian,
German, French

Latvia
Area: 24,942 sq mi
(64,599 sq km)
Population: 2,416,000
Capital: Riga
Languages: Latvian,
Lithuanian, Russian

Liechtenstein
Area: 62 sq mi
(160 sq km)
Population: 33,000
Capital: Vaduz
Languages: German,
Alemannic dialect

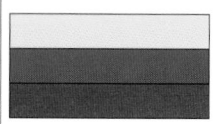

Lithuania
Area: 25,174 sq mi
(65,200 sq km)
Population: 3,697,000
Capital: Vilnius
Languages: Lithuanian,
Polish, Russian

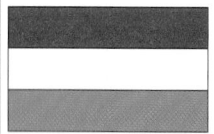

Luxembourg
Area: 998 sq mi
(2,586 sq km)
Population: 438,000
Capital: Luxembourg
Languages:
Luxembourgian, German,
French

Macedonia
Area: 9,928 sq mi
(25,713 sq km)
Population: 2,033,000
Capital: Skopje
Languages: Macedonian,
Albanian

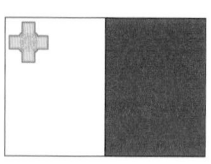

Malta
Area: 122 sq mi
(316 sq km)
Population: 390,000
Capital: Valletta
Languages: Maltese,
English (both official)

Moldova
Area: 13,217 sq mi
(33,999 sq km)
Population: 4,276,000
Capital: Chişinău
Languages: Moldavian,
Russian

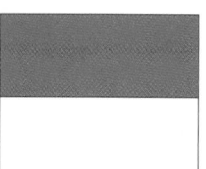

Monaco
Area: 0.6 sq mi
(1.9 sq km)
Population: 34,000
Capital: Monaco
Languages: French,
English, Italian

Netherlands
Area: 16,023 sq mi
(41,499 sq km)
Population: 15,921,000
Capital: Amsterdam
Language: Dutch

Norway
Area: 125,182 sq mi
(324,220 sq km)
Population: 4,487,000
Capital: Oslo
Language: Norwegian

Poland
Area: 120,725 sq mi
(312,677 sq km)
Population: 38,648,000
Capital: Warsaw
Language: Polish

Portugal
Area: 35,672 sq mi
(92,389 sq km)
Population: 10,013,000
Capital: Lisbon
Language: Portuguese

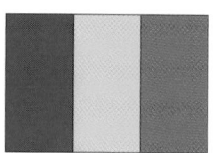

Romania
Area: 91,699 sq mi
(237,499 sq km)
Population: 22,432,000
Capital: Bucharest
Languages: Romanian,
Hungarian, German

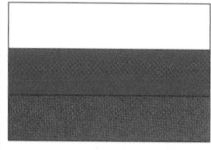

Russia
Area: 6,592,692 sq mi
(17,074,993 sq km)
Population: 145,231,000
Capital: Moscow
Language: Russian

San Marino
Area: 24 sq mi
(61 sq km)
Population: 27,000
Capital: San Marino
Language: Italian

Slovakia
Area: 18,921 sq mi
(49,006 km)
Population: 5,401,000
Capital: Bratislava
Languages: Slovak,
Hungarian

Slovenia
Area: 7,819 sq mi
(20,251 sq km)
Population: 1,968,000
Capital: Ljubljana
Languages: Slovene,
Serbo-Croat

Spain
Area: 194,897 sq mi
(504,782 sq km)
Population: 39,466,000
Capital: Madrid
Languages: Spanish,
Catalan, Galician, Basque

Sweden
Area: 173,732 sq mi
(449,964 sq km)
Population: 8,866,000
Capital: Stockholm
Language: Swedish

Switzerland
Area: 15,941 sq mi
(41,288 sq km)
Population: 7,142,000
Capital: Bern
Languages: German,
French, Italian, Romansch

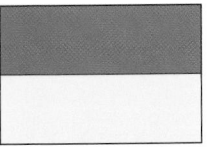

Ukraine
Area: 233,206 sq mi
(604,001 sq km)
Population: 49,509,000
Capital: Kiev
Languages: Ukrainian,
Russian, Romanian

United Kingdom
Area: 94,248 sq mi
(24,101 sq km)
Population: 59,750,000
Capital: London
Languages: English, Welsh,
Gaelic

Vatican City
Area: 0.2 sq mi
(0.4 sq km)
Population: 1,000
Languages: Italian, Latin

Yugoslavia
Area: 39,450 sq mi
(102,173 sq km)
Population: 10,662,000
Capital: Belgrade
Languages: Serbo-Croat,
Albanian

AFRICA

Algeria
Area: 919,595 sq mi
(2,381,741 sq km)
Population: 31,471,000
Capital: Algiers
Languages: Arabic, French,
Berber dialects

Angola
Area: 481,354 sq mi
(1,246,700 sq km)
Population: 12,878,000
Capital: Luanda
Languages: Portuguese,
Bantu

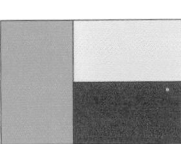

Benin
Area: 43,484 sq mi
(112,622 sq km)
Population: 6,396,000
Capitals: Porto-Novo,
Cotonou
Languages: French, Fon,
Yoruba, indigenous languages

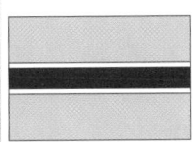

Botswana
Area: 231,805 sq mi
(600,372 sq km)
Population: 1,576,000
Capital: Gaborone
Languages: English, Setswana

Burkina Faso
Area: 105,869 sq mi
(274,200 sq km)
Population: 11,946,000
Capital: Ouagadougou
Languages: French,
indigenous languages

Burundi
Area: 10,747 sq mi
(27,834 sq km)
Population: 6,054,000
Capital: Bujumbura
Languages: Kirundi,
French (both official)

Cameroon
Area: 183,569 sq mi
(475,442 sq km)
Population: 15,422,000
Capital: Yaoundé
Languages: French, English
(both official), 24 major
African language groups

Cape Verde
Area: 1,557 sq mi
(4,033 sq km)
Population: 401,000
Capital: Praia
Languages: Portuguese,
Crioulo

Central African Republic
Area: 240,535 sq mi
(622,984 sq km)
Population: 3,513,000
Capital: Bangui
Languages: French,
Sango, Arabic, Hunsa

Chad
Area: 495,755 sq mi
(1,284,000 sq km)
Population: 7,977,000
Capital: N'Djamena
Languages: French, Arabic
(both official), Sara, Sango,
more than 100 different
languages and dialects

Comoros
Area: 719 sq mi
(1,862 sq km)
Population: 578,000
Capital: Moroni
Languages: Arabic, French
(both official), Comoran

Congo
Area: 132,047 sq mi
(342,000 sq km)
Population: 2,831,000
Capital: Brazzaville
Languages: French,
Lingala, Monokutuba, many
local languages, dialects

Congo, Democratic Republic of the
Area: 905,568 sq mi
(2,345,409 sq km)
Population: 51,965,000
Capital: Kinshasa
Languages: French,
Lingala, Kingwana

Côte d'Ivoire
Area: 124,504 sq mi
(322,463 sq km)
Population: 15,980,000
Capitals: Yamoussoukro,
Abidjan
Languages: French,
Dioula, 60 native dialects

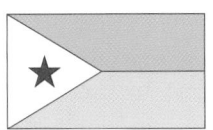

Djibouti
Area: 8,958 sq mi
(23,200 sq km)
Population: 638,000
Capital: Djibouti
Languages: French, Arabic
(both official)

Egypt
Area: 386,662 sq mi
(1,001,449 sq km)
Population: 68,344,000
Capital: Cairo
Languages: Arabic,
English, French

Equatorial Guinea
Area: 10,831 sq mi
(28,051 sq km)
Population: 453,000
Capital: Malabo
Languages: Spanish,
French (both official), pid-
gin English, Fang, Bubi, Ibo

Eritrea
Area: 46,842 sq mi
(121,320 sq km)
Population: 4,142,000
Capital: Asmara
Languages: Afar, Amharic,
Arabic, Tigre

Ethiopia
Area: 424,934 sq mi
(1,100,574 sq km)
Population: 64,117,000
Capital: Addis Ababa
Languages: Amharic,
Tigrinya, Orominga,
Guaraginga, Somali, Arabic

Gabon
Area: 103,347 sq mi
(267,667 sq km)
Population: 1,226,000
Capital: Libreville
Languages: French, Fang,
Myene, Bateke, Bapounou/
Eschira,Bandjabi

Gambia
Area: 4,361 sq mi (11,295 sq km)
Population: 1,305,000
Capital: Banjul
Languages: English, Mandinka, Wolof, Fula

Ghana
Area: 92,100 sq mi (238,537 sq km)
Population: 19,534,000
Capital: Accra
Languages: English, African languages (including Akan, Moshi-Dagomba, Ewe and Ga)

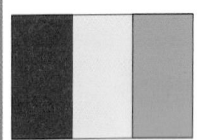

Guinea
Area: 94,926 sq mi (245,857 sq km)
Population: 7,466,000
Capital: Conakry
Languages: French, indigenous languages

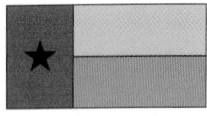

Guinea-Bissau
Area: 13,948 sq mi (36,125 sq km)
Population: 1,213,000
Capital: Bissau
Languages: Portuguese, Crioulo, indigenous languages

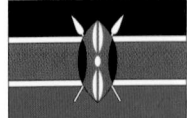

Kenya
Area: 228,861 sq mi (592,747 sq km)
Population: 30,340,000
Capital: Nairobi
Languages: English, Swahili (both official), indigenous languages

Lesotho
Area: 11,720 sq mi (30,355 sq km)
Population: 2,143,000
Capital: Maseru
Languages: English, Sesotho, Zulo, Xhosa

Liberia
Area: 43,000 sq mi (111,369 sq km)
Population: 3,164,000
Capital: Monrovia
Languages: English, indigenous languages

Libya
Area: 679,362 sq mi (1,759,540 sq km)
Population: 5,114,000
Capital: Tripoli
Languages: Arabic, Italian, English

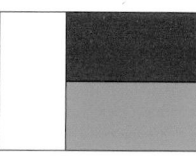

Madagascar
Area: 226,658 sq mi (587,041 sq km)
Population: 14,858,000
Capital: Antananarivo
Languages: French, Malagasy (both official)

Malawi
Area: 45,747 sq mi (118,484 sq km)
Population: 10,385,000
Capital: Lilongwe
Languages: Chewa, English (both official)

Mali
Area: 478,841 sq mi (1,240,192 sq km)
Population: 11,234,000
Capital: Bamako
Languages: French, Bambara, numerous African languages

Mauritania
Area: 397,955 sq mi (1,030,700 sq km)
Population: 2,670,000
Capital: Nouakchott
Languages: Hasaniya Arabic, Wolof (both official), Pula, Soninke, French

Mauritius
Area: 788 sq mi (2,040 sq km)
Population: 1,189,000
Capital: Port Louis
Languages: English, Creole, French, Hindi, Urdu, Hakka, Bojpoori

Morocco
Area: 275,117 sq mi (712,550 sq km)
Population: 28,778,000
Capital: Rabat
Languages: Arabic, Berber dialects, French

Mozambique
Area: 308,642 sq mi (799,380 sq km)
Population: 19,105,000
Capital: Maputo
Languages: Portuguese, indigenous dialects

Namibia
Area: 318,261 sq mi (824,292 sq km)
Population: 1,771,000
Capital: Windhoek
Languages: English, Afrikaans, German, indigenous languages

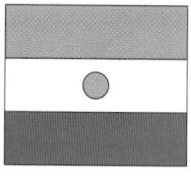

Niger
Area: 489,191 sq mi (1,267,000 sq km)
Population: 10,076,000
Capital: Niamey
Languages: French, Hausa, Djerma

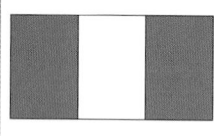

Nigeria
Area: 356,669 sq mi (923,768 sq km)
Population: 123,338,000
Capital: Abuja
Languages: English, Hausa, Yoruba, Igbo

Rwanda
Area: 10,169 sq mi (26,338 sq km)
Population: 7,229,000
Capital: Kigali
Languages: Kinyarwanda, French, English (all official), Kiswahili (Swahili)

Sao Tome and Principe
Area: 372 sq mi (964 sq km)
Population: 160,000
Capital: São Tomé
Language: Portuguese

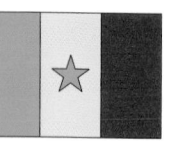

Senegal
Area: 75,955 sq mi (196,722 sq km)
Population: 9,481,000
Capital: Dakar
Languages: French, Wolof, Pulaar, Diola

Seychelles
Area: 175 sq mi (453 sq km)
Population: 82,000
Capital: Victoria
Languages: English, French (both official), Creole

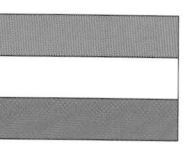

Sierra Leone
Area: 27,699 sq mi (71,740 sq km)
Population: 5,233,000
Capital: Freetown
Languages: English, Mende, Temne, Krio

Somalia
Area: 246,201 sq mi (637,657 sq km)
Population: 7,253,000
Capital: Mogadishu
Languages: Somali, Arabic, Italian, English

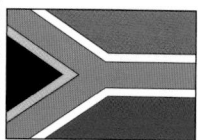

South Africa
Area: 471,445 sq mi (1,221,037 sq km)
Population: 43,421,000
Capitals: Pretoria (administrative), Cape Town (legislative), Bloemfontein (judicial)
Languages: Afrikaans, English, Ndebele, Pedi, Sotho, Swazi, Tsonga, Tswana, Venda, Xhosa, Zulu (all official)

Sudan
Area: 963,600 sq mi
(2,495,712 sq km)
Population: 29,490,000
Capital: Khartoum
Languages: Arabic,
Nuban, Ta Bedawie

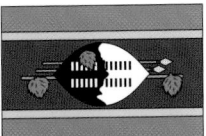

Swaziland
Area: 6,704 sq mi
(17,364 sq km)
Population: 1,004,000
Capital: Mbabane
Languages: English, Swazi
(both official)

Tanzania
Area: 364,900 sq mi
(945,087 sq km)
Population: 35,306,000
Capital: Dar es Salaam
Languages: Swahili, English
(both official), Arabic, many
local languages

Togo
Area: 21,925 sq mi
(56,785 sq km)
Population: 5,019,000
Capital: Lomé
Languages: French, Ewe,
Mina, Kabye, Dagomba

Tunisia
Area: 63,170 sq mi
(163,610 sq km)
Population: 9,619,000
Capital: Tunis
Languages: Arabic, French

Uganda
Area: 91,134 sq mi
(236,036 sq km)
Population: 23,318,000
Capital: Kampala
Languages: English, Ganda
or Luganda

Zambia
Area: 290,586 sq mi
(752,614 sq km)
Population: 9,582,000
Capital: Lusaka
Languages: English,
indigenous languages

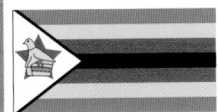

Zimbabwe
Area: 150,804 sq mi
(390,580 sq km)
Population: 11,343,000
Capital: Harare
Languages: English,
Shona, Sindebele

ASIA

Afghanistan
Area: 251,773 sq mi
(652,090 sq km)
Population: 26,668,000
Capital: Kabul
Languages: Pashto, Dari,
Turkic languages

Armenia
Area: 11,583 sq mi
(30,000 sq km)
Population: 3,809,000
Capital: Yerevan
Languages: Armenian,
Russian

Azerbaijan
Area: 33,591 sq mi
(87,000 sq km)
Population: 7,734,000
Capital: Baku
Languages: Azeri, Russian,
Armenian

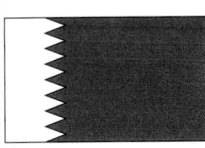

Bahrain
Area: 267 sq mi
(691 sq km)
Population: 691,000
Capital: Manama
Languages: Arabic,
English, Persian, Urdu

Bangladesh
Area: 55,598 sq mi
(143,998 sq km)
Population: 128,133,000
Capital: Dhaka
Languages: Bengali,
English

Bhutan
Area: 18,147 sq mi
(47,001 sq km)
Population: 877,000
Capital: Thimphu
Languages: Dzonkha,
Tibetan, and Nepali
dialects

Brunei
Area: 2,226 sq mi
(5,765 sq km)
Population: 331,000
Capital: Bandar Seri
Begawan
Languages: Malay, English,
Chinese

Cambodia
Area: 69,898 sq mi
(181,035 sq km)
Population: 12,127,000
Capital: Phnom Penh
Languages: Khmer, French

China
Area: 3,705,820 sq mi
(9,598,032 sq km)
Population:
1,264,536,000
Capital: Beijing
Languages: Chinese,
Mandarin, dialects

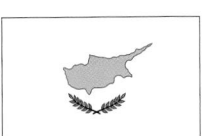

Cyprus
Area: 2,277 sq mi
(5,897 sq km)
Population: 882,000
Capital: Nicosia
Languages: Greek, Turkish,
English

Georgia
Area: 27,027 sq mi
(70,000 sq km)
Population: 5,454,000
Capital: T'bilisi
Languages: Georgian,
Russian, Armenian

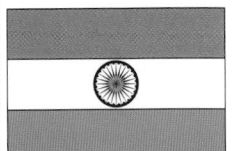

India
Area: 1,269,346 sq mi
(3,287,591 sq km)
Population: 1,002,142,000
Capital: New Delhi
Languages: Hindi, 14
other official languages,
English

Indonesia
Area: 741,101 sq mi
(1,919,443 sq km)
Population: 212,207,000
Capital: Jakarta
Languages: Bahasa
Indonesia, English, Dutch,
Javanese and other local
dialects

Iran
Area: 636,296 sq mi
(1,647,999 sq km)
Population: 67,411,000
Capital: Tehran
Languages: Persian, Turkic,
Kurdish, Luri

Iraq
Area: 169,235 sq mi
(438,317 sq km)
Population: 23,115,000
Capital: Baghdad
Languages: Arabic,
Kurdish (official in Kurdish
regions), Assyrian,
Armenian

Israel
Area: 8,019 sq mi
(20,770 sq km)
Population: 6,227,000
Capital: Jerusalem
Languages: Hebrew,
Arabic, English

Japan
Area: 145,875 sq mi
(377,815 sq km)
Population: 126,876,000
Capital: Tokyo
Language: Japanese

Jordan
Area: 35,467 sq mi
(91,860 sq km)
Population: 5,083,000
Capital: Amman
Languages: Arabic, English understood

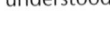

Kazakhstan
Area: 1,049,039 sq mi
(2,716,998 sq km)
Population: 14,865,000
Capital: Astana
Languages: Kazakh, Russian

Korea, North
Area: 46,540 sq mi
(120,538 sq km)
Population: 21,688,000
Capital: Pyongyang
Language: Korean

Korea, South
Area: 38,230 sq mi
(99,016 sq km)
Population: 47,275,000
Capital: Seoul
Languages: Korean, English widely taught

Kuwait
Area: 6,880 sq mi
(17,818 sq km)
Population: 2,190,000
Capital: Kuwait
Languages: Arabic, English

Kyrgyzstan
Area: 76,834 sq mi
(198,999 sq km)
Population: 4,929,000
Capital: Bishkek
Languages: Kirghiz, Russian (both official)

Laos
Area: 91,429 sq mi
(236,800 sq km)
Population: 5,218,000
Capital: Vientiane
Languages: Lao, French, English, ethnic

Lebanon
Area: 4,015 sq mi
(10,399 sq km)
Population: 4,202,000
Capital: Beirut
Languages: Arabic, French, English

Malaysia
Area: 127,317 sq mi
(329,749 sq km)
Population: 23,253,000
Capital: Kuala Lumpur
Languages: Malay, English, Chinese

Maldives
Area: 115 sq mi
(298 sq km)
Population: 286,000
Capital: Male
Languages: Maldivian Divehi, English

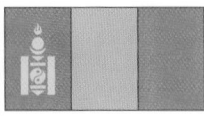

Mongolia
Area: 604,250 sq mi
(1,565,000 sq km)
Population: 2,472,000
Capital: Ulaanbaatar
Languages: Khalkha Mongol, Turkic, Russian, Chinese

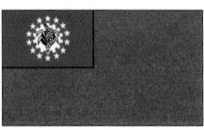

Myanmar
Area: 261,218 sq mi
(676,552 sq km)
Population: 48,852,000
Capital: Yangon (Rangoon)
Languages: Burmese, minority ethnic

Nepal
Area: 54,362 sq mi
(140,797 sq km)
Population: 23,930,000
Capital: Kathmandu
Languages: Nepali, 20 other languages

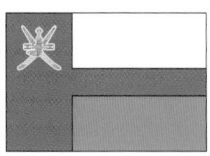

Oman
Area: 82,030 sq mi
(212,457 sq km)
Population: 2,353,000
Capital: Muscat
Languages: Arabic, English, Baluchi, Urdu

Pakistan
Area: 307,374 sq mi
(796,095 sq km)
Population: 150,648,000
Capital: Islamabad
Languages: Urdu, English, Punjabi, Sindhi

Philippines
Area: 115,831 sq mi
(300,001 sq km)
Population: 80,298,000
Capital: Manila
Languages: Tagalog, English (both official)

Qatar
Area: 4,247 sq mi
(11,000 sq km)
Population: 591,000
Capital: Doha
Languages: Arabic, English

Saudi Arabia
Area: 830,000 sq mi
(2,149,690 sq km)
Population: 21,607,000
Capital: Riyadh
Language: Arabic

Singapore
Area: 239 sq mi
(618 sq km)
Population: 4,001,000
Capital: Singapore
Languages: Chinese, Malay, Tamil, English

Sri Lanka
Area: 25,332 sq mi
(65,610 sq km)
Population: 19,169,000
Capitals: Colombo, Sri Jayewardenepura Kotte
Languages: Sinhalese, Tamil, English

Syria
Area: 71,044 sq mi
(184,004 sq km)
Population: 16,482,000
Capital: Damascus
Languages: Arabic, Kurdish, Armenian

Tajikistan
Area: 55,213 sq mi
(143,001 sq km)
Population: 6,374,000
Capital: Dushanbe
Languages: Tajik, Russian

Thailand
Area: 198,457 sq mi
(514,001 sq km)
Population: 62,043,000
Capital: Bangkok
Languages: Thai, English, regional dialects

Turkey
Area: 300,948 sq mi
(779,452 sq km)
Population: 65,311,000
Capital: Ankara
Languages: Turkish, Kurdish, Arabic

Turkmenistan
Area: 188,418 sq mi
(488,000 sq km)
Population: 5,239,000
Capital: Ashgabat
Languages: Turkmenian, Russian, Uzbek

United Arab Emirates
Area: 32,278 sq mi
(83,600 sq km)
Population: 2,835,000
Capital: Abu Dhabi
Languages: Arabic,
Persian, English, Hindi,
Urdu

Uzbekistan
Area: 172,588 sq mi
(447,001 sq km)
Population: 24,760,000
Capital: Tashkent
Languages: Uzbek,
Russian, Tajik

Vietnam
Area: 127,242 sq mi
(329,556 sq km)
Population: 78,697,000
Capital: Hanoi
Languages: Vietnamese,
Chinese, English, French,
Khmer, indigenous languages

Yemen
Area: 203,850 sq mi
(527,968 sq km)
Population: 17,030,000
Capital: Sanaa
Language: Arabic

AUSTRALIA & OCEANIA

Australia
Area: 2,968,000 sq mi
(7,687,000 sq km)
Population: 19,195,000
Capital: Canberra
Languages: English,
indigenous languages

Fiji Islands
Area: 7,056 sq mi
(18,274 sq km)
Population: 811,000
Capital: Suva
Languages: English, Fijian,
Hindi

Kiribati
Area: 277 sq mi
(717 sq km)
Population: 92,000
Capital: Tarawa
Languages: English,
Gilbertese

Marshall Islands
Area: 70 sq mi
(181 sq km)
Population: 68,000
Capital: Majuro
Languages: English, local
dialects, Japanese

Micronesia
Population: 271 sq mi
(702 sq km)
Population: 119,000
Capital: Palikir
Languages: English,
Trukese, Pohnpeian

Nauru
Area: 8 sq mi
(21 sq km)
Population: 12,000
Capital: Yaren
Languages: Nauruan,
English

New Zealand
Area: 103,883 sq mi
(269,057 sq km)
Population: 3,836,000
Capital: Wellington
Languages: English, Maori

Palau
Area: 188 sq mi
(487 sq km)
Population: 19,000
Capital: Koror
Languages: English,
Palaun, 3 local official

Papua New Guinea
Area: 178,260 sq mi
(461,691 sq km)
Population: 4,810,000
Capital: Port Moresby
Languages: 715 indige-
nous languages

Samoa
Area: 1,093 sq mi
(2,831 sq km)
Population: 176,000
Capital: Apia
Languages: Samoan
(Polynesian), English

Solomon Islands
Area: 10,985 sq mi
(28,450 sq km)
Population: 434,000
Capital: Honiara
Languages: Melanesian
pidgin, 120 indigenous
languages, English

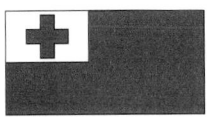

Tonga
Area: 270 sq mi
(699 sq km)
Population: 108,000
Capital: Nuku'alofa
Languages: Tongan,
English

Tuvalu
Area: 10 sq mi
(26 sq km)
Population: 10,000
Capital: Funafuti
Languages: Tuvalu, English

Vanuatu
Area: 5,700 sq mi
(14,760 sq km)
Population: 195,000
Capital: Port-Vila
Languages: English,
French, pidgin (Bislama)

Glossary

Note: Terms defined within the main body of the atlas text are not listed below.

Alkaline term describing soil or natural body of water that has a high salt content; most often found in dry areas where soluble salts have not been washed away or where evaporation rates are high (p. 84)

Arid climate type of dry climate in which annual precipitation is often less than 10 inches (25 cm); experiences great daily variations in day-night temperatures (pp. 18–19)

Boundary line established by people to separate one political or mapped area from another; physical features, such as mountains and rivers, or latitude and longitude lines sometimes act as boundaries (p. 10)

Breadbasket geographic region that is a principal source of grain (p. 34)

Brine solution containing a much higher concentration of salt than seawater (p. 84)

Canadian Shield region containing the oldest rock in North America; areas are exposed in much of eastern Canada and some bordering U.S. regions (p. 42)

Coastal plain any comparatively level land of low elevation that borders the ocean (p. 50)

Continental climate midlatitude climate zone occurring on large landmasses in the Northern Hemisphere and characterized by great variations of temperature, both seasonally and between day and night; continental cool summer climates are influenced by nearby colder subarctic climates; continental warm summer climates are influenced by nearby mild or dry climates (pp. 18–19)

Culture hearth center from which major cultural traditions spread and are adopted by people in a wide geographic area (p. 86)

Desert and dry shrub vegetation region with either hot or cold temperatures that annually receives 10 inches (25 cm) or less of precipitation (pp. 22–23)

Ecosystem term for classifying Earth's natural communities according to how all the things in an environment, such as a forest or a coral reef, interact with each other (p. 10)

Fault break in Earth's crust along which movement up, down, or sideways occurs (pp. 14–15)

Flooded grassland wetland dominated by grasses and covered by water (pp. 22–23)

Fossil fuel group of nonrenewable mineral resources—coal, oil, natural gas—formed over millions of years from plant and animal remains (pp. 38–39)

Geothermal energy heat energy generated within Earth (p. 39)

Glacier large, slow-moving mass of ice that forms over time from snow (p. 42)

Gondwana name given to the southern part of the supercontinent Pangaea; made up of what we now call Africa, South America, Australia, Antarctica, and India (pp. 14, 84)

Hemisphere one-half of the globe; the Equator divides Earth into Northern and Southern Hemispheres; the prime meridian and the 180 degree meridian divide it into Eastern and Western Hemispheres (p. 5)

Highland/upland climate region associated with mountains or plateaus that varies depending on elevation, latitude, continental location, and exposure to sun and wind; in general, temperature decreases and precipitation increases with elevation (pp. 18–19)

Humid subtropical climate region characterized by hot summers, mild to cool winters, and year-round precipitation that is heaviest in summer; generally located on the southeastern margins of continents (pp. 18–19)

Ice cap climate one of two kinds of polar climate; summer temperatures rarely rise above freezing, and what little precipitation occurs is mostly in the form of snow (pp. 18–19)

Indigenous native to or occurring naturally in a specific area or environment (p. 102)

Infiltration process that occurs in the water, or hydrologic, cycle when gravity causes surface water to seep down through the soil (p. 36)

Isthmus narrow strip of land that connects two larger landmasses and has water on two sides (p. 56–57)

Landform physical feature shaped by uplifting, weathering, and erosion; mountains, plateaus, hills, and plains are the four major types (p. 20)

Language family group of languages that come from a common ancestry (pp. 30–31)

Latin America cultural region generally considered to include Mexico, Central America, South America, and the West Indies; Portuguese and Spanish are the principal languages (pp. 28–29)

Llanos extensive, mostly treeless grasslands in the Orinoco River basin of northern South America (p. 58)

Lowlands fairly level land at a lower elevation than surrounding areas (p. 12)

Mangrove vegetation tropical trees and shrubs with dense root systems that grow in tidal mud flats and extend coastlines by trapping soil (pp. 22–23)

Marine west coast type of mild climate common on the west coasts of continents in midlatitude regions; characterized by small variations in annual temperature range and wet, foggy winters (pp. 18–19)

Median age midpoint of a population's age; half the population is older than this age; half is younger (p. 27)

Mediterranean climate type of mild climate common on the west coasts of continents, named for the dominant climate along the Mediterranean coast; characterized by mild rainy winters and hot dry summers (pp. 18–19)

Mediterranean shrub low-growing, mostly small-leaved evergreen vegetation, such as chaparral, that thrives in Mediterranean climate regions (p. 22–23)

Melanesia one of three major island groups that make up Oceania; includes the Fiji Islands, New Guinea, Vanuatu, the Solomon Islands, and New Caledonia (pp. 102–103)

Melanesian indigenous to Melanesia (p. 102)

Mestizo person of mixed Native American and European ancestry; most commonly used in Latin America (p. 53)

Microclimate climate of a very limited area that varies from the overall climate of the surrounding region (p. 20)

Micronesia one of three major island groups that make up Oceania; made up of some 2,000 mostly coral islands, including Guam, Kiribati, the Mariana Islands, Palau, and the Federated States of Micronesia (pp. 102–103)

Micronesian indigenous to Micronesia (p. 102)

Monsoon seasonal change in the direction of the prevailing winds, which causes wet and dry seasons in some tropical areas (p. 90)

Mountain grassland vegetation region characterized by clumps of long grass that grow beyond the limit of forests at high elevations (pp. 22–23)

Nonrenewable resource elements of the natural environment, such as metals, minerals, and fossil fuels, that form within Earth by geological processes over millions of years and thus cannot be readily replaced (pp. 38–39)

Northern coniferous forest vegetation region composed primarily of cone-bearing, needle-leafed or scale-leafed evergreen trees that grow in regions with long winters and moderate to high annual precipitation; also called boreal forest or taiga (pp. 22–23)

Oceania name for the widely scattered islands of Polynesia, Micronesia, and Melanesia; often includes Australia and New Zealand (pp. 96–107)

Pampas temperate grassland primarily in Argentina between the Andes and the Atlantic Ocean; one of the richest agricultural regions in the world (pp. 56, 58)

Patagonia cool, windy, arid plateau region primarily in southern Argentina between the Andes and the Atlantic Ocean (p. 58)

Plain large area of relatively flat land; one of the four major kinds of landforms (p. 16)

Plate tectonics study of the interaction of slabs of Earth's crust as molten rock within Earth causes them to slowly move across the surface (pp. 14–15)

Plateau large, relatively flat area that rises above the surrounding landscape; one of the four major kinds of landforms (pp. 16–17)

Polar climates climates that occur at very high latitudes; generally too cold to support tree growth; include tundra and ice cap (pp. 22–23)

Polynesia one of three major regions in Oceania made up mostly of volcanic and coral islands, including the Hawaiian Islands, the Society Islands, Samoa, and French Polynesia (pp. 102–103)

Polynesian indigenous to Polynesia (p. 102)

Predominant economy main type of work that most people do to meet their wants and needs in a particular country (pp. 32–33, 47, 63, 73, 83, 93, 103)

Province land governed as a political or administrative unit of a country or empire; Canadian

provinces, like U.S. states, have substantial powers of self-government (p. 49)

River basin area drained by a single river and its tributaries (p. 58)

Sahel in Africa the semi-arid region of short tropical grassland that lies between the dry Sahara and the humid savanna and that is prone to frequent droughts (p. 78)

Savanna tropical tall grassland with scattered low trees (p. 23)

Selva Portuguese word referring to tropical rain forests, especially in the Amazon Basin (p. 64)

Semiarid dry climate region that experiences great daily variation in day-night temperatures; receives enough rainfall to support grasslands (pp. 18–19)

Silt mineral particles that are larger than grains of clay but smaller than grains of sand (p. 65)

Sisal tropical plant with leaves made up of strong fibers that are used to make rope (p. 84)

Steppe Slavic word referring to relatively flat, mostly treeless temperate grasslands that stretch across much of central Europe and central Asia (p. 88)

Subarctic climate region characterized by short, cool, sometimes freezing summers and long, bitter cold winters; most precipitation falls in summer (pp.18–19)

Subcontinent large landmass such as India that, although part of a continent, is considered a separate feature either geographically or politically (p. 84)

Subtropical climate region between tropical

and continental climates characterized by distinct seasons but with milder temperatures than continental climates (pp. 18–19)

Temperate broadleaf forest vegetation region with distinct seasons and dependable rainfall; predominant species include oak, maple, and beech, all of which lose their leaves in the cold season (pp. 22–23)

Temperate coniferous forest vegetation region that has mild winters with heavy precipitation; made up of mostly evergreen, needleleaf trees that bear seeds in cones (pp. 22–23)

Temperate grassland vegetation region where grasses are dominant and the climate is characterized by hot summers, cold winters, and moderate rainfall (pp. 22–23)

Territory land under the jurisdiction of a country but that is not a state or a province (p. 43)

Tropical coniferous forest vegetation region that occurs in a cooler climate than tropical rain

forests; has distinct wet and dry seasons; made up of mostly evergreen trees with seed-bearing cones (pp. 22–23)

Tropical dry climate region characterized by year-round high temperatures and sufficient precipitation to support savannas (pp. 18–19)

Tropical dry forest vegetation region that has distinct wet and dry seasons and a cooler climate than tropical moist forests; has shorter trees than rain forests and many shed their leaves in the dry season (pp. 22–23)

Tropical grassland and savanna vegetation region characterized by scattered individual trees; occurs in warm or hot climates with annual rainfall of 20 to 50 inches (50–130 cm) (pp. 22–23)

Tropical moist broadleaf forest vegetation region occurring mostly in a belt between the Tropic of Cancer and the Tropic of Capricorn in areas that have at least 80 inches (200 cm) of rain annually and an average annual temperature of 80°F (20°C) (pp. 22–23)

Tropical wet climate region characterized by year-round warm temperatures and rainfall ranging from 60 to150 inches (150–400 cm) annually (pp. 18–19)

Troposphere region of Earth's atmosphere that is closest to the surface; where weather occurs (p. 5)

Tundra vegetation region at high latitudes and high elevations characterized by cold temperatures, low vegetation, and a short growing season (pp. 22–23)

Tundra climate region with one or more months of temperatures slightly above freezing when the ground is free of snow (pp. 18–19)

Upland climate see *Highland/upland climate*

Web Sites (Web Link)

Antarctica: http://www.nsf.gov/od/opp/antarct/start.htm

Earth's Climates: http://www.worldclimate.com

Earth's Geologic History:

    Earthquakes: http://earthquake.usgs.gov/

    Volcanoes: http://www.geo.mtu.edu/volcanoes/

Earth's Vegetation: http://www.earthobservatory.nasa.gov/Library/LandCover/

Map Projections: http://www.colorado.edu/geography/gcraft/notes/mapproj/mapproj.html

Political World: http://www.cia.gov/cia/publications/factbook/index.html

Predominant World Economies: http://www.wto.org/english/res_e/statis_e/overvwf_e.htm

Types of Maps: http://magma.nationalgeographic.com/education/

World Cities: http://www.un.org/esa/population/urbanization.htm

World Cultures: http://highschoolhub.org/hub/language.htm

World Energy: http://www.bp.com/worldenergy/

World Food: http://www.cgiar.org/areas.htm

World Population: http://www.census.gov/ipc/www/idbnew.html

World Water: http://water.usgs.gov/

Thematic Index

Boldface indicates illustrations

A

Agriculture 34–35, **37**
  irrigation **36**
  slash-and-burn 64, **65**
  subsistence **32, 84**
Alaska (state), U.S. 54
Amazon (river), Brazil **65**
Amazon rain forest 64–65, **65**
  map 64–65
Angkor Wat, Cambodia **94**
Antarctica
  map 25
Arabian Peninsula, Asia **84**
Arctic regions
  map 24
Arizona **36**
Austria 74

B

Belgium 74
Brazil
  Amazon rain forest 64–65
British Columbia (province), Canada 54
Bulgaria 74

C

California (state), U.S. **39,** 54
Cambodia **94**
Canada 54
Central America **36**
Cities 28
Climate 18
  controls 20–21
  graphs 18, **18–19**
  map 18–19
  zones 18–19
Columbia (river), British Columbia-Washington **32**
Continents 13
Corn 34, **34**
  map 34
Côte d'Ivoire
  population pyramid 27

Culture hearths 31
  map 31
Cultures 30–31
Cypress 74
Czech Republic 24, 74

D

Date line 107
Denmark 74
Desert shrub **22**
Djibouti
  volcanoes **84**
Dominican Republic 54

E

Earth 4–5
  climate map 18–19
  cross section **16–17**
  geologic history 14–15
  rotation **5**
  satellite map 16–17
Earthquakes 54, map 55
Economies
  Europe 74–75
  map 32–33
Elevation 20
Energy resources
  hydroelectric **37**
  map 38–39
Estonia 74
Euro (currency) 74, 75, **75**
European Union (EU) 74–75, map 75

F

Farming **34,** 34–35, **84**
Fertilizer use 35
  map 35
Fiji 106
Finland 74
Fishing **32**
Flags and facts 112–119
Flamingos **84**
Floods **54,** map 55
Food 34
  map 34–35
Forests
  temperate **22**
  tropical **23,** 64–65
France 74

G

Germany 24, 74
Globes 10, **10**
Gondwana 14, **84**
Grasslands **23**
Great Rift Valley, Africa 84–85
  map 85
Greece 74
Guatemala 54

H

Hungary 74
Hurricanes 54, map 55

I

Iceland
  geothermal power plant **39**
Illinois (state), U.S. 54
Internet 33, **33**
Iowa (state), U.S. 54
Ireland 74
Irrigation 36
Itaipú Dam, South America **37**
Italy 74
  population pyramid 27

J

Japan
  fishing **32**
JASON Project **33**

K

Kansas (state), U.S. 54
Köppen, Wladimir 18

L

Languages
  map 30–31
Latitude 8, 20
Latvia 74
Lithuania 74
Logging **32**
Longitude 8
Louisiana (state), U.S. 54

M

Maastricht Treaty 74
Mangroves **23**
Maps
  cartograms 10, **11**
  choropleth 10, **10**
  physical 10, **10**
  political 10, **11**

projections 6–7, **6–7**
  reading 8–9
  satellite 11, 16–17
  scale 8, **8**
  symbols 9, **9**
  thematic 10–11
  types 10
Mariana Trench, North Pacific Ocean 12
Mexico 54
Mid-Atlantic Ridge, Atlantic Ocean 12
Minerals **65**
  map 38
Mississippi (river), U.S.
  floods 54, **54**
Missouri (state), U.S. 54

N

Natural hazards 54–55
Natural resources 64
  energy 38–39
  water 36–37
Nebraska (state), U.S. 54
Netherlands 74
New York, New York 28
North America
  natural hazards 54–55, map 55
North Pole 24
Nuclear power plants **39**

O

Ocean floor 21
  map 18–19
Ocean floor
  map 12
Oklahoma (state), U.S. 54
Organization of Petroleum Exporting Countries (OPEC) 38
  map 38–39

P

Panama 54
Pangaea 14, **84**
  map 14
Peru
  farmers **32**
Philippines
  reefs **95**
Planets 4, **4**
Plate tectonics 14–15, **84**
  map 14–15

Poland 74
Population 26–27
  map 26–27
  urban areas 28–29
Portugal 74
Prime meridian 8, 106

R

Rain forests 64–65
Religions
  map 30
Rice 34, **34**
  map 34–35
Romania 74
Rotterdam, Netherlands **74**
Ruhr Valley, Germany 74
Rural areas and populations 28–29

S

Sacramento, California
  power plants **38**
San Pedro Valley, Arizona **36**
Schuman, Robert 74
Seasons **5**
Shanghai, China **26**
Sloth **64**
Slovakia 24, 74
  manufacturing **33**
Slovenia 74
Solar energy **39**
Solar system 4
South Dakota (state), U.S. 54
South Pole 25
Spain 74
St. Helens, Mount, Washington **54**
Suva, Fiji 106
Sweden 74

T

Taj Mahal, India **95**
Tehachapi, California
  windmills **39**
Texas (state), U.S. 54
Time zones 106
  map 106–107
Tornadoes 54, map 55
Trade 75
Trains 106, **106**
Trewartha, Glenn 18
Tubbataha Reef Marine Park, Philippines **95**
Tundra **22**
Turkey 74, **94**

Place-name Index

Due to limited space, only countries, their capitals, cities with populations of one million or more, and selected physical features are listed here.

C

Cairo, Egypt 79, 82, 83
Calcutta, India 89, 92, 93
Cali, Colombia 59, 62, 63
Cambodia 89, 90, 91, 92, 93
Cameroon 79, 80, 81, 82, 83
Canada 43, 44, 45, 46, 47, 48, 49
Canadian Shield, Canada 42, 47, 48
Canberra, Australia 99, 103, 104
Cantabrian Mountains, Spain 68
Cape Town, South Africa 79, 82, 83
Cape Verde 79
Caracas, Venezuela 59, 62, 63
Caroline Islands, North Pacific Ocean 98, 99
Carpathian Mountains, Europe 68
Casablanca, Morocco 79, 82, 83
Cascade Range, U.S. 42, 50
Caspian Sea 68, 69, 70, 71, 72, 88
Castries, St. Lucia 43
Caucasus Mountains, Asia-Europe 68
Central African Republic 79, 80, 81, 82, 83
Central Lowland, U.S. 42, 50
Central Plateau, Mexico 52
Central Russian Upland, Russia 68
Chad 79, 80, 81, 82, 83
Charlotte, North Carolina 43, 46, 47, 51
Chengdu, China 89, 92
Chennai, India 89, 92, 93
Chicago, Illinois 43, 46, 47, 51
Chile 59, 60, 61, 62, 63

China 89, 90, 91, 92, 93
Chişinău, Moldova 69, 72
Chongqing, China 89, 92
Cleveland, Ohio 43, 46, 51
Coast Mountains, British Columbia 42, 48
Coast Ranges, U.S. 50
Coastal Plain, U.S. 42, 50
Cologne, Germany 72
Colombia 59, 60, 61, 62, 63
Colombo, Sri Lanka 89
Colorado (river), Argentina 58
Colorado (river), Mexico-U.S. 42, 50, 52
Columbia Plateau, U.S. 50
Columbus, Ohio 46, 51
Comoros 79, 80, 81, 82, 83
Conakry, Guinea 79, 82
Congo 79, 80, 81, 82, 83
Congo (river), Africa 78
Congo Basin, Africa 78
Congo, Democratic Republic of the 79, 80, 81, 82, 83
Cook Islands, South Pacific Ocean 98, 99, 100, 101, 102, 103
Copenhagen, Denmark 69, 72
Córdoba, Argentina 59, 62
Costa Rica 43, 44, 45, 46, 47
Côte d'Ivoire 79, 80, 81, 82, 83
Croatia 69, 70, 71, 72, 73
Cuba 42, 43, 44, 45, 46, 47
Curitiba, Brazil 59, 62
Cyprus 89, 90, 91, 92, 93
Czech Republic 69, 70, 71, 72, 73

D

Dakar, Senegal 79, 82
Dallas, Texas 43, 46, 47, 51
Damascus, Syria 89
Dar es Salaam, Tanzania 79, 82
Dardanelles, Turkey 68
Darling (river), Australia 98
Dead Sea, Israel-Jordan 88
Death Valley, California 42, 50
Deccan Plateau, India 88
Delhi, India 89, 92
Denmark 69, 70, 71, 72, 73
Denver, Colorado 43, 46, 47, 51
Detroit, Michigan 43, 46, 47, 51
Dhaka, Bangladesh 89, 92
Djibouti 79, 80, 81, 82, 83
Djibouti, Djibouti 79
Dnipropetrovs'k, Ukraine 69, 72
Doha, Qatar 89
Dominica 43, 46
Dominican Republic 43, 44, 45, 46, 47
Donets'k, Ukraine 69, 72
Douala, Cameroon 79, 82
Drakensberg (mountains), South Africa 78
Dublin, Ireland 69, 72
Dushanbe, Tajikistan 89

E

Ecuador 59, 60, 61, 62, 63
Egypt 79, 80, 81, 82, 83
El Gîza, Egypt 82
El Salvador 43, 44, 45, 46, 47
El'brus (peak), Republic of Georgia-Russia 68
Ellesmere Island, Nunavut 42, 49
Ellsworth Land, Antarctica 110

Ellsworth Mountains, Antarctica 110
Enderby Land, Antarctica 110
Equatorial Guinea 79, 80, 81, 82, 83
Eritrea 79, 80, 81, 82, 83
Essen, Germany 72
Estonia 69, 70, 71, 72, 73
Ethiopia 79, 80, 81, 82, 83
Ethiopian Highlands, Ethiopia 78, 83
Euphrates (river), Asia 88
Everest, Mount, China-Nepal 88
Eyre, Lake, Australia 98

F

Falkland Islands, South Atlantic Ocean 58, 59
Federal District, Mexico 53
Fiji 98, 99, 100, 101, 102, 103
Filchner Ice Shelf, Antarctica 110
Fimbul Ice Shelf, Antarctica 110
Finland 69, 70, 71, 72, 73
Fortaleza, Brazil 59, 62
France 69, 70, 71, 72, 73
Frankfurt, Germany 69, 72
Freetown, Sierra Leone 79
French Guiana 59, 60, 61, 62, 63
Funafuti (island), Tuvalu 99

G

Gabon 79, 80, 81, 82, 83
Gaborone, Botswana 79
Gambia 79, 80, 81, 82, 83
Ganges (river), Bangladesh-India 88
Georgetown, Guyana 59
Georgia, Republic of 69, 70, 71, 72, 73, 89, 90, 91, 92, 93

Germany 69, 70, 71, 72, 73
Ghana 79, 80, 81, 82, 83
Glasgow, Scotland 69, 72
Gobi (desert), China-Mongolia 88, 93
Good Hope, Cape of, South Africa 78
Gran Chaco (region), Argentina-Paraguay 58
Grande de Chiloé, Isla, Chile 58
Great Artesian Basin, Australia 98
Great Basin, Nevada 50
Great Bear Lake, Northwest Territories 42, 48
Great Dividing Range, Australia 98
Great Indian Desert, India 88
Great Lakes, Canada-U.S. 42
Great Plains, Canada-U.S. 42, 48, 50
Great Rift Valley, Africa 78, 85
Great Salt Lake, Utah 42, 50
Great Sandy Desert, Australia 98
Great Slave Lake, Northwest Territories 42, 48
Great Victoria Desert, Australia 98
Greece 69, 70, 71, 72, 73
Greenland 42, 43, 44, 45, 46, 47, 48, 49
Grenada (island), Caribbean Sea 43, 46
Guadalajara, Mexico 43, 46, 47, 53
Guam (island), Mariana Islands 99, 100, 101, 102, 103
Guangzhou, China 89, 92
Guatemala 43, 44, 45, 46, 47
Guatemala, Guatemala 43, 46
Guayaquil, Ecuador 59, 62, 63

National Geographic Society

John M. Fahey, Jr.
President and Chief Executive Officer

Gilbert M. Grosvenor
Chairman of the Board

Nina D. Hoffman
President, Books and School Publishing Group

William R. Gray
Vice President and Director of the Book Division

Ericka Markman
Vice President and Director, School Publishing

Staff for this book

Children's Books

Nancy Laties Feresten
Publishing Director, Children's Books

Suzanne Patrick Fonda
Project Editor

Carl Mehler
Director of Maps

Marianne R. Koszorus
Design Director

Dorrit Green
Art Director and Designer

Martha B. Sharma
Writer and Chief Consultant

Marilyn Mofford Gibbons
Illustrations Editor

Jerome N. Cookson
Map Production Manager

Matt Chwastyk
Thomas L. Gray
Nicholas P. Rosenbach
Gregory Ugiansky
Martin S. Walz
National Geographic Maps
XNR Productions
Map Research and Production

Marcia Pires-Harwood
Text Research

Marilyn "Minh" Le
Jessica Ann Peterson
Anjali M. Shenai
Research Assistance

Stuart Armstrong
Graphs

Sharon K. Berry
Illustrations Assistant

Connie B. Binder
Indexer

Ellen Teguis
Director
Trade Sales and Marketing

Lawrence M. Porges
Marketing Specialist

R. Gary Colbert
Production Director

Lewis R. Bassford
Production Manager

Vincent R. Ryan
Manufacturing Manager

School Publishing Division

Steve Mico
Editorial Director

Richard Easby
Editorial Manager

Carolyn Hatt
Lydia Lewis
Editors

Jean Stringer
Anika Trahan
Associate Editors

Education Foundation

Lanny Proffer
Executive Director

Joe Ferguson
Director of Programs
Geography Education Outreach

Christopher Shearer
Program Officer

Consultants

Deborah Batchelor
Specialist
Baltimore City Public School System
Baltimore, Maryland

Sari J. Bennett
Department of Geography & Environmental Systems
University of Maryland
Baltimore County

Acknowledgments: We are grateful for the assistance of Richard W. Bullington, Jan D. Morris, Karla H. Tucker, and Alfred L. Zebarth of NG Maps; the National Geographic Image Collection; and Jo H. Tunstall, Robert W. Witt, and Lyle Rosbotham, NG Book Division

Illustrations Credits: Abbreviations for terms appearing below: (t) top; (b) bottom; (l) left; (r) right; (c) center; NGS: National Geographic Staff

Locator globes on pages 2–3 and in chapter openers created by Theophilus Britt Griswold

Graphs created by Stuart Armstrong

Continent chapter openers: NASA/JPL/California Institute of Technology/Advanced Very High Resolution Radiometer Project/Cartographic Applications Group

Cover: NOAA satellite mosaic prepared for National Geographic Television by NASA/ JPL, color enhanced by Alfred L. Zebarth; background art digitally created by Slim Films

Back cover: photograph, Steve Raymer; satellite image map, NOAA/NESDIS/NGDC

About The Earth
4 (art) © NGS; 4–5 (t) Shusei Nagaska; (b) Earth Satellite Corporation; 5 (bl) Robert Hynes; 6–7 (art) Shusei Nagaska; 10 (l) Vlad Kharitonov NGS; 11 (t–b) NASA/GISS, NOAA/NESDIS/NGDC, NASA/GSFC, University of Miami; 14–15 (t) NASA/JPL/CalTech/CAG, (b) Christopher R. Scotese/PALEOMAP Project, U. of TX, Arlington; 16–17 (t) NOAA/NESDIS/NGDC; 22–3 (l–r) Jen & Des Bartlett; Raymond Gehman; Cosmo Condina/stone; Walter M. Edwards; Tom Bean/stone; Steve Jackson; Timothy G. Lamar; Medford Taylor; 26 Stuart Franklin; 32 (graph) Theophilus Britt Griswold, revised by Stuart Armstrong; 32–3 (l–r) Martin Rogers; James P. Blair; Phil Schermeister; James L. Stanfield; Mark Thiessen NGS; © NGS; 34 (l) Steve Raymer; (c) Sisse Brimberg; (r) Stephen G. St. John; 36–7 (l–r) Steve Winter; Annie Griffiths Belt; Loren McIntyre; Jim Brandenburg; 39 (tl) James A. Sugar/Black Star; (tr) Marc Moritsch; (bl) Bob Krist; (r) stone

North America
54 (tl) Roger Werth/Woodfin Camp Inc; (tr) Ravi Miro Fry; (b) Chris Stewart/Black Star

South America
65 (bl, br) Michael Nichols NGS; (tr) Bill Curtsinger; (c) Mattias Klum

Europe
74 Bert Blokhuis/stone; 75 (br) Index Stock

Africa
84 (l) Paul Zahl; (tr, br) Chris Johns NGS

Asia
94 (t) James L. Stanfield; (b) Steve McCurry; 95 (l) James P. Blair; (r) Lynn Funkhouser

Australia
106 (l) Bob Sacha; (r) The Granger Collection; 107 Shusei Nagaska

The world's largest nonprofit scientific and educational organization, the National Geographic Society was founded in 1888 "for the increase and diffusion of geographic knowledge." Since then it has supported scientific exploration and spread information to its more than nine million members worldwide.

The National Geographic Society educates and inspires millions every day through magazines, books, television programs, videos, maps and atlases, research grants, the National Geographic Bee, teacher workshops, and innovative classroom materials.

The Society is supported through membership dues and income from the sale of its educational products. Members receive National Geographic magazine—the Society's official journal—discounts on Society products, and other benefits.

For more information about the National Geographic Society and its educational programs and publications, please call 1-800-NGS-LINE (647-5463), or write to the following address:

National Geographic Society, 1145 17th Street N.W., Washington, D.C. 20036-4688 U.S.A.

Visit the Society's Web site: www.nationalgeographic.com

Library of Congress Cataloging-in-Publication Data

National Geographic Society (U.S.)
National Geographic student atlas of the world.
p. cm.
Includes index and glossary.
ISBN 0-7922-7221-8 (pbk.)
ISBN 0-7922-7235-8 (hc.)
 1. Children's atlases. 2. Earth—remote-sensing images. 3. Physical geography—Maps for children. [1.Atlases.] I. Title: Student atlas of the world. II. Title.
G1021 .N42 2001
912–dc21   00-030006

Published by the National Geographic Society
1145 17th St. N.W.
Washington, D.C. 20036-4688
Copyright © 2001 National Geographic Society